THE FILMS OF APICHATPONG WEERASETHAKUL

THE FILMS OF APICHATPONG WEERASETHAKUL

EDITED BY

ANIK SARKAR AND JAYJIT SARKAR

LIVERPOOL UNIVERSITY PRESS

First published 2024 by
Liverpool University Press
4 Cambridge Street
Liverpool
L69 7ZU

Copyright © 2024 Anik Sarkar and Jayjit Sarkar

Anik Sarkar and Jayjit Sarkar have asserted the right to be identified as
the editors of this book in accordance with the Copyright, Designs and
Patents Act 1988.

All rights reserved. No part of this book may be reproduced, stored
in a retrieval system, or transmitted, in any form or by any means,
electronic, mechanical, photocopying, recording, or otherwise, without
the prior written permission of the publisher.

British Library Cataloguing-in-Publication data
A British Library CIP record is available

ISBN 978-1-83764-513-8 cased

Typeset by Carnegie Book Production, Lancaster

... that there is never a concrete thing in life.

—Apichatpong Weerasethakul

Contents

Acknowledgement	ix

Introduction
Open Cinema: The Films and Installations of
Apichatpong Weerasethakul   1
> *Anik Sarkar and Jayjit Sarkar*

Time

1. Time, Social Reproduction and the Precarious Body in
the Films of Apichatpong Weerasethakul   27
> *Patrícia Sequeira Brás*

2. Representing Memory through Slowness: The
Time-Images of Apichatpong Weerasethakul's
Syndromes and a Century and *Cemetery of Splendour*   47
> *Francesco Quario*

Nonhuman

3. Stray Dogs and Strange Beasts: Apichatpong
Weerasethakul's Queer Animal Ethics   69
> *Duncan Caillard*

4. Imagining the Nonhuman in the Cinema of
Apichatpong Weerasethakul   89
> *Çağatay Emre Doğan*

viii CONTENTS

Mind

5. The Stillness Wandering Within: Notes on the Caesura of the Cinematic Image in Apichatpong Weerasethakul's *Primitive* Project 115

    Elizabeth Sikes

6. Dreams, Abstractions and Spectatorship in Apichatpong Weerasethakul's Films and Videos 133

    Alessandro Ferraro

7. *EFFULGENCES* Particles in Motion: *Cycling the Mindscapes of* Apichatpong Weerasethakul 155

    Jeffner Allen

Forms and Representations

8. Transmedia Plot in Apichatpong Weerasethakul's *Primitive* 181

    Jade de Cock de Rameyen

9. Home Away From Home: Apichatpong Weerasethakul's Filmed Images of Home and Homeland Envisioned 207

    Palita Chunsaengchan

10. Between an Erased Past and an Uncertain Future: Hybrid Forms in the Films of Apichatpong Weerasethakul 229

    Sivaranjini

11. Post-Interstitial Authorship in Apichatpong Weerasethakul's Cinema 249

    Anchalee Chaiworaporn

Notes on Contributors 277

Index 281

Acknowledgement

We greatly appreciate the support of John Berra (Renmin University, China) and May Adadol Ingawanij (Westminster School of Arts, UK). We are also grateful to the commissioning editors Ally Lee and John Atkinson of Liverpool University Press for their incessant support. *The Films of Apichatpong Weerasethakul* is a collaborative project which would not have been possible without the cooperation, scholarship, and support of our contributors. We extend our heartfelt gratitude to all of them for this shared experience. And last, but not the least, our family, friends, and colleagues for their constant support and encouragement.

Anik Sarkar
Jayjit Sarkar
Darjeeling, India
7 May 2023

Introduction
Open Cinema: The Films and Installations of Apichatpong Weerasethakul

Anik Sarkar and Jayjit Sarkar

Film is still like an entity by itself.
—Apichatpong Weerasethakul[1]

The mind loves the unknown. It loves images whose meaning is unknown, since the meaning of the mind itself is unknown.
—René Magritte[2]

Over the years, a steady and diverse corpus of scholarship has been dedicated to the works of Apichatpong Weerasethakul. His nickname "Joe" being familiar now, more than ever—as his films have acquired transnational audiences: "a celebrated figure amongst a small group of transnational art-house cinephiles"[3] to "the preeminent Thai filmmaker—and one of the freshest voices in cinema anywhere".[4] His

---

[1] Ji-hoon Kim, "Learning About Time: An Interview with Apichatpong Weerasethakul", *Film Quarterly* 64, no. 4 (2011): 48–52. doi:10.1525/FQ.2011.64.4.48.
[2] Suzy Gablik quotes René Magritte in her book *Magritte* (1970) published by New York Graphic Society, Greenwich, Conn. p. 12.
[3] Nicholas Mercer, "Between the Global and the Local: The Cultural Geopolitics of Apichatpong Weerasethakul's Film Aesthetics", *Linguistics, Literature and Culture: Millennium Realities and Innovative Practices in Asia* (Newcastle: Cambridge Scholars Publishing, 2012), 191–216.
[4] James Quandt, "Exquisite Corpus: The Films of Apichatpong Weerasethakul", *Artforum International Magazine*, 1 May 2005, https://www.artforum.com/print/200505/exquisite-corpus-the-films-of-apichatpong-weerasethakul-8835.

works that are labelled as "dreamlike",[5] "surreal",[6] "ambiguous"[7] have been frequenting Cannes (*Memoria* starring Tilda Swinton being the most recent one) and end up becoming rigorous subjects of discourse at home and abroad.

With what could be asserted as a "fresh style"—stylistically innovative, unconventional and offbeat—Apichatpong's rise to prominence was through his earliest feature film, *Mysterious Objects at Noon* (2000). Enigmatic and evocative, this part-documentary, part-fantasy arguably solidifies some of the signature templates of later Apichatpong, although, these are permeable stratifications and with each new project his perplexing style slips on and off, inhibiting particular forms of hybridity that exhausts rigid categorization.

His first filmmaking venture involved a silent, experimental documentary called *Bullet* (1993), that plays with lights and time, something he frequently indulges with, and a similar experiment-heavy framework had been followed in *Kitchen and Bedroom* (1994), *0016643225059* (1994) and *Like the Relentless Fury of Pounding Waves* (1996).[8] His major projects after *Mysterious Objects* included his *Un Certain Regard* winning film *Blissfully Yours* (2002), a romance that centres on a girl and her Burmese lover who is an illegal immigrant. He made *The Adventure of Iron Pussy* (2003) with Michael Shaowanasai, which falls in the category of action–comedy–musical and is a parody on older Thai action films and melodramas. He followed it with *Tropical Malady* (2004) a romance between two men that surrogates mid-way into a spellbinding tale of fantasy and animism. Next, basing on a story inspired by his parents, he made *Syndromes and a Century* (2006), which is a poignant tale on the idea of transformation, shot centrally in a hospital and a medical centre. His surreal *Palme d'Or* winning film, *Uncle Boonmee Who Can Recall His Past Lives* (2010) depicts the life of Boonmee, a farmer who is slowly dying from kidney failure, and his

---

[5] Benoit Pavan, "Memoria, the New Sensory Journey from Apichatpong Weerasethakul", Festival de Cannes 2021, 19 July 2021, https://www.festival-cannes.com/en/festival/actualites/articles/memoria-the-new-sensory-journey-from-apichatpong-weerasethakul.

[6] James Balmont, "Meet the 'David Lynch of Thailand' and His Queer, Surrealist Cinema", *Dazed*, 6 January 2021, https://www.dazeddigital.com/film-tv/article/51589/1/apichatpong-weerasethakul-david-lynch-of-thailand-queer-surrealist-cinema.

[7] Patrick Langley, "Apichatpong Weerasethakul", *Frieze*, accessed 1 October 2021, https://www.frieze.com/article/apichatpong-weerasethakul.

[8] K. Kuiper, "Apichatpong Weerasethakul", *Encyclopedia Britannica*, 12 July 2021, https://www.britannica.com/biography/Apichatpong-Weerasethakul.

INTRODUCTION

reunion with now "transformed" members. Primarily, the film appears to divulge into multiple storylines: one that includes Boonmee and his last days, the second that captures a princess, her servant and a catfish, and the final one being about Jen, Roong and Tong after he becomes a monk. Through a disjointed narrative, the film explores themes of identity, political violence and reincarnation and, as he laments cinema's movement from "celluloid" to digital, the filming of *Uncle Boonme* on a growingly "outdated" medium also embodies the "death of cinema". This was part of his *Primitive* installations, a multimedia project that he had previously set up with London-based "Animate" centring on Nabua.[9] Following *Uncle Boonme*, his recurring exploration of spectrality and mysticism features in a film titled *Mekong Hotel* (2012). *Cemetery of Splendour* (2015) is a breath-taking fantasy based on a group of soldiers who are suffering from a mysterious sleeping sickness. Apart from these he had a series of short films in between, among which the noteworthy ones include *Worldly Desires* (2005), *The Anthem* (2006), *Phantoms of Nabua* (2009), *Empire* (2010), *Ashes* (2012), *Blue* (2018), etc.

Through his installations Apichatpong creates a multifaceted realm where narratives and perspectives entwine like interwoven rhizomes through his expert use of multichannel video projections. When many screens or surfaces are strategically arranged, viewers are invited to simultaneously traverse through a rich mosaic of feelings and ideas, immersing them in a world where various stories coexist. His installations are centred on the liminalities of memory, time, space, and the interaction between the past and present, reflecting Deleuze's investigation of how time folds and unfolds. His artistic creations evoke a profound sense of reflection and melancholy through the subtle fusing of individual and collective experiences. By revealing time's cyclical character and highlighting the relationship between the material and immaterial aspects of existence, Apichatpong undermines the linear understanding of time. As the past and present merge in these works, viewers are encouraged to test their own memories as they consider how fleeting life is and how entrenched notions of reality might be. Some of his notable installations include *Primitive* (2009), *Fireworks (Archives)* (2014), *Fever Room* (2016), *Invisibility* (2020) and *Memoria* (2021), which shares its name with his film.

---

[9] Steve Rose, "You Don't Have to Understand Everything: Apichatpong Weerasethakul", *The Guardian*, 11 November 2010, https://www.theguardian.com/film/2010/nov/11/apichatpong-weerasethakul-director-uncle-boonmee-interview.

The Style

Born in Bangkok in 1970, but living in Khon Kaen, Apichatpong's fondness for the rural expanses close at home resonate with distinct facets of the "local": the daily commuters, the human–animal kinship, the frequenting Thai troops, people going about their daily lives while nature and objects too participating in a symbiosis, the light-hearted gossips and sharing over dinner and the serene, wondrous jungles that frighten and delight. The curation, assemblage and play of spaces, places, nonhuman and humans inhabiting them reflect his training in Khon Kaen University, where he had pursued a bachelor's degree in architecture in 1994, following it later with a master's degree in filmmaking at the School of the Art Institute of Chicago in 1997. Known for his featuring of the northeast part of Thailand, and the frequent using of superstition, spirits and mysticism, his films have also been termed as "ghost cinema".[10] He explains that the interconnected presence of all that is around manifested in forms such as fables, Buddhist tales, comics, Thai horror films, old television shows and Thai novels—something which had become outdated overtime. His filmic style reincorporates the rich legacy of these presences, in a land where beliefs in such parallel existences, rituals and animity continue to matter[11]: "Thailand's atmosphere is unique. It might be hard to understand for foreigners. I actually feel a presence of the spirits when I am at home. When I am abroad, the dimensions change."[12]

Folklores pervade the figurative landscapes in his films, where characters narrate tales of human greed and karma: in *Tropical Malady* a lady who introduces herself to the two lead characters of the film (Keng and Tong), talks about a small monk offering a boon to two poor farmers, while a similar kind of tale is uttered by the doctor's companion (Pa Jane) in *Syndromes* when they are enjoying a delightful picnic at a park. Both these tales are of excessive greed, in accumulation of gold and silver: the farmers return to stock up the excess only to discover later that the gold turned into frogs and, in the second tale, the greedy farmer is shot by thieves. Folktales across his oeuvre offer a feeling of disconnect in connectivity, carrying superstition, like a game of Chinese whispers that

---

[10] Travis Jeppesen, "Ghost Cinema", *ARTnews.com*, 22 September 2020, https://www.artnews.com/art-in-america/features/ghost-cinema-63193/.

[11] Rose, 2010.

[12] Ryan Inouye, "Unknown Forces: Apichatpong Weerasethakul", *Redcat*, 2007, http://www.redcat.org/sites/redcat.org/files/gallery/linked-files/2011-06/0411unknown_09.pdf.

INTRODUCTION

begin one way and end up with retellings. In the sense, the connective elements present across films, where characters remember their past: in *Cemetery of Splendour* the mind reader recalls her previous life where she was a boy, who fell from a tree and died. In a particular scene from *Syndromes and a Century* where the monk is talking to the dentist, the latter recalls his childhood when he forced his brother to climb a tree, which results in a tragic death—a moment that still haunts him with guilt. These connective elements across his body of work spreads tentacularly, like nodes of network that carry, collect and bridge fragments of experiences. Memories, dreams, fantasies, longings and many such enigmas of the mind occupy the filmic labyrinth of Apichatpong's works: "Stories morph, change course, or start over; genre slips moment to moment from fiction to fantasy to documentary; characters shift shape, male to female, human to animal, extraterrestrial to earthling, and what they report is often unreliable; time becomes suspended, and setting ebbs from landscape into dreamscape."[13] More often, the rural Thailand features as the backdrop of Apichatpong's films, with its multitudes of life: the daily interactions, the humdrum affairs, the tedious tasks, the necessary rituals and customs. And all these reverberate with a distinct southeast Asian palette. On the surface, there are these local images of Isan, the livelihood of villagers and the continuing migration: some of the recurring subjects of his films that give his works a "national" character, enabling a global audience to explore the society, culture, politics and practices of both the rural and urban population of Thailand. While, on the other hand, his films also unearth concerns that are universal and complex. As Matthew Barrington observes, "When Weerasethakul uses his camera to focus on Isan and the exploration of the voiceless Thai inhabitants it becomes useful to place Weerasethakul as a transnational filmmaker whose films provide an international audience for the documenting of the marginalised individuals who populate Isan."[14]

Several of his works are dipped in the notion of the *body*—the various adventures and misadventures of bodilyness, the bliss, the pangs, the illnesses and the suffering. As memory (or the lack of it) takes the centre-stage in his oeuvre, bodies—young and old, male and female, rural and urban, real and ethereal—are often forgotten,

[13] Quandt, 2005.
[14] Matthew Barrington, "The Ethnographic Everyday in the Cinema of Apichatpong Weerasethakul— Photogénie", *Cinea*, 22 August 2017, https://cinea.be/ the-ethnographic-everyday-the-cinema-apichatpong-weerasethakul/.

remembered and reremembered in both quick and slow succession. Such embodied characters, in their varied entanglements with mnemonic and topographical occupations, haunt and are haunted by the setting. Various types of bodies inhabit these narratives, each with their own peculiarities, and very often they transform to become something or someone else, be it the various ill bodies, the shape-shifting shaman-tiger in *Tropical Malady*, the nonhuman "otherworldly" bodies like that of the spirit-cow in *Tropical Malady* or the sister spirits who can appear as humans in *Cemetery of Splendour*, the transformed "ape" body of Boonme's son or Uncle Boonme himself, whose soul seems to be a tenant in different bodies across time.

The "unhurried", hallucinatory quality of his films invites a patiently curious audience to traverse the mindscapes of Apichatpong: his dreams, memories and imagination splash unexpected visual combinations that stir up new vistas of thought, destabilizing grounded forms of rationality, offering a purview of boundless consciousness that flutter in an open world. The possibilities appear in duality, the modernity fusing in local myth, technology juxtaposed with superstition, science and spectrality accompanying one another to map trippy, fluid territories. This transfiguring fluidity and ease permeate the often-ethereal narrative, captured across still frames and in typical long shots, allowing contemplation and mindfulness to partake in a medium that otherwise characterizes a rapid, turbulent flow of images. Although these fluidities and seemingly ambiguous patterns that repeat in his films should not be read as meaningless abstractions. In the article, "The politics and aesthetics of non-representation" Marrero-Guillamón Issac develops the idea of "non-representation" wherein the world of Apichatpong's films is "not given in advance, but is rather a performative achievement, continuously (re)made" resulting in an "inventive, performative, world-making activity" as in, "enabling other ways to see the world" or "enacting other worlds to be seen".[15] In what he calls "open cinema",[16] one can also envisage images unbounded and freed from immediate rationality, having Dionysiac impulses that shock and shatter conventions, in the process of making and unmaking,

[15] Isaac Marrero-Guillamón, "The Politics and Aesthetics of Non-Representation: Re-Imagining Ethnographic Cinema with Apichatpong Weerasethakul", *Antípoda. Revista de Antropología y Arqueología* 33 (2018): 13–32, https://doi.org/10.7440/antipoda33.2018.02.

[16] Steve Rose, "'You Don't Have to Understand Everything': Apichatpong Weerasethakul", *The Guardian*, 11 November 2010, https://www.theguardian.com/film/2010/nov/11/apichatpong-weerasethakul-director-uncle-boonmee-interview.

INTRODUCTION

as in the introduction of *Nocturnal Fabulations*, Erin Manning writes how Apichatpong becomes an intercessor, where in his films the "intercessions" are "wildly layered", "activating cinema's potential for coming-between in times as yet uncharted".[17]

Apichatpong is also credited with the use of non-actors in his films, which preserves the rawness, authenticity and flavor of the land and its people. The non-actors, without having to depersonalize themselves, advocate a closer-to-self earthliness, as "non-professional" and "amateurish" as trees, orchids or rivers that lay bare in his filmic landscapes, separating themselves and us from the conventions of how we are used to seeing acting in films. This trajectory always renders a very discrete performance on screen and its subsequent affect/receptive experience. By other means too, the natural, gritty and unapologetic vision of Apichatpong is seen through a shot of breeze blowing through the trees, followed by a man openly defecating in a jungle; an innocent conversation among three women around a sleeping soldier in the hospital ends up with one of them attempting to settle an erection as the others are curiously amused at the peculiarity.

The films also have a tendency to move across genres, not as a means to complicate narratives or tangle up plotlines in some "kooky avant-garde" experiment, but to unravel deeply submerged personal, cultural and collective histories, pertaining to the highly intertextual framework that he employs across a plethora of local media where "even in the interior of each story emerges an adventure, an alternate route, inhabiting and multiplying points of view".[18]

Surreal Prognosis: *Syndromes and a Century* and *Cemetery of Splendour*

Premiering in 2006, *Syndromes and a Century* was majorly shot at a rural hospital and a medical centre in Bangkok. Dedicated to his parents who were both doctors, Apichatpong's childhood memories are entwined here with scenes from hospitals, as the film proceeds to capture fractions of routine procedures albeit odd incidents. Light-hearted comic scenes are infused with delightful romance, as interviews and medical check-ups repeat themselves across two halves of the film—one held at a rural

---

[17] Érik Bordeleau et al., *Nocturnal Fabulations: Ecology, Vitality and Opacity in the Cinema of Apichatpong Weerasethakul* (London: Open Humanities Press, 2017), 11.

[18] Bordeleau et al., 2017.

hospital and the other at a modern facility. The film had also suffered cuts by the Thai Board of Censors, where controversies were levied against four scenes: the monk playing guitar, two monks playing with toy UFOs, a doctor kissing his girlfriend at his place of work and a group of doctors drinking during working hours. He had protested it by leaving a black screen in the places of cuts, as it opened in Thailand with a limited screening. Later, he had formed the "Free Thai Cinema Movement" to appeal against the censorship, as well as petitioning for an age-based rating system. He wrote for *The Guardian*: "There will be those who wonder why this matters; why an independent film-maker's movie getting shelved should be of concern to anyone. It's because what happens in the film industry shows us more than how the board of censors works. It shows us how Thailand works. And that really is important".[19]

Cemetery of Splendour, released in 2015, had premiered in *Un Certain Regard* at Cannes. Shot at a school that acts as a clinic for soldiers consumed by a mysterious sleeping sickness, this film has a particularly rare infusion of science-fiction and magical realism pertaining to the presence of colour-changing tubes connected to the beds of soldiers and the frequent invocation of ghosts and a spirit talker. The plot, which has been deemed as subtly political, follows Jen (Jenjira Pongpas Widner), who is a volunteer at a temporary clinic, sheltering soldiers down with a mysterious sleeping sickness. The clinic is housed on the site of a school, which was in turn built on a cemetery of an ancient kingdom. Their beds have been equipped with machines having tall tubes that alter color, while filtering in good dreams in the form of a treatment. The symbolism in the film comments on the socio-political scenario of the region, as good dreams are fed artificially while the agents of action remain dormant and passive.[20]

As denoted in the essay "The Politics of Health in the Films of Apichatpong Weerasethakul", his films that frequently feature hospitals and health also allow for an inspection of medical surveillance, production of knowledge and the well-being of the Thai nation state, which in that sense shapes in an understanding of how the hierarchy of power functions in the projections of care.[21] These structures of power

---

[19] Apichatpong Weerasethakul, "Who Can Save My Flying Saucer?", *The Guardian*, 14 September 2007, https://www.theguardian.com/film/2007/sep/14/1.

[20] Violet Lucca, "Dream State: Cemetery of Splendour: Apichatpong Weerasethakul", *Film Comment*, 2016, https://www.filmcomment.com/article/apichatpong-weerasethakul-cemetery-of-splendor/.

[21] Noah Viernes, "The Politics of Health in the Films of Apichatpong

INTRODUCTION

in the manner of biopolitics that regulate and determine exclusion is also seen in *Blissfully Yours*, with Min as the immigrant, dependent on Roong and Orn for his treatment.[22]

Love, Transformation, and Transformations of Love: *Blissfully Yours, The Adventures of Iron Pussy* and *Tropical Malady*

Blissfully Yours, released in 2002, is a critically acclaimed film by Weerasethakul. It follows Min (Min Oo), an illegal Burmese immigrant living in Thailand with his girlfriend Roong (Kanokporn Tongaram), as they look to heal the rash that Min had incurred. With the help of Orn (Jenjira Jansuda), they get the prescribed medicines required to heal Min, meanwhile exposing the difficulties of living as an "alien" in a land different from one's own.

The Adventures of Iron Pussy premiered in 2003 and was made at a time when Weerasethakul faced a delay in funding for *Tropical Malady*. This action–musical comedy starring Michael Shaowanasai has been termed a hasty knockoff of *Tears of the Black Tiger* (2000), directed by Wisit Sasanatieng. It introduces a cross-dressing character, Iron Pussy, played by Shaowanasai, who switches between a female secret agent and a male clerk. Although lampooning and sketchy, he manages to subvert and ridicule the conventions of pop culture.

The 2004 film *Tropical Malady* (*Sud Pralad* in Thai, meaning "strange animal") bewildered many critics. Soldiers are posted at a small city to investigate the mysterious death of cattle in nearby farms, wherein one of them from the infantry Keng develops feelings for a local, Tong. The first section of the film captures their gradually developing romance, until the disappearance of Tong and departure of Keng. In the second half, the film frizzles into a dreamy, hallucinatory chase through a jungle, blending unorthodox and unfamiliar trajectories that lead onto a different narrative than the film began with. Keng is tasked to track down a shaman who can shape-shift into a tiger (Tong), the roles of which are played by the same actors. In the English title *Tropical Malady*, the highly suggestive term "malady" could be that of desire—the urge of being with someone in a world where the stigma associated with same-sex persists. The "tabooed" love that exists between the two men erupts in an atypical, hesitant fashion: the fear of being watched, the shame of being confronted, maybe even the guilt of being different—all

Weerasethakul", *AIU Global Review* 5 (2014): 1–28.

[22] Viernes, 2014.

these interrupting the "normalcy" of romance. After the split between the characters and the plotline, we find that the setting has shifted to a dark, uncertain and sometimes frightening "tropicality", something resembling the unconscious, where dreams and apprehensions muddle with the mysteries of the forest. It is harder still to render it as unrequited love and a narrative of repression:

> *Tropical Malady's* narrative of love between the two men cannot be reduced to a simple story of sexual repression, desire and death. Weerasethakul's deliberate staging of a mix of styles, his barely visible night times scenes, and his reference to shamanism and the spirit world – all of these suggest he is primarily interested in posing questions about what it means to be human.[23]

The Motley of Fact and Fiction: *Mysterious Objects at Noon* and *Mekong Hotel*

Weerasethakul's first major work was an independently produced experimental film that premiered in January 2000. Shot in Thailand, *Mysterious Objects at Noon* borrows a documentary style rendition, as locals collaborate to continue a story that has been passed on to them, similar to the French Surrealist game *corps exquis*, translated as "exquisite corpse", where an incomplete painting is passed from one painter to another so that they may improvise and add on, to complete the painting. The film too carries forward a story whose narrative evolves exponentially, through these various unscripted additions, making it an ever-expanding multi-genre project, with each layering complicating the intricacies of a single documentation with any singular ideology, as the emergent ideas that flow into function as a displacement of "conventional authorship".[24]

Mekong Hotel, which premiered in 2012, appeared at the Special Screenings section at Cannes, in the same year. The film was shot on hotel premises near the Mekong river that borders Thailand and Laos, and was based on a story "Ecstasy Garden" that he had written

[23] Barbara Creed, "Tropical Malady: Film & the Question of the Uncanny Human-Animal", *ETropic: Electronic Journal of Studies in the Tropics* 10 (2011), https://doi.org/10.25120/etropic.10.0.2011.3414.

[24] Michael Pattison, "Shapeshifter: Close-up on Apichatpong Weerasethakul's 'Mysterious Object at Noon'", *MUBI*, accessed 2 October 2021, https://mubi.com/notebook/posts/shapeshifter-close-up-on-apichat-pong-weerasethakul-s-mysterious-object-at-noon.

INTRODUCTION

in 2002. As a recurrent trope in his oeuvre, horror and supernatural presence makes way in the film, denoted by the girl's mother, who is a vampire-like spirit, feeding on human and animal flesh. The film contains rehearsals and interviews of "Ecstasy Garden" enmeshed with other fantastical genres that combine to express an absorbing yet perplexing tale. *Mekong Hotel*'s cast includes Jenjira Pongpas, also cast in *Cemetery, Blissfully Yours, Uncle Boonmee, Syndromes*, etc, and Sakda Kaewbuadee in the male lead, who is also seen in *Tropical Malady, Cemetery, Uncle Boonmee, Syndromes*, and in numerous other shorts by Weerasethakul. Both these films, while using a documentary style, capture not just the rich, imaginative textures of fictional storytelling but also act as a factual repository of life, livelihood, and pertinent issues of the north-eastern part of Thailand.

In Remembrance of Distant Dreams and Aberrant Memories: *Memoria* and *Uncle Boonme Who Can Recall His Past Lives*

The investigation of memory, sound, and its effects on how we make sense of the hidden depths of the world in *Memoria* (2021) is one of the film's remarkable achievements. The line between personal memories and a location's shared history becomes fuzzy as the movie probes the depths of both individual and collective retentions. In a way that transports the audience to a hypnotic state, Apichatpong deftly weaves together the protagonist's sensory experiences with the eerie Colombian rainforest landscape. The elusive nature of memory itself, wherein bits and pieces of impressions drift in and out of consciousness, is reflected in this ethereal exploration.

The *Palme d'Or* winner in 2010, *Uncle Boonme* was the first southeast Asian film to win the award. The film had been inspired by the book *A Man Who Can Recall His Past Lives* by Tibetan Buddhist monk, Phra Sripariyattiweti. It follows a farmer called Boonmee who is dying of kidney failure while undergoing dialysis and his strange ability to recall his past lives. It is an exploration of individual and collective past, specially surrounding the Nabua valley, where there had been accounts of trouble, violence and disappearances related to the brutal crackdown on Communism in the 1960s.[25] The film, like many among Weerasethakul's previous works, does not offer facial clarifications,

---

[25] "Uncle Apichatpong Who Ruminates on the Past, Present and Future", *Asia Society*, accessed 3 October 2021, https://asiasociety.org/uncle-apichatpong-who-ruminates-past-present-and-future.

although a familiarity with some of his previous installations and films assist in decrypting its manifold layers. Although *Uncle Boonme* had garnered major critical acclaim, it had also been shunned by some as being boring, pointless and obscure.[26] In the article titled "Apichatpong: Staging the Photo Session", J. Suter argues that there had been an odd reception for *Uncle Boonme* by international critics: "The critical discourse is being framed not by an understanding of local situation within the *actual* film, but in a curious way, Apichatpong's *prior* films' critical discourses are framing the discourse of *this* particular film, becoming a kind of quick paratextual aid in interpretation of *Uncle Boonmee*."[27] Referring to Apictahpong's own interview on *Uncle Boonme* wherein he speaks of remembrance in connection to Nabua and then to Pandit Chanrochanakit who writes on "history/political repression/ power of invisible forces in the Primitive Project and in the 2010 feature film *Uncle Boonmee*" she builds a case on the relatively misunderstood symbolism of the film and its "obscure" process of representation, as it embodies a distinct, subversive rewriting of the past, while also doubling up as a voice against censorship.[28]

The Significance of Apichatpong's Filmmaking

Thematically classified, the sections in this book elaborate on viewpoints that have been overlooked in academic assessments of Apichatpong's body of work, stimulating fresh discussions and in-depth analyses. Given that a sizable portion of his films are set in non-Western settings and frequently have enigmatic and challenging elements, they had eluded research and scrutiny for several years, sometimes even being (unfavourably) demarcated as "slow". In fact, Apichatpong was not relatively well-known in Thailand. In terms of significance, it is worth noting that Apichatpong's films cover a wide range of subject matter, from animism and spirituality to topics such as ethnicity, censorship, migration and repressed history. His works delve into the complexities of life and living, including themes of rebirth, transmi-gration, death and dying, and often probe the boundaries of reality,

---

[26] Lizzy Davies, "Cannes Winner Uncle Boonmee Panned by French Film Critics", *The Guardian*, 1 September 2010, https://www.theguardian.com/film/2010/sep/01/palme-dor-winner-uncle-boonmee.

[27] J. Suter, "Apichatpong: Staging the Photo Session", *Asian Cinema* 24, no. 1 (2013): 51–67, doi: 10.1386/ac.24.1.51_1.

[28] J. Suter, 2013.

venturing into the realms of surrealism and magical realism. Most of what is considered a "bizarre" element of Apichatpong comes from the fact that his films follow a non-traditional, radically innovative, and multilayered approach across cinematography, narrative technique and storyline. The unconventional methods that recur as a hallmark of "Apichatpong-esque" filmmaking could be traced over time, from the experimental documentary *Mysterious Objects at Noon* to his more recent *Memoria*. Being a quintessential filmmaker from southeast Asia, his films announce a radical departure from mainstream cinema, as many aspects which appear weird, bizarre or random to non-Thai audiences are laden with deep-rooted implications and resonate closely with those who are acquainted with the local folklore, history, mythology, superstition, Thai culture and intermingling sub-cultures. His surrealist tendencies are consequently linked to history, culture and politics of the land, and the moving image takes the character of active vocalization of these muffled memories and interspersed histories that have remained submerged for ages; meanwhile, as articulated across multiple works, his films also inhabit "transnational"[29] and "glocal"[30] characteristics. Surrealist artists used techniques like automatism and freeform to shock people into thinking about their society and social orientations. Their "bizarre" art pieces were designed to deviate the mind from the ordinary life and push them into contemplation where connections, situations and socio-historical conditions would be multivocally reconsidered. The cinematic style of Apichatpong is characterized by uncompromising rejections of representation, displaying an inherent unconventionality. His works project an unmatched style that embraces an original aesthetic vision. His films defy accepted cinematic norms and upend preconceived ideas about how a story ought to be delivered. Although some stylistic aspects of his films have been compared to other contemporaries, such as the slow and contemplative cinema of Lav Diaz and Tsai Ming-liang, the visual qualities of Chantal Akerman, to the dream-like quality of legendary directors such as Tarkovsky, Apichatpong invites us to explore the limitless potential of the moving image as he keeps pushing the limits of cinematic art.

---

[29] Brenda Hollweg and Krstić Igor, *World Cinema and the Essay Film: Transnational Perspectives on a Global Practice* (Edinburgh: Edinburgh University Press, 2021).

[30] Nenad Jovanovic, "Nostalgic from the Hip: Apichatpong Weerasethakul's Lomokino Short", *Quarterly Review of Film and Video* (2021), doi: 10.1080/10509208.2021.1966289.

The Chapters

The chapters in this volume have been divided into four sections corresponding to four broad areas: Time, Nonhuman, Mind, and Forms and Representations. In the first section "Time", Patrícia Sequeira Brás and Francesco Quario reflect upon the aspect of temporality in general and the debate surrounding "slow cinema" in particular. In the second section "Nonhuman", Duncan Caillard and Çağatay Emre Doğan locate the nonhuman, animate or inanimate, in the select works of Apictahpong and underscore the fluid binary between the human and the nonhuman in those works. In the third section "Mind", Elizabeth Sikes, Alessandro Ferraro and Jeffner Allen delve into the deep recesses of the mindscape and try to map the difficult terrain of Apichatpong's topological spaces. And in the fourth section, "Forms and Representations", Jade de Cock de Rameyen, Palita Chunsaengchan, Sivaranjini and Anchalee Chaiworaporn help us in understanding the making and unmaking of cinematic sutures in Apichatpong, and discuss in depth the production, politics and poetics of representation in his cinema.

In Chapter 1 Patrícia Sequeira Brás analyzes Apichatpong Weerasethakul's use of extended duration to argue that his aesthetic strategy seems to enhance the precariousness nature of his films' on-screen bodies. The chapter engages with some of the discussions that position Apichatpong's films under the term "slow cinema", as well as those that identify a dialectical tension between Apichatpong's depictions of urban and rural, global and local landscapes. The term "slow cinema" is often applied to films that use extended duration as an aesthetic paradigm within contemporary cinema. Its proponents argue that slow cinema evolve "from spaces that have been indirectly affected or left behind by globalization" in an attempt to rescue "extended temporal structures from the accelerated tempo of late capitalism". Accordingly, extended duration appears to be a stylistic device in direct opposition to fast-paced capitalist flows. A similar argument can be found, however, among the detractors of slow cinema and/or contemplative cinema, including Steven Shaviro. For him, extended duration is a "cliché" device, essentially retrograde and negligent to the ways in which globalization and technological innovation have profoundly changed the world in the last decades. However, the assumption that extended filmic temporalities are nostalgic of a pre-industrial era is imprecise, since capitalism is capable of capturing a variety of temporalities and intensities. If not, how would capital expropriate value from social reproduction? Following this argument, the chapter discusses how his use of extended duration evidences not only the ways in which time is secreted from the films' on-screen bodies, but also how ordinary bodily gestures are subjected to the relentless repetition of social reproduction. Contrary to the argument of the proponents and detractors of "slow cinema", the chapter posits that these gestures are not outside fast-paced capitalists flows but instead captured by the logic of capital to worn out the bodies that perform them.

Due to their recurring portrayals of everyday situations framed through static, long takes, the films of Apichatpong Weerasethakul can be said to belong to the trend of "slow cinema", a style defined by its ability to exacerbate the spectator's awareness of the passing of time. As such, slow films engender a type of time-image: a category of cinematic images described by philosopher Gilles Deleuze as being evoked by pure optical and sound situations, which are eschewals of montage and narrative progression that cause spectators to experience time in its pure state. Referring to the theories of Henri Bergson, Deleuze interprets time as *durée*, a flux wherein the past constantly interpenetrates the present. When experiencing *durée*, the viewer is made at once aware of the past (recollection), the present and the future (anticipation), which would otherwise appear separated if inscribed in a linearized narrative. Through his slow cinema, Apichatpong is therefore able to evoke multiple temporalities at once. His subject matters work in tandem with this, as the director often draws inspiration from his personal memories as well as Thailand's collective memory in order to craft his narratives.

In Chapter 2 Francesco Quario looks at two of Apichatpong's films, *Syndromes and a Century* and *Cemetery of Splendour*, in order to individuate in them this inscription of memory within cinematic time. Both films are set in hospitals, evoking his childhood, as he grew up with two doctors as parents. *Syndromes and a Century*'s main characters are deliberately based on the director's parents, while *Cemetery of Splendour* is set in his hometown of Khon Kaen. Despite this personal framework, both films also rely on imaginary elements. *Syndromes and a Century* portrays two alternative realities through two narrative strands set, respectively, in an old countryside hospital and a modern city hospital. Meanwhile, *Cemetery of Splendour* depicts a group of soldiers afflicted by a supernatural sickness, caused by ancient spirits that haunt their dreams. Thus, both films create a direct dialogue between the present and the past, the real and the imaginary. Moreover, both films address (and implicate) the spectator's own experience of time through their shared use of slowness.

In Chapter 3 Duncan Caillard considers the recurrence of stray animals across the work of Apichatpong Weerasethakul and addresses the ways in which he frames an ethical intersection between the experiences of animals, migrants and queer characters across his films. In her book *Stray*, Barbara Creed theorizes the stray as a being who—due to rising threats of political repression, economic inequality and ecological disaster—has diverged from or been rejected by their community, applying equally to human and non- human animals. Forced to the spatio-cultural margins of society, strays form tactical relationships with other marginal beings in order to survive, and therefore not only frame the ways in which migrant, queer and animal experiences can be considered in continuum with one another, but also stage new ethical relations between them in their shared state of precarity. For Apichatpong, strays and straying recur across his films, but also impact his filmmaking process itself. His characters, from wandering dogs and chickens to queer, impoverished and dislocated humans, exist in uncertain spaces, frequently leaving behind the restrictive structures of urban life behind for the open possibilities of rural life and the wilderness. Yet considering Apichatpong's filmmaking more broadly, straying also serves as a creative practice, as—like the recurrent images of dogs moving in uncertain ways within a frame—his plots are often spasmodic and unfixed. In linking his stray practice and representation with the human–animal ethics of Creed, Emmanuel Levinas and Jacques Derrida, this chapter restages the ethical encounters between humans and animals experienced in his films, concentrating on their manifestations in his key three early films: "stray intimacy" in *Tropical Malady*, "stray temporality" in *Blissfully Yours*, and concluding with analysis of Apichatpong's "stray creative practice" in his first feature film, *Mysterious Object at Noon*. Through this analysis, the chapter establishes straying as a key component of his ethics and creative practice, providing a unifying concept through which to understand the intersecting migrant, animal and queer subjectivities that define his work.

In one of his interviews, Apichatpong Weerasethakul explains a sequence in *Cemetery of Splendour* in which the protagonists walk through a place where a palace once stood. He states that, apart from the layers of memory and traces of the past, there is an influence of animist culture, in the creation of the scene where "the trees and every object have other spirits". *Cemetery of Splendour* alludes to a strong sense of genius loci, and how layers of memory, traces of past lives fill the otherwise ordinary leftover spaces. This emphasis on space and objects is not an exception in his films. In fact, in Chapter 4 Çağatay Emre Doğan argues that Apichatpong's cinema gives power to the objects, spaces, and relationality to challenge the authority of the camera and anthropocentric imagination of the viewer. One can see this, for instance, in *Uncle*

Boonmee, where the jungle, free of visible action or spatial hierarchies, becomes open to expectations and possibilities. Here, the nonhuman world ceases to be a prop for an action, nor a décor, a background for the events but instead, through static camera and a patient gaze, the jungle becomes the main experience itself, asking the viewer to stop searching for a place of authority as an anthropocentric agent. Instead, we have bodies in space that relate to each other in multitudes of ways. Wide-angle landscape-like long takes of interiors show how bodies redefine themselves in a set of dynamic relations with each other, objects and nature. In this emphasis on objects and their nonhierarchical relationality, Apichatpong's cinema gives us the much needed tools to think about the major questions that New Materialist philosophies and speculative realism raise. Indeed, Karen Barad's conception of intra-action between objects that undoes the relationship between a human subject and a passive object and Gilbert Simondon's emphasis on the individual lives of the objects are two planes that we can use to think about the question of space and objective relations raised by Apichatpong's cinema, where neither the landscapes nor the buildings are the passive receivers of our gaze. By exploring how built and unbuilt spaces and the objects are put into relations of becoming through subverting cinematic gaze towards an object-oriented plane, especially salient in *Uncle Boonmee Who Can Recall His Past Lives*, *Cemetery of Splendour* and *Syndromes and a Century*, this chapter claims that Apichatpong's cinema opens up questions of the possibility of another form of objective relation, one that emphasizes the individual moments of the nonhuman and demands another perspective that seeks to involve the experience of this objectivity in its multiple relations.

In Chapter 5 Elizabeth Sikes explores the role of cinematic caesura and its relationship to memory or, better, a kind of nonmemory that blows open the future, in Apichatpong Weerasethakul's film, *Uncle Boonmee Who Can Recall His Past Lives*, and his video installation project, *Primitive*, which the film was a part of. The film is a ghost story, one that also shows us what Derrida claimed, namely that cinema, when combined with psychoanalysis, is an art and science of ghosts. The chapter connects the figure of the ghost and phantom in the *Primitive* project with Apichatpong's use of the cinematic caesura, a cut that produces a counter-rhythmic interruption in the movement of the narrative image. The most radical of these cuts produces an excellent example of what Deleuze calls a "pure time image", an image uncoupled from its subordination to movement. The automatism of film—that it makes its own movement, untying itself from the mind or body for its motility—has been much theorized in film literature.

For Deleuze, this has the power to generate in us a *spiritual automaton*, that is, thought, which reacts in turn on movement. For this thought to be generated by movement that actually opens up the future as the very possibility for becoming-other, rather than a repetition locked mainly in the past of habit or memory, time must be introduced into thinking; the movement-image must become a time-image. The chapter illustrates the introduction of the time-image in several examples from the *Primitive* project and *Uncle Boonmee*. Here we see better how the caesura works its effects on the sensorimotor unity of the image by shocking the spiritual automaton with something disjointed within the image itself—whether it be the self-conscious play of styles, the recursive use of a particular image in order to decouple it from the movement of the play, the insertion of still images, or the use of a split screen. In both cases we might argue that these qualify as examples of what Deleuze calls the "time-image" in cinema. At the end of the chapter, Sikes turns to Bracha Ettinger's work on the uncanny and her efforts in *The Matrixial Borderspace* to trace out the intergenerational transmission of trauma, a kind of non-memory, or memory encrypted in amnesia, that is linked to the womb and earth, and which the chapter suggests is the stillness wandering within the caesura of the image in Apichatpong's *Primitive* project.

Focused on an analysis of the meaning of social and collective dream in Apichatpong's films, the aim of Chapter 6 by Alessandro Ferraro is to establish a relation between the way to consider the sleeping condition and, consequently, the act of dreaming, with the physical concreteness of the body able to produce the dream itself. The dialectic between something physical, as the reality of the illness in *Cemetery of Splendour*, and something immaterial, as the absorbed yet precarious conditions of the Thai soldiers, can be intended as a concrete abstraction—"so physically grounded yet truly immaterial" (Luetticken, Malik, Galison): this dialectic condition can be found of course in lots of other works by the Thai filmmaker, where his interest in spiritual animism is often combined with a bodily materialism. Besides a reflection on the corporeity and the intangibility of the dreaming-body, in *Cemetery of Splendour* there is also a peculiar declination of the political and the collective, presented through a layering of metaphors: it is the purpose to demonstrate how the sleeping condition, as well as the act of dreaming, can be considered both as an "escapist" solution and also a concrete political act. Particular attention is going to be dedicated to the case-study of the SLEEPCINEMAHOTEL (Rotterdam-International Film Festival) where he displayed—through a peculiar curatorial methodology that can be considered a truly artistic solution—films and

INTRODUCTION 19

videos in order to induce the audience to altered states of consciousness and to propose an intimate and sincere way of experiencing movies. In order to create an interdisciplinary and dialectic approach, the chapter considers contemporary art films and videos such as the solipsistic ode to memory, dream and the self shown in *I ... Dreaming* by Stan Brakhage (1988) and also *Dreamland: The Coney Island Psychoanalitic Society Amateur Dream Films* by Zoe Beloff (2012), a study on the meaning of displaying dreams through film.

In Chapter 7 Jeffner Allen's lyrical and poetic essay paddles through the moving images, drawing on the synapses that connect Apichatpong's mind to his films. She calls Apichatpong "an architect of beautiful images in film and writing", and thereupon in the oscillatory looping of filmmaking and meditation across and beyond the region of Isan, in northeast Thailand, she highlights the Cambodian Khmer and animist roots of Apichatpong's productions. Tracing the immersions in motile relations between *Sakda (Rousseau), Primates' Memories*, the multivalent *Primitive*, and *Luminous People*, she projects how our minds linger amid *Cactus River, Mekong Hotel, Photophobia*, and *Fireworks (Archives)*, motivated by a cinema described by its maker as "not meant to be monumental, but weightless". She shows how the performances of decomposition in a landscape of ghosts coexist with the living, collaborative transformations among hybrid beings, dreaming and awakening to the dehiscent, though utterly simple, cohabitation of film and meditation. Ruminating on themes like reincarnation, the play of shimmering light and darkness, the ideation of river and waters, Jeffner also outlines the historical, factual and often mythological signif-icance, illuminating the connections as she moves along, following Apichatpong's camera.

Seven videos, two online shorts, an artist book filled with story bits and drawings, two photographs, and the prize-winning feature film *Uncle Boonmee Who Can Recall His Past Lives*: those are the miscel-laneous ingredients composing Apichatpong's multiplatform project *Primitive*. Although the whole stubbornly resists dispersion, one would be at pains to understand its narrative configuration. While critics generally agree on Apichatpong's features' narrativity and on how they challenge traditional narrative schemes, they are at pains to describe its logics. Understanding the narratives of his cinema requires us to take a detour by his museum installations. Apichatpong's *Primitive* illustrates a recent phenomenon in artists' cinema, where feature and installation are embedded into a single filmic universe extending across platforms and media (e.g. Salome Lamas, Dora Garcia and Ben Rivers). How do works shot in distinct locations, reflecting a strong generic, stylistic and medial diversity intersect? *Uncle Boonmee* has received extensive critical attention, but little has been said on its narrative articulation with the more overtly political videos of *Primitive*. In Chapter 8 Jade de Cock de Rameyen examines the workings of plot in Apichatpong's *Primitive*. If, according to postclassical narratology, plots involve storyworld virtualities rather than the logical planification of story, then the concept is particularly adequate to evaluate worldly construction in transmedia storytelling. How does Apichatpong's installation intrigue us? The analysis is informed by the erotization of loss in Buddhist melancholia and Buddhadasa Bikkhu's *suññatā*—the void of self as means of interspecies transformation. In turn, *Primitive* shows the limits of narratology, for its disciplinary focus on chronology does not reflect museum visitors' experience of looping films, nor the dynamics of screenic and acoustic contamination.

In one of his interviews in 2010, Apichatpong Weerasethakul referred to the influence of his training in architecture on the vision of his films as following: "Eisenstein, Dmytryk, Lang, they all came from architecture or engineering ... I think that the time element in architecture and film is shared. You decide the angles, the openings, the relationship of time to space, the light."[31] Apichatpong's cinematic designs of time, space and light are of course one of the topics most discussed by scholars and cinephiles alike. In Chapter 9, Palita Chunsaengchan turns to another important aspect of architecture—the relational symbiosis between space and inhabitants. The chapter argues that the distinct way in which Apichatpong worked with camera (cinematography), mise-en-scène and editing allows traumatic or uninhabitable spaces to emerge as a political venue for vulnerable communities. This chapter is most interested in spaces that are foreign to the director, and yet instil potentials for political critique. Thus, it first traces the role of Nabua, a town in the northeast of Thailand that has inspired a 2009 art installation prior to the making of the Cannes-awarded *Uncle Boonmee Who Can Recall His Past Lives*, and then it examines spaces and communities near Mekong river as they were significantly evoked in Apichatpong's documentary-style shorts, *Cactus River* (*Khong Lang Nam*, 2012) and *Ashes* (2012). By analyzing his cinematic design of spaces, this chapter underlines not only the political commitment of the director but also the significance of communities both in his cinematic world and in reality that lies beyond his cinema.

Apichatpong Weerasethakul's cinema dwells at the margin. It possesses a liminal, transcendent aura within and around, both in

---

[31] https://filmmakermagazine.com/19141-past-tense/.

INTRODUCTION

literal and metaphorical realms. Contradictions coexist in his cineverse; differences merge, an aleatoric portal emerges anywhere, anytime. A river separates two lands, *Sud Pralad* (the Thai title of *Tropical Malady*); a hybrid monster born to two species wanders between the nocturnal jungle landscapes of Isan to a fleeting afternoon at an urban construction site in Bangkok. Personal to political, memory to reincarnation, man to animal—letters finding their way back home. Analog dissolves to digital; moving image attains stillness. The idea of the real is questionably tossed between narrated memories, staged photographs and meta-references. In his first feature, *Mysterious Objects at Noon*, a cinéma vérité beginning is abruptly broken to the construction of a labyrinthine narrative juxtaposed with its re-enactments. The *Primitive* project, a collaborative work with the teens of Isan, revisits a consciously forgotten past of the nation through collective memory. In *Worldly Desires* and *Mekong Hotel*, an unfinished film project runs as a parallel narrative breaking the fourth wall. Through a music track playing in the background leaking out of a rehearsal session, *Mekong Hotel* creates a meta-cinema with actors reading out of scripts and looking directly at the camera. The staged photographs from the *Primitive* in the coda sequence of *Uncle Boonmee Who Can Recall His Past Lives* present the "immaterial" as Barthes puts in *Camera Lucida*, the photographic image as a "return of the dead", embalming time that gets lost in the fleeting of moving images. A set of non-professional actors, whose real names are taken by the characters, continue their presence from film to film and, as their real stories find their way into the cinematic narrative, the blending of real-reel becomes uncanny. In Chapter 10, Sivaranjini discusses some of the hybrid tendencies in Apichatpong's cinema by identifying, analyzing and creating parallels to ethnofiction, docufiction, participatory or collaborative cinema in the context of socio-political realities, national identity and the self.

The final chapter, by Anchalee Chaiworaporn, explores the contemporary portrayal of global film finance and its effect on the construction of cinematic authorship in Apichatpong's works, in which the author prefers to define it as "(post)-interstitial" authorship. In this study, the author proposes two dimensions of Apichatpong's "(post)-interstitial" mode of production: the first part explores the characteristics of local and global film financing surrounding Apichatpong's filmmaking trajectories in order to see how the interstitial mode of production is characterized nowadays, especially in relation to global arts cinema. In the final part, the hybrid identity and aesthetics that have been accentuated in Apichatpong's cinema is analysed by using both textual and contextual methods.

Bibliography

Balmont, James. "Meet the 'David Lynch of Thailand' and His Queer, Surrealist Cinema". *Dazed.* 5 January 2021. https://www.dazeddigital.com/film-tv/article/51589/1/apichatpong-weerasethakul-david-lynch-of-thailand-queer-surrealist-cinema.

Barrington, Matthew. "The Ethnographic Everyday in the Cinema of Apichatpong Weerasethakul—Photogénie". *Cinea.* 22 August 2017. https://cinea.be/the-ethnographic-everyday-the-cinema-apichatpong-weerasethakul/.

Bordeleau, Érik, Toni Pape, Ronald Rose-Antoinette and Adam Szymanski. *Nocturnal Fabulations: Ecology, Vitality and Opacity in the Cinema of Apichatpong Weerasethakul.* London. Open Humanities Press. 2017.

Creed, Barbara. "Tropical Malady: Film & the Question of the Uncanny Human–Animal". *ETropic: Electronic Journal of Studies in the Tropics* 10 (2011). https://doi.org/10.25120/etropic.10.0.2011.3414.

Davies, Lizzy. "Cannes Winner Uncle Boonmee Panned by French Film Critics". *The Guardian.* 1 September 2010. https://www.theguardian.com/film/2010/sep/01/palme-dor-winner-uncle-boonmee.

Feinstein, Howard. "Past Tense". *Filmmaker.* 24 January 2011. https://filmmakermagazine.com/19141-past-tense/.

Hollweg, Brenda and Krstić Igor. *World Cinema and the Essay Film: Transnational Perspectives on a Global Practice.* Edinburgh. Edinburgh University Press. 2021.

Inouye, Ryan. "Unknown Forces: Apichatpong Weerasethakul". *Redcat.* 2007. http://www.redcat.org/sites/redcat.org/files/gallery/linked-files/2011-06/0411unknown_09.pdf.

Jeppesen, Travis. "Ghost Cinema". *ARTnews.com.* 22 September 2020. https://www.artnews.com/art-in-america/features/ghost-cinema-63193/.

Jovanovic, Nenad. "Nostalgic from the Hip: Apichatpong Weerasethakul's Lomokino Short". *Quarterly Review of Film and Video* (2021): 1–17. https://doi.org/10.1080/10509208.2021.1966289.

Kuiper, K. "Apichatpong Weerasethakul". *Encyclopedia Britannica.* 12 July 2021. https://www.britannica.com/biography/Apichatpong-Weerasethakul.

Langley, Patrick. "Apichatpong Weerasethakul". *Frieze.* 2014. Accessed 1 October 2021. https://www.frieze.com/article/apichatpong-weerasethakul.

Lucca, Violet. "Dream State: Cemetery of Splendour: Apichatpong Weerasethakul". *Film Comment.* 2016. https://www.filmcomment.com/article/apichatpong-weerasethakul-cemetery-of-splendour/.

Marrero-Guillamón, Isaac. "The Politics and Aesthetics of Non-Representation: Re-Imagining Ethnographic Cinema with Apichatpong Weerasethakul". *Antípoda. Revista de Antropología y Arqueología* 22 (2018): 13–32. https://doi.org/10.7440/antipoda33.2018.02.

Mercer, Nicholas. "Between the Global and the Local: The Cultural Geopolitics of Apichatpong Weerasethakul's Film Aesthetics". *Linguistics, Literature and Culture: Millennium Realities and Innovative Practices in Asia*. Newcastle. Cambridge Scholars Publishing. 2012. 191–216.

Pattison, Michael. "Shapeshifter: Close-up on Apichatpong Weerasethakul's 'Mysterious Object at Noon'". *MUBI*. Accessed 3 October 2021. https://mubi.com/notebook/posts/shapeshifter-close-up-on-apichatpong-weerasethakul-s-mysterious-object-at-noon.

Pavan, Benoit. "Memoria, the New Sensory Journey from Apichatpong Weerasethakul". Festival de Cannes 2021. 19 July 2021. https://www.festival-cannes.com/en/festival/actualites/articles/memoria-the-new-sensory-journey-from-apichatpong-weerasethakul.

Quandt, James. "Exquisite Corpus: The Films of Apichatpong Weerasethakul". *Artforum International Magazine*. 1 May 2005. https://www.artforum.com/print/200505/exquisite-corpus-the-films-of-apichatpong-weerasethakul-8835.

Rose, Steve. "'You Don't Have to Understand Everything': Apichatpong Weerasethakul". *The Guardian*. 11 November 2010. https://www.theguardian.com/film/2010/nov/11/apichatpong-weerasethakul-director-uncle-boonmee-interview.

Suter, Jacquelyn. "Apichatpong: Staging the Photo Session". *Asian Cinema* 24, no. 1 (2013): 51–67. https://doi.org/10.1386/ac.24.1.51_1.

"Uncle Apichatpong Who Ruminates on the Past, Present and Future". *Asia Society*. Accessed 3 October 2021. https://asiasociety.org/uncle-apichatpong-who-ruminates-past-present-and-future.

Viernes, Noah. "The Politics of Health in the Films of Apichatpong Weerasethakul". *AIU Global Review* 5 (2014): 1–28.

Weerasethakul, Apichatpong. "Who Can Save My Flying Saucer?". *The Guardian*. 14 September 2007. https://www.theguardian.com/film/2007/sep/14/1.

Time

1

Time, Social Reproduction and the Precarious Body in the Films of Apichatpong Weerasethakul

Patrícia Sequeira Brás

In this chapter, I discuss the use of extended duration in the films of Apichatpong Weerasethakul, examining at length *Blissfully Yours* (2002) and *Syndromes and a Century* (2006) but also reflecting upon films such as *Mysterious Object at Noon* (2000), *Tropical Malady* (2004), *Uncle Boonmee Who Can Recall His Past Lives* (2010) and *Cemetery of Splendour* (2015). I argue that in his films, durational aesthetics enhances the precariousness of the bodies onscreen thus revealing the enduring nature of social reproduction. In my argument, I engage with the theoretical debates that shaped the concept of "slow cinema" and with the economic category of social reproduction "used to describe the institutionalized separation between productive and reproductive activities" within a capitalist economy.[1] In this way, I intend to conclude that in the films of Apichatpong durational aesthetics renders visible the ways social reproduction is captured by the logic of late capitalism.

Slow Cinema

The term 'slow cinema' comprehends a variety of films that use extended duration as aesthetic practice. It is often deployed in theoretical debates that attempt to redress duration as an aesthetic paradigm within contemporary cinema. Its proponents have highlighted the possibilities of cinematic temporality to amplify the "awareness of the viewing" experience[2] as well as argued that because extended duration challenges

---

[1] Emma Dowling, *The Care Crisis* (London and New York: Verso, 2021), 38.
[2] Tiago de Luca, "Slow Time, Visible Cinema: Duration, Experience, and Spectatorship", *Cinema Journal* 56, no. 1 (Fall 2016): 25.

meaning, it demands a type of unproductive labouring from the film audience.[3] Others have also explicated that the "distinctive aesthetics of slow cinema tend to emerge from spaces that have been indirectly affected or left behind by globalisation".[4] According to Matthew Flanagan, filmmakers associated with *slow* have turned their cameras to people living in remote areas, and with livelihoods dependent on "the performance of (waged or unwaged) agricultural and manufacturing work that is increasingly obscured by the macro volatility of finance-capital's huge speculative flows".[5] In addition, Flanagan argues that slow cinema belongs to the aesthetic legacy of modern cinema and, as such, it is in direct opposition to Hollywood action films, and their use of fast camera moves and speedy montage.

Horacio Muñoz Fernández, on the other hand, identifies a nostalgic tendency within slow films, but expounds that Apichatpong and others employ formal characteristics without "implying a kind of apology for a primitive, idyllic, pure pre-industrial time".[6] Accordingly, these filmmakers have used prolonged duration instead because they either "value the haptic qualities of sensorial images" or, they aim to "capture the quotidian in its temporal integrity or even, offer a critique of the reason of History".[7] I will argue, then, that in the case of Apichatpong the use of prolonged duration is capable of not only capturing "the

---

[3] Karl Schoonover, "Wastrels of Time: Slow Cinema's Labouring Body, the Political, the Spectator and the Queer", in *Slow Cinema*, eds. Tiago de Luca and Nuno Barradas Jorge (Edinburgh: Edinburgh University Press, 2016).

[4] Matthew Flanagan, "'Slow Cinema': Temporality and Style in Contemporary Art and Experimental Film", D.Phil. thesis, University of Exeter, 2012, 118.

[5] Flanagan, 2012.

[6] "Algunos de los cineastas a los que se ha incluido dentro del Slow Cinema sí que responden a los parámetros enunciados y defendidos por Flanagan, Tuttle o Mai, a pesar de sus diferencias. Sin embargo, otros muchos, como Pedro Costa, Wang Bing, Lisandro Alonso, Apichatpong Weerasethakul, Jia Zhang-ke o Raya Martin emplean las características formales con las que se define el Slow Cinema sin que la lentitud y la duración supongan una especie de apología de un tiempo preindustrial primitivo, edénico y puro, ni un intento de convertir a la imagen cinematográfica en un sucedáneo de la imagen pictórica." Horacio Muñoz Fernández, "Cierta tendencia (nostálgica) del slow cinema", *Aniki* 4, no. 2 (2017): 308; my translation.

[7] "la lentitud se emplea aquí para favorecer la hapticidad de las imagines sensoriales, para captar lo cotidiano en su integridad temporal, o para hacer crítica de la razón de la Historia." Fernández, 2017; my translation.

quotidian" but also making intelligible the ways in which "its temporal integrity" is seized by global capitalism. Later in the chapter, I will engage with Foucault's argument regarding the disciplining of bodies since the temporal integrity of the quotidian, which constitutes reproductive time, is intricately tied to the body politics.

Still, Tiago de Luca and Nuno Barradas Jorge argue that slow cinema has a political potential in so far as it shares "its discursive genesis with a much larger socio-cultural movement whose aim is to rescue extended temporal structures from the accelerated tempo of late capitalism".[8] Accordingly, the term *slow* has "become a convenient prefix for a number of grass-roots movements such as 'slow media', 'slow travel' and 'slow food'".[9] Despite recognizing that the filmmakers associated with durational aesthetics are not necessarily "engaged with, or even aware of these movements",[10] Luca and Jorge conclude that extended duration has a political effect because it is capable of rendering visible the marginal spaces that subsist outside capital's circulation. In my view, however, their argument, far from confirming cinema's political possibilities, ignores the commodification of the prefix *slow*. I would even argue that such commodification evidences instead the creative capacity of late capitalism to capture different temporalities as well as different subjectivities.

According to Jacques Rancière, art is political when it produces an "aesthetic experience" that "disturbs the way in which bodies fit their functions and destinations".[11]As the French philosopher expounds, the political effect of an artistic aesthetic experience resides in the possibility of "a multiplication of connections and disconnections that reframe the relation between bodies, the world where they live and the way in which they are 'equipped' for fitting it".[12] Luca and Jorge argue, however, that slow cinema's political potential resides in the deployment of temporal structures that are seemingly in opposition to fast-pace capitalist financial flows. Yet this assumption is imprecise, since capitalism is capable of capturing a variety of temporalities and intensities. Otherwise, how could capital expropriate value from social reproduction?

[8] Tiago de Lucas and Nuno Barradas Jorge, "Introduction: From Slow Cinema to Slow Cinemas", in *Slow Cinema* (Edinburgh: Edinburgh University Press, 2016), 3.
[9] de Lucas and Nuno Barradas, 2016.
[10] de Lucas and Nuno Barradas, 2016.
[11] Jacques Rancière, *The Emancipated Spectator* (London, New York: Verso, 2008), 72.
[12] Rancière, 2008.

Among the detractors of slow cinema and contemplative cinema, terms that often collapse, Steven Shaviro argues that extended duration is a cliché device, essentially retrograde and negligent to the ways in which globalization and technological innovation have profoundly changed the world in the last decades.[13] His accusation originates from the fact that slow cinema and other "slow" movements appear to "blame directly or indirectly technology [...], or [be] against what it appears to generate: speed".[14]However, the reason why these filmmakers can deploy prolonged duration as a formal procedure is precisely because of the development of audio-visual technology that made HD video cameras ubiquitous[15]; because of this, these filmmakers can hardly be blamed for "entertaining Luddite sentiments".[16]

Contrary to the argument of both the proponents and detractors of slow cinema, Apichatpong's films are neither nostalgic of a pre-industrial era, nor show any attempt to rescue extended temporalities from fast-paced capitalist flows. On the other hand, the Thai filmmaker often depicts the plight of migrants coming from Thailand's neighbouring countries, as in the case of the undocumented Burmese migrant Min in *Blissfully Yours* and the case of the Laotian carer in *Uncle Boonmee Who Can Recall His Past Lives*. Accordingly, rather than negligent, his films evidence instead a cautious observation on the impact of globalization.

In this respect, I return to some extent to my argument vis-à-vis the use of extended duration in *Jeanne Dielman, 23 quai du Commerce, 1080 Bruxelles* (Chantal Akerman, 1975) and *Three Sisters* (Wang Bing, 2012) discussed elsewhere,[17] in which I argued that durational aesthetics emphasizes the relentless and repetitive character of the reproductive labor performed by the protagonists of both films, Jeanne and Yingying,

---

[13] Stephen Shaviro, "Slow Cinema vs. Fast Films", *The Pinocchio Theory*, 2010, http://www.shaviro.com/Blog/?p=891.

[14] "culpa, directa o indirectamente, a la tecnología de aquello contra lo que se opone, o contra lo que en apariencia surge: la velocidad." Fernández, 2017, 301; my translation.

[15] Fernández in his article cites Pedro Costa, who is an advocate of the digital because in his words, provides him time and the possibility of "being more patient, and available for other at any given moment"; my translation from: "el digital le proporciona tiempo y la posibilidad 'de ser mas paciente, de estar disponible para los outros en cualquier momento'". Fernandez, 2017, 303; my translation.

[16] Lutz Koepnick, *On Slowness: Toward an Aesthetic of the Contemporary* (New York: Colombia University Press, 2014), 13.

[17] Patrícia Sequeira Brás, "Time and Reproductive Labour in *Jeanne Dielman, 23 quai du Commerce, 1080 Bruxelles* (1975) and *Three Sisters* (2012)", in "Work" (Spring 2019) 9 *Parse*, ed. Marina Vishmidt.

TIME, SOCIAL REPRODUCTION AND THE PRECARIOUS BODY   31

respectively. In the case of the films of Apichatpong, however, women and migrants, and male and female doctors perform these chores associated with care and social reproduction. Illness is a recurrent theme (i.e., *Blissfully Yours, Uncle Boonmee Who Can Recall His Past Lives* and *Cemetery of Splendour*); and hospitals are frequently used as set locations (i.e., *Syndromes and a Century* and *Cemetery of Splendour*) evidencing a concern with the precarious nature of living bodies. The use of prolonged duration in his films expose in turn the ways through which time is secreted from on-screen bodies, because these bodies are either unwell or are often seen performing domestic chores, sleeping or having sex. The depiction of doctor–patient interactions seems to disclose, on the other hand, inherent power relations as well as the purpose of health care for the control of the social body.

Time and the Laboring of Viewership

Filmic temporality is often discussed vis-à-vis representations of labor and of laboring bodies yet the role of reproductive labor is often disregarded. This is surprising since the films associated with slow cinema tend to depict the quotidian and show characters performing menial domestic chores, like cooking, but also eating, sleeping and having sex, as mentioned previously. These are the activities that comprise social reproduction; but, in the theoretical debates regarding durational aesthetics, reproductive labor is reduced to unproductive labor, while laboring is often narrowly related to viewership.

Karl Schoonover's chapter "Wastrels of Time: Slow Cinema's Labouring Body, the Political, the Spectator and the Queer" evidences the latter. For the author, "slow art film anticipates a spectator not only eager to clarify the value of wasted time and uneconomical temporalities but also curious about the impact of broadening what counts as productive human labour".[18] Schoonover criticizes *Sight and Sound* editor Nick James for arguing that slow and/or contemplative cinema beseeches "an indulgent temporality in the viewer"[19]; thus, accusing James of overturning André Bazin's argument, who in turn argued that the "dilation of time encourages a more active and politically present viewing practice" by means of rendering time visible.[20] Schoonover probes what non-productivity may look like by staging a discussion

[18] Schoonover, 2016, 153.
[19] Schoonover, 2016, 154.
[20] Schoonover, 2016.

concerning the laboring of viewership, while also alluding to the distinction between "time wasted" and "time labored".[21] But, under late capitalism, the distinction between labor time and leisure time has become less plausible, which complicates his argument.

For Theodor Adorno, "leisure" was the predecessor expression of "free time".[22] It had previously "denoted the privilege of an unconstrained, comfortable life-style"; in the same way that free time is today reliant on "the totality of social conditions, which continues to hold people under its spell".[23]Still, Schoonover argues that slow cinema anticipates a certain type of viewer willing to speculate about "what counts as productive human labour".[24] As I understand it, the available time for such musings may reflect instead the social privilege of the viewer. Moreover, following his argument closely, I would add that Schoonover seems to disregard the fact that free time is defined by labor time itself. As Adorno explicates "the expression 'hobby' amounts to a paradox" since it "is a continuation of the forms of profit-oriented social life".[25] According to a Marxist feminist critique of social reproduction, on the other hand, free time corresponds to the period in which workers reproduce themselves. Free time is not only defined by labour time—spare time outside working hours—but also corresponds to the time necessary for the reproduction of the labor force. This is not simply idle time but instead organized outside working hours with the single purpose of productivity. Despite still broadly ignored in these discussions about cinematic temporality and labor and/or depictions of labor in cinema, Marxist feminist theory offers compelling objections to the ways in which reproductive and unproductive labor mistakenly coincide. Accordingly, waged or unwaged reproductive labor is never unproductive since it produces surplus value; and, even when unwaged, reproductive labour is still dependent on the salary of the male breadwinner therefore it is not "outside the wage relation".[26]

As suggested earlier, the distinction between working hours and leisure time, productive and unproductive labour is far more tenuous under late capitalism. When we consider the time spent in social

---

[21] Schoonover, 2016, 155.

[22] Theodor Adorno, "Free Time", in *The Culture Industry: Selected Essays on Mass Culture*, ed. J.M. Bernstein (London and New York: Routledge, 1991), 187.

[23] Adorno, 1991.

[24] Schoonover, 2016, 153.

[25] Adorno, 1991, 189.

[26] Silvia Federici, "Permanent Reproductive Crisis: An Interview with Silvia Federici", in *Mute*, ed. Marina Vishmidt, 7 March 2013.

TIME, SOCIAL REPRODUCTION AND THE PRECARIOUS BODY 33

media and streaming platforms, is it possible to claim that our leisure is anything but productive? Do we not produce surplus value for tech companies (and for ourselves) when we generate content in social media? As Isabel Lorey puts it:

> Through communication and services, production becomes social in a new way. This transformation of production is accompanied by practices of subservient self-government, of which the self-exposure of the seemingly private self in (social) media is only one symptom. As all the experiences of individuals tend to become part of the production process, self-realization takes place as a performance in public.[27]

Despite its ubiquity, not everyone in the world has access to social media and streaming platforms. This does not mean that they are "indirectly affected or left behind by globalization",[28] but instead that many endure the effects of global capitalism without relishing its fruits. Global capitalism produces inequality and is impossible to escape its claws. Still, when considering the use of streaming platforms, such as Netflix, it is the subscribers' viewing that feeds the algorithm. By watching films and series, viewers inattentively produce information about their viewing tastes, which are then subsumed and presented to them as viewing recommendations. Here, the distinction between producer and consumer collapse in so far as viewers end up generating surplus value for streaming platforms. In this regard, the distinction between private and public, and between producer and product, subside within the post-Fordist regime of production.[29] This is felt more acutely by those who perform immaterial labor, and specially within the context of Western countries, since in the last decades a process of deindustrialization has intensified the tertiary sector in the Western world, but not only. This type of argument may disregard those whose work is to produce tangible products like Roong, a young factory worker in *Blissfully Yours*; but still, it is useful to point out that surplus value not only resides in the production of these tangible products but also

---

[27] Isabel Lorey, *State of Insecurity: Government of the Precarious*, trans. Aileen Derieg (London and New York: Verso, 2015), 73.

[28] Flanagan, 2012, 118.

[29] Paolo Virno, *A Grammar of the Multitude* (Los Angeles and New York: Semiotexte, 2004).

"in the discrepancy between paid and unpaid work",[30] as much as in immaterial and reproductive labor.

Blissfully Yours

Before escaping the factory to spend an idyllic afternoon in the jungle with Min, Roong is seen painting a line of miniature Bugs Bunnies. According to Jonathan L. Owen, this scene in *Blissfully Yours* alludes "to the corporate practice of outsourcing labour to developing countries (from Bugs Bunnies produced in Thai factories to Mickey Mouses in Bangladesh",[31]therefore placing Roong and her boyfriend and migrant Min within the global flux of capital. In this sense, contrary to Shaviro's argument, the use of extended duration does not prevent Apichatpong to observe in detail the ways globalization affects contemporary Thailand.

The rolling credits that interrupt 30 minutes into the film split *Blissfully Yours* in two parts. In the second part, Roong and Min spend the afternoon walking through the jungle, looking for a place to have a picnic and lazing around streams of water. The depiction of their intimacy (they eat, sleep and have sex) in this natural setting and the use of prolonged scenes and sequences seem to imply that they are enjoying a moment away from the cycle of production—the factory where Roong works. Moreover, Roong is seen earlier lying to her employer, claiming that she has fallen ill with malaria in order to break away from her menial tasks and go on this day trip with Min.

Blissfully Yours opens with the main characters Min, Roong and Orn at a female doctor's practice. Orn is a middle-aged woman who is trying to help Min obtain a health certificate to work in Thailand. While the doctor examines Min's heart and lungs as well as his skin ailment, Roong and Orn claim that his sore throat prevents him to speak; however, Min simulates his muteness in order not to expose his foreign accent. This opening sequence intertwines two of the director's familiar tropes: the migrant, which reappears in *Uncle Boonmee Who Can Recall His Past Lives* and in *Mekong Hotel* (2012), as well as doctor-patient relations. The way in which these familiar tropes intertwine

---

[30] Sylvère Lotringer, "Introduction", in Paolo Virno, *A Grammar of the Multitude* (Los Angeles and New York: Semiotexte, 2004), 13.

[31] Jonathan L. Owen, "The Migrations of Factory Style: Work, Play, and Work-as-Play in Andy Warhol, Chantal Akerman, and Apichatpong Weerasethakul", in *Work in Cinema: Labor and the Human Condition*, ed. Ewa Mazierska (New York: Palgrave MacMillan, 2013), 564.

exposes the ways in which medical practice functions to regulate the social body, including the flux of migration and border control. The use of fixed camera angles in his films enhances, on the other hand, the strenuous dialogue and the prolonged duration of the sequence.

In his first feature film *Mysterious Object at Noon*, Apichatpong uses the surrealist storytelling method *cadaver exquisite* to weave a national narrative without openly making reference to Thailand's violent historical past. Moreover, a brief comical scene in the film, in which a woman and her elderly father argue during a doctor's appointment, indicates that Thai society is "still bound by close communal relations, where personal ties may overlap with more formal professional ones".[32] The father complains to the doctor that his daughter broke his hearing aid, while the daughter claims instead that he is only trying to deceive her in order to acquire a new one. During the argument, the father also claims that he would prefer a male offspring, exposing a gender prejudice at the core of this generational conflict. The scene is restaged in *Blissfully Yours* when, earlier in the film, Orn refuses to leave the practice in the hope to convince the doctor to provide Min's health certificate. Here, a cut-away shot, in which we see Min and Orn standing still, abruptly interrupts the father and daughter's argument, as though they were witnessing the conflict. For James Quandt, the two shots do not match, and the strenuous stare of Min and Orn, "suddenly perusing the audience", produces a Brechtian effect.[33]

This restaged scene exposes, on the other hand, existing generational tensions within Thai modern society, while the doctor, as a representative of the state, is assigned to moderate these same tensions. The conflict between father and daughter also appears to question the common understanding that democratic processes are made of consensus when depicting intimate moments "weaved together in everyday forms of disagreement".[34] These social tensions are also substantiated in the director's use of dichotomies: rural and urban, and traditional and modern in films, such as *Syndromes and a Century* and *Tropical Malady* that are, likewise, divided into diptychs.

---

[32] Owen, 2013, 561.
[33] James Quandt, *"Blissfully Yours"*, in *Apichatpong Weerasethakul*, ed. James Quandt (Vienna: Synema, 2009), 46.
[34] Viernes, 2014, 7.

Syndromes and a Century

The leitmotif of *Syndromes and a Century* is inspired by the story of how Apichatpong's parents, both physicians, met in a hospital. His childhood memories (his parents' profession and the family's move from Bangkok to the region of Isan in the northeast of Thailand) have nourished the imagery and imaginary of his filmography. Yet, in an interview, Apichatpong explains that his interest regarding doctor-patient interactions goes beyond his childhood references. Accordingly, he states: "I am also very interested in hospitals—Thai hospitals—and how class power are reflected in them, the authority of the doctors and submissiveness of the patients. I am very concerned about class, codes we often don't recognize: doctors and patients, maids and masters."[35] Like *Blissfully Yours*, *Syndromes and a Century* is divided into two parts. The first is set in a rural clinic in the province of Khon Kaen, and the second is set in a military hospital in Bangkok. The film was "submitted for domestic release seven months after the military coup" in September 2006.[36] Then, the Thai Censorship Board demanded the cutting out of one scene, among others, in which doctors gather in an impromptu meeting in the basement of a military hospital. The attempt to censor this particular scene demonstrates that "under the guise of martial law, the medical institution falls within, and contributes to, this oversight"[37]; thus, evidencing the role of health care in engineering and controlling the social body.

In the scene, Dr Nong, the male protagonist meets two senior female doctors. In conversation with Dr Nong, Dr Wan reaches for a bottle of whiskey[38] from a pile of prosthetic limbs, while Dr Nan swiftly closes the door. Their conversation seems to expose the "anxiety of their moral guardianship" as a symptom of the surveillance they are likely subjected under a military coup.[39] When another doctor comes in with a patient who has suffered from carbon monoxide poisoning, Dr Wan begins to

---

[35] James Quandt, "Exquisite Corpus: An Interview with Apichatpong Weerasethakul", in *Apichatpong Weerasethakul*, ed. James Quandt (Vienna: Synema, 2009), 125.

[36] Noah Viernes, "The Politics of Health in the Films of Apichatpong Weerasethakul", *Akita International University Global Review* 5 (2014): 9.

[37] Viernes, 2014, 19–20.

[38] Accordingly, the bottle of whiskey was considered "as the most problematic narrative device" as it thwarted the moral integrity of the medical community. See Viernes, 2014, 20.

[39] Viernes, 2014, 18.

TIME, SOCIAL REPRODUCTION AND THE PRECARIOUS BODY 37

examine the patient, using the traditional method of "Chakra healing".[40] After this, the camera begins to move, framing Dr Nan looking into the lens. Similarly to the cut-away shot in *Blissfully Yours*, in which Min and Orn witness the argument between father and daughter, Dr Nan's gaze also produces a Brechtian effect. Here, self-reflexivity appears to "challenge potential censors of the film"; while the overall scene suggests the possibility of subversive encounters happening "beyond the watchful eye of the state".[41]

In *Discipline and Punish: The Birth of the Prison*, Michel Foucault contends that through the history of the body, historians have "shown to what extend historical processes were involved in what might seem to be the purely biological base of existence".[42] According to Foucault, the body has been subjected to a political investment, not only through violent force but also through the use of more elusive forms capable of turning the body docile, and more productive. This mastery over the body corresponds to what Foucault designates as a "political technology" employed through the use of techniques and disciplines, and practiced within state institutions, such as, prisons, schools and hospitals, in order to engineer the social body.[43] It is in this sense that Noah Viernes argues that in *Syndromes and a Century*, the "hospital is not simply an institution of medical authority, but one with diagnostic weight in the social engineering of the nation-state".[44]

Following the scene of the impromptu gathering, the camera leaves the basement behind to then travel through a deserted fluores-cent-lit hospital corridor,[45] stopping only at a "large vacuum device whose ominous black maw threatens to suck the viewer in".[46] For Owen, this tracking shot alludes "to a technologized future society in which work has lost its organic, communal character and human

[40] Viernes, 2014, 19.
[41] Viernes, 2014, 20.
[42] Michel Foucault, *Discipline and Punish: The Birth of the Prison*, trans. Alan Sheridan (New York: Vintage Books, 1995), 25.
[43] Foucault, 1995, 26.
[44] Viernes, 2014, 11.
[45] Fernandez argues that this tracking shot seems to recreate the closing tracking shot of *L'Eclisee* (Michelangelo Antonioni, 1962) when the camera leaves the narrative and the characters behind. See Fernandez, 2017, 293; my translation. Still, in relation to *L'Eclisee*, the inclusion of a building mushroom-shaped in Antonioni's famous tracking shot suggests an allusion to the nuclear threat felt during the Cold War, thus offering a dystopian future in which humans are made redundant, not unlike the tracking shot in *Syndromes and a Century*.
[46] Owen, 2013, 562.

workers have become reified, even redundant".[47] The camera's mobility versus the doctors' inertness and the referencing to the traditional healing method in the abovementioned scene seem to corroborate this reading; still, according to Owen, the final scene of the film set in an outdoor aerobic class appears to "ostensibly returns us to vigorous human activity" despite "equally mindless, alienated, and dominated by machines".[48] But, as I argued before, if the scene in the basement hospital seems to imply that the scrutiny of the medical gaze functions to engineer the social body, then I would argue that, in this last scene, the vigour of a mass of bodies moving to the tempo of a blasting sound system in a kind of post-state violence normality suggests instead that the medical scrutiny has been replaced by the self-governing of the social body.

The Self-Governing of the Social Body

Foucault's study of places of confinement in the eighteenth and nineteenth centuries informs the reading of this conclusive scene. In disciplinary societies, Foucault argues, the *panopticon* is the organizing model, thus functioning to allocate bodies in space, and distribute individuals "in relation to one another".[49] The awareness of our permanent and excessive visibility becomes then an instrument of power, and the exercise of control becomes self-inflicted. The closing scene in *Syndromes and a Century* points then to a transition from a violent military coup to a society in which control is self-inflicted. In its apparent normality, the scene suggests that individuals are made responsible for their well-being; as such, individuals exercise during their leisure time in an attempt to self-govern their own bodies. Self-governing "arises at those moments when the social conditions of the precariousness of the body and the whole of life are perceived by the individual as capable of being treated and formed".[50] This is in turn a characteristic of our late capitalist societies wherein the state has withdrawn from its social responsibility. In *Syndromes and a Century*, the closing scene suggests further that state violence (military) and control (medical care) generated the conditions for the self-governing of the social body in a post-dictatorship society.

[47] Owen, 2013.
[48] Owen, 2013.
[49] Foucault, 1995, 216.
[50] Lorey, 2015, 26.

Foucault's disciplinary model is also brought to mind in *Cemetery of Splendour*. The film is set in a hospital in which a group of soldiers are interned, and begin to suffer from an unexplained sleeping disease. In the film, it is suggested that the hospital was built on the grounds of a royal cemetery, and it is this that is causing the soldiers' sleeping disease. Regarding the scene in which Jen, the film's main character, and a soldier "stand still in darkness", Masato Fukushima argues that this signifies for "the absence of the king or a portrayal of a black hole of power".[51] Similarly, in another scene, Jen describes the previously existing royal palace as having "only cornfields" at the centre, suggesting then that the centre is divested of power.[52] Consequently, this means that it is the subjects' compliance that confers power to the king, which is analogous to the disciplinary model of the *panopticon*. This is because under the panoptical model, bars and chains become outmoded since the belief that we are scrutinized by others, as much as we scrutinize others, results in a self-imposed surveillance as the mechanism through which social control is exercised.

So far, I have argued that films such as *Blissfully Yours*, *Syndromes and a Century* and *Cemetery of Splendour* appear to make intelligible the ways in which the medical gaze functions to engineer the social body. I have also argued that the conclusive scene of *Syndromes and a Century* signifies that, in the aftermath of the military coup, social control becomes self-inflicted under a *supposed* normality. Yet this concern with medical scrutiny also implies a careful attention to the physicality and therefore fragility of on-screen bodies. As such, in the following section, I address the precariousness and vulnerability of these bodies, in an attempt to offer a critique to the ways global capitalism captures social reproduction.

Precarious Bodies and Queer Temporalities

Following a meeting with her lover, Orn runs into Min and Roong in the jungle at the end of *Blissfully Yours*. In reference to one particular scene in which the three characters bathe in the river, Apichatpong explains: "I just thought about how the three were so fragile that they

---

[51] Masato Fukushima, "Sick Bodies and the Political Body: The Political Theology of Apichatpong Weerasethakul's *Cemetery of Splendour*", in *2 or 3 Tigers*, ed. Anselm Franke and Hyunjin Kim (Berlin: Haus der Kulturen der Welt, 2017), 6.

[52] Fukushima, 2017, 7.

need the water to support them, to float, to be happy. The way Roong felt towards Orn was more a play on simple triangle love found in soap operas. She suddenly felt possessive. The water scene heightened the vulnerability of the three characters".[53] When resting on the margins of the river, a lethargic Roong strokes Min's penis, while Orn cries in her solitude, not too far from them. This scene evidences a shared precariousness precisely because they seem to be together apart. Here, precariousness is understood as "something that is existentially shared, and endangerment of bodies that is ineluctable and hence not to be secured, not only because they are mortal, but specifically because they are social".[54] Co-vulnerability is further inferred since water suggests interconnectedness between characters, and between characters and the natural environment that surrounds them.

Interconnectedness is also found in the superimposition of temporalities, as evidenced in the last sequence of *Uncle Boonmee Who Can Recall His Past Lives*. The film won the *Palme d'Or* in Cannes on 19 May 2010, two days after the second military intervention, aimed at suppressing anti-coup protests.[55] In the film, the homonymous character suffers from a kidney disease and his carer is a Laotian migrant, evidencing once again the figure of the migrant and the precariousness of living bodies as Apichatpong's customary tropes. At the beginning of the film, his sister-in-law Jen visits Boonmee in his farm. At night, the ghost of his wife Huay and his son Boonsong join them at the dinner table. In conversation with Jen, Boonmee also reveals that he killed communists in the army; because of that, he seeks redemption, before dying. The memory of the country's violent history resurfaces in the film, while the superimposition of distinct temporalities is emphasized by the fact that, as the title suggests, Boonmee recalls his past lives.

In the film's last sequence, Jen and a young woman watch TV in a hotel room, after attending the funeral of uncle Boonmee. Buddhist monk Tong, who previously visited Boonmee, along with Jen in his farm, knocks on their door; after having a shower, he is seen folding his clothes in a corner of the room. At the bottom of the frame, we see Jen moving on the bed, and when Tong turns to speak to her, he sees both women and himself watching TV. Tong seems briefly startled but goes for dinner with Jen's double soon after. According to Quandt, this sequence demonstrates the way that Apichatpong treats "time as malleable, flowing rather than fixed and linear" and employ different

---

[53] Quandt, 2009, 131.
[54] Lorey, 2015, 12.
[55] Viernes, 2014, 21.

strategies to complicate filmic temporality, including the superimposition and "co-existence of various times".[56]

Karl Schoonover and Rosalind Galt argue, on the other hand, that Apichatpong's use of double narratives and superimposed temporalities implies a queer temporality that troubles simultaneously linearity and heterosexual normativity.[57] The depiction of same-sex, and human and nonhuman romantic relationships renders his films explicitly queer. For example, *Uncle Boonmee* features a sex scene between a princess and a fish; and, when visiting his father, Boonsong tells him about his obsession with a female ghost-ape, before becoming a ghost-ape himself. However, according to Schoonover and Galt, the way nonhuman figures become objects of "queer desire" in his films is less "about bestiality but [instead] about altering the constitution of the human subject".[58] Queerness is also implicit within the ghostly figures that haunt the characters of his films, not only because they traverse different temporalities but also because they refuse to be placed into a single category and, following Foucault's previous argument, to become docile, akin queer bodies.

Queer desire is explicitly depicted in *Tropical Malady*. The film is turned into a diptych after the rolling of credits change its title into *A Spirit's Path*. Both sections have the same actors, making indiscernible whether or not they are playing the same characters. The first part depicts a romantic relationship between a soldier and a local young man, while in the second the same actor who played the soldier ventures into the jungle, searching for a shaman-tiger. The possibility that the tiger may eat the man/soldier infers an erotic relationship between them that mirrors the relationship between the soldier and the young man in the first part.

Schoonover has argued before that slow cinema provides the means to question "what it means to live queerly",[59] but in *Queer Cinema in the World*, Schoonover and Galt also expound that the theoretical discussions regarding slow cinema have dismissed the counter productivity of queer temporalities.[60] Accordingly, they claim:

---

[56] James Quandt, "Resistant to Bliss: Describing Apichatpong", in *Apichatpong Weerasethakul*, ed. James Quandt (Vienna: Synema, 2009), 25.

[57] Quandt, 2009, 272.

[58] Karl Schoonover and Rosalind Galt, *Queer Cinema in the World* (Durham: Duke University Press, 2016), 162.

[59] Schoonover, 2016, 162.

[60] Schoonover and Galt, 2016, 276.

> Slow cinema wastes our time, asking us to spend time in visibly unproductive ways, outside efficient narrative economies of production and reproduction. As such, slow films are interesting to consider in light of queer theory's debates around negative aesthetics, particularly in how they resist reproductive futurity. Like the wilfully unproductive queer, slow cinema refuses to labor along socially sanctioned narrative pathways.[61]

The reasoning behind their argument that slow cinema resists "reproductive futurity", while also demanding an unproductive laboring from the viewer, is found in Lee Edelman's argument, according to which "reproductive futurity" is epitomized in the figure of the Child, and onto whom "remains the perpetual horizon of every acknowledged politics.[62] In this way, Edelman argues that reproductive futurity imposes "an ideological limit on political discourse as such, [...] by rendering unthinkable, by casting outside the political domain, the possibility of a queer resistance to" heterosexual normativity.[63] Queerness, however, not only rejects the future that the Child epitomizes but also subverts the very possibility of meaning since it disrupts the "signifying chain"[64] "through which we experience ourselves as subjects".[65] It is possible then to establish a correlation between Edelman's argument and the notion that queer temporality disrupts linearity and heterosexual normativity that in the case of Apichatpong's films is expressed both in content and in form.

In both arguments (Edelman and Schoonover and Galt, alike), reproduction seems, however, analogous with heterosexuality and child rearing. But I choose to rescue reproduction from heteronormativity, since Apichatpong tends to depict his characters performing activities, such as cooking, eating, sleeping, and/or having sex, which are in turn the activities that comprise social reproduction; or rather, "all the supporting activities that take place to make, remake, maintain, contain and repair the world we live in".[66] These activities are in turn depicted through the use of prolonged duration, rendering visible the time necessary for social reproduction. Through the depiction of the quotidian, prolonged duration is capable of not only exposing the

---

[61] Schoonover and Galt, 2016, 277.
[62] Lee Edelman, *No Future: Queer Theory and the Death Drive* (Durham and London: Duke University Press, 2004), 3.
[63] Edelman, 2004, 2.
[64] Edelman, 2004, 24.
[65] Edelman, 2004, 25.
[66] Dowling, 2021, 21.

precarious relations between bodies but also question their capacity to fit their social function,[67] since in their precariousness they are neither docile nor productive. This is why I argue that Apichatpong produces an aesthetic filmic experience through duration capable of generating a political effect; rather than demanding unproductive laboring from the film audience or rescue pre-capitalist temporal structures, in his films extended duration uncovers instead the ways through which our quotidian and reproductive capacity are seized by capital.

Bibliography

Adorno, Theodor. "Free Time". In *The Culture Industry: Selected Essays on Mass Culture*. Ed. J.M. Bernstein. London and New York. Routledge. 1991. 187–197.

Dowling, Emma. *The Care Crisis*. London and New York. Verso. 2021.

Edelman, Lee. *No Future: Queer Theory and the Death Drive*. Durham and London. Duke University Press. 2004.

Federici, Silvia. "Permanent Reproductive Crisis: An Interview with Silvia Federici". In *Mute*. Ed. Marina Vishmidt. 7 March 2013. https://www.metamute.org/editorial/articles/permanent-reproductive-crisis-interview-silvia-federici.

Fernández, Horacio Muñoz. "Cierta tendencia (nostálgica) del slow cinema". *Aniki* 4, no. 2 (2017): 289–314. doi:10.14591/aniki.v4n2.283.

Flanagan, Matthew. "'Slow Cinema': Temporality and Style in Contemporary Art and Experimental Film". D.Phil. thesis. University of Exeter. 2012.

Foucault, Michel. *Discipline and Punish: The Birth of the Prison*. 2nd edition. Trans. Alan Sheridan. New York. Vintage Books. 1995.

Fukushima, Masato. "Sick Bodies and the Political Body: The Political Theology of Apichatpong Weerasethakul's Cemetery of Splendour". In *2 or 3 Tigers*. Ed. Anselm Franke and Hyunjin Kim. Berlin. Haus der Kulturen der Welt. 2017. https://www.hkw.de/de/tigers_publication/.

Koepnick, Lutz. *On Slowness: Toward an Aesthetic of the Contemporary*. New York. Colombia University Press. 2014.

Lorey, Isabel. *State of Insecurity: Government of the Precarious*. Trans. Aileen Derieg. London and New York. Verso. 2015.

Lotringer, Sylvère. "Foreword: We, the Multitude". In *A Grammar of the Multitude*. Ed. Paolo Virno. Los Angeles and New York. Semiotexte. 2004. 7–20.

---

[67] Rancière, 2008.

Luca, Tiago de. "Slow Time, Visible Cinema: Duration, Experience, and Spectatorship". *Cinema Journal* 56, no. 1 (Fall 2016): 23–42. doi:10.1353/cj.2016.0052.

Luca, Tiago de and Nuno Barradas Jorge. "Introduction: From Slow Cinema to Slow Cinemas". In *Slow Cinema*. Edinburgh. Edinburgh University Press. 2016. 1–21.

Owen, Jonathan L. "The Migrations of Factory Style: Work, Play, and Work-as-Play in Andy Warhol, Chantal Akerman, and Apichatpong Weerasethakul". In *Work in Cinema: Labor and the Human Condition*. Ed. Ewa Mazierska. New York. Palgrave MacMillan. 2013. 521–572.

Quandt, James. "*Blissfully Yours*". In *Apichatpong Weerasethakul*. Ed. James Quandt. Vienna. Synema. 2009. 43–56.

Quandt, James. "Exquisite Corpus: An Interview with Apichatpong Weerasethakul". In *Apichatpong Weerasethakul*. Ed. James Quandt. Vienna. Synema. 2009. 125–131.

Quandt, James. "Resistant to Bliss: Describing Apichatpong". In *Apichatpong Weerasethakul*. Ed. James Quandt. Vienna. Synema. 2009. 13–30.

Rancière, Jacques. *The Emancipated Spectator*. Trans. Gregory Elliot. London and New York. Verso. 2008.

Schoonover, Karl. "Wastrels of Time: Slow Cinema's Labouring Body, the Political, the Spectator and the Queer". In *Slow Cinema*. Ed. Tiago de Luca and Nuno Barradas Jorge. Edinburgh. Edinburgh University Press. 2016. 158–168.

Schoonover, Karl and Rosalind Galt. *Queer Cinema in the World*. Durham. Duke University Press. 2016.

Sequeira Brás, Patrícia. "Time and Reproductive Labour in *Jeanne Dielman, 23 quai du Commerce, 1080 Bruxelles* (1975) and *Three Sisters* (2012)". In "Work", (Spring 2019) 9 *Parse*. Ed. Marina Vishmidt. https://parsejournal.com/article/time-and-reproductive-labour-in-jeanne-dielman-23-quai-du-commerce-1080-bruxelles-1975-and-three-sisters-2012/.

Shaviro, Stephen. "Slow Cinema vs. Fast Films". In *The Pinocchio Theory*. 2010. http://www.shaviro.com/Blog/?p=891.

Viernes, Noah. "The Politics of Health in the Films of Apichatpong Weerasethakul". *Akita International University Global Review* 5 (2014): 1–28.

Virno, Paolo. *A Grammar of the Multitude*. Los Angeles and New York. Semiotexte. 2004.

Filmography

Blissfully Yours. Dir. Apichatpong Weerasethakul. 2002.
Cemetery of Splendour. Dir. Apichatpong Weerasethakul. 2015.

Jeanne Dielman, 23 quai du Commerce, 1080 Bruxelles. Dir. Chantal Akerman. 1975.
Ne Change Rien. Dir. Pedro Costa. 2009.
Syndromes and a Century. Dir. Apichatpong Weerasethakul. 2006.
Three Sisters. Dir. Wang Bing. 2012.
Tropical Malady. Dir. Apichatpong Weerasethakul. 2004.
Uncle Boonmee Who Can Recall His Past Lives. Dir. Apichatpong Weerasethakul. 2010.

2

Representing Memory through Slowness
The Time-Images of Apichatpong Weerasethakul's
Syndromes and a Century and *Cemetery of Splendour*

Francesco Quario

Apichatpong Weerasethakul's penchant for episodic narratives, his attention for the commonplace and everyday, and his frequent use of static, long takes effectively place his work in the elusive category of "slow cinema". The category was first defined by French critic Michel Ciment as a reaction to "the bombardment of sound and image" and to the "fetishim of technology" embodied by Hollywood.[1] Then, in 2010, it was famously criticized by *Sight & Sound*'s Nick James as "passive-aggressive", sparking a critical debate on the validity of quiet contemplation as an aesthetic and political tool.[2] Here, I am interested in the concept of slowness in so far as it enables the spectator to achieve an awareness of duration and how this can, in turn, facilitate the portrayal of memories and multiple temporalities within the image. As Tiago de Luca and Nuno Barradas Jorge note: "slowness, understood as a mode of temporal unfolding and as an awareness of duration, is a fundamentally subjective experience".[3] In other words, the rhythm of the image shapes the viewer's perception of time, but it likewise has different aesthetic effects on different viewers.

The words *slowness* betrays a feeling of boredom, which most cinema goers would associate with a negative cinematic experience. However, as Emre Çağlayan states in his analysis of boredom in the films of Nuri Bilge Ceylan, "a temporally extended [therefore, often boring] mode of consciousness can yield acts of subjective introspection and enhance

---

[1] Michel Ciment, "The State of Cinema", speech at the 46th San Francisco International Film Festival, in *Unspoken Cinema*, blog, accessed 29 January 2021, https://unspokencinema.blogspot.com/2006/10/state-of-cinema-m-ciment.html.

[2] Nick James, "Passive-Aggressive", *Sight & Sound* 20, no. 4 (2010): 5.

[3] Tiago de Luca and Nuno Barradas Jorge, "Introduction: From Slow Cinema to Slow Cinemas", in *Slow Cinema*, ed. Tiago de Luca and Nuno Barradas Jorge (Edinburgh: Edinburgh University Press, 2016), 4.

individual creativity"[4] One should consider boredom as capable of enabling the phenomenological viewer's conscious engagement with the image, rather than shutting it down. There already exists extensive research on the stylistic means through which slow cinema achieves this effect. One of the most influential books on slow cinema theory is Song Hwee Lim's *Tsai Ming Liang and a Cinema of Slowness*, where the author argues: "cinematic stillness can be achieved even when there is bodily movement within the static shot because the movement is primarily of an everyday nature, contributing not so much to the drive of the narrative as to a sense of 'nothing happening'".[5] Again, this understanding of slowness implicates the phenomenological spectator and their affective experience of time in the aesthetics of slow cinema. Here, as Vivian Sobchack argues in her theory of cinematic phenomenology, it is useful to consider the spectator as "embodied", meaning that the cinematic image is capable of directly affecting their full sensorial experience beyond merely sight and sound.[6] Slowness has the power to induce bodily reactions such as sleep/relaxation or restlessness/frustration on the spectator. However, in order to address the portrayal of memories and multiple temporalities in Apichatpong's cinema, my reading must also make use of the concept of duration and how the cinematic image harnesses it independently of the spectator's body.

This idea harkens back to the philosophy of Henri Bergson who, in the essay "Time and Free Will", describes duration as "a process of organization or interpenetration of conscious states" which occurs within the subject.[7] One of these conscious states is the subject's memory, which, as Bergson phrases in *Creative Evolution*, "conveys something of the past into the present" in a constant interpenetration of the former into the latter.[8] The most famous application of Bergson's philosophy to film theory is Gilles Deleuze's concept of the "time-image", actualized when the correlation between shots or character actions is not mediated by a

---

[4] Emre Çağlayan, *Poetics of Slow Cinema: Nostalgia, Absurdism, Boredom* (Cham: Palgrave Macmillan, 2018), 198.

[5] Song Hwee Lim, *Tsai Ming Liang and a Cinema of Slowness* (Honolulu: University of Hawai'i Press, 2016), 93.

[6] Vivian Sobchack, *The Address of the Eye: A Phenomenology of Film Experience* (New Jersey: Princeton University Press, 1992), 17.

[7] Henri Bergson, *Time and Free Will: An Essay on the Immediate Data of Consciousness*, trans. F.L. Pogson (Abingdon and New York: Routledge, 2013 (1889)), 108.

[8] Henri Bergson, *Creative Evolution*, trans. Arthur Mitchell (Mineola: Dover Publications, 1998 (1907)), 2.

cause-and-effect relation. This is a contrast to movement-images, which are constituted by the sensorimotor schema of perception, affection and action.[9] Such schema, which finds its most prolific application in pre-war American cinema, subordinates time to movement. The circuit of images, or shots, in the movement-image aims to establish direct cause-and-effect relations. To reduce this circuit in the simplest possible terms, one can say: a character's perception causes an affection, which in turn produces an action. Thus, temporality is linearized as a series of presents coming one after another.

Meanwhile, time-images are *pure optical and sound situations*, which arise when the sensory-motor schema is broken or negated. In the time-image, the character's body becomes "the developer of time, [and] shows time through its tiredness and waitings".[10] Slow films often operate outside of the sensorimotor schema by avoiding continuity editing, sidelining character action, and extending the duration of a single event past the point of character action. Again, to simplify the definition: pure optical and sound situations arise from the interruption or negation of the sensorimotor schema. Deleuze finds plenty of hetero-geneous examples of this in post-war European cinema. From the neorealism of Vittorio de Sica and Roberto Rossellini, which highlight a certain lack of agency and uncertainness leading to the interruption of linear circuits of cause-and-effect; to the cinema of Alain Resnais, who lays out the contradictoriness of memory (both subjective and collective) disrupting the circuit of recollection. While these two examples are not mutually exclusive, the former is more reminiscent of the stylistic techniques associated to slow cinema. Through these techniques, slow films open up their temporality across different planes of potentiality as there is no linear cause-and-effect correlation between images. As D.N. Rodowick puts it in his book *Gilles Deleuze's Time Machine*: "When a pure optical image or sound displaces an image based on motor action, the distinction between objective and subjective also loses relevance in favor of a principle of indeterminability or indiscernibility."[11]

Moreover, slow films tend to eschew narrative-motivated action in favour of what various scholars of slow cinema, such as de Luca and

---

[9]   See Gilles Deleuze, *Cinema 1: The Movement-Image*, trans. Hugh Tomlinson and Barbara Habberjam (Minneapolis: University of Minnesota Press, 1997 (1983)).

[10] Gilles Deleuze, *Cinema 2: The Time-image*, trans. Hugh Tomlinson and Robert Gaeta (London and New York: Bloomsbury Academic, 2013 (1985)), xiii.

[11] D.N. Rodowick, *Gilles Deleuze's Time Machine* (Durham and London: Duke University Press, 1997, repr. 2003), 81.

Çağlayan, describe as *dead time*.[12] This popular term bespeaks slow cinema's antagonistic relation to Hollywood modes of production, as it quantifies time in a capitalistic sense, its supposed deadness being due to a lack of activity and productivity. However, I avoid using the term in this chapter, as my Deleuzian approach implies time (as duration) to be in a constant state of becoming, rather than still or inactive. Going back to Rodowick's book:

> [Close] attention to the present shows that there is real movement, a movement of becoming which is the pure form of time as change. Here there is no present distinguishable from a present-becoming-past, on the one hand, and the present-becoming-future on the other. Rather than a chronological and successive addition of spatial movements, time continually divides into a present that is passing, a past that is preserved, and an indeterminate future.[13]

This relationship between slow cinema and Deleuzian philosophy lends itself particularly well to a reading of Apichatpong's cinema. In an appraisal of the work of Andy Warhol, Apichatpong claims: "[Warhol] changed my way of looking at time ... He showed me the importance of looking at scenes (such as an old man walking his fat pug) which, in fact, can be any moment when you are just aware of your existence."[14] These scenes constitute pure optical and sound situations, which enable the spectator's awareness of duration and, through slowness, directly affect them on a phenomenological level. As Elena del Rio argues, Deleuze and phenomenology have a shared desire to suspect and undermine the "drive to determine a clear dividing line between subject and world, perceiver and perceived, objective reality and subjective experience"; a desire which is undoubtedly shared by director Apichatpong.[15]

In this chapter, I mainly explore how Apichatpong uses style to consciously represent multiple temporalities flowing into each other, with particular attention to the director's portrayal of personal and collective memory. The two case studies that I selected are the features *Syndromes and a Century (Sæng Satawat*, 2006) and *Cemetery of Splendour*

---

[12] See Tiago de Luca, "Slow Time, Visible Cinema: Duration, Experience and Spectatorship", *Cinema Journal* 56, no. 1 (Fall 2016): 56; and Çağlayan, 2018, 7.

[13] Rodowick, 2003, 81.

[14] Quoted in James Quandt, "Resistant to Bliss: Describing Apichatpong", in *Apichatpong Weerasethakul*, ed. James Quandt (Vienna: Synema, 2009), 15.

[15] Elena del Rio, "Film", in *Handbook of Phenomenological Aesthetics*, ed. Hans Reiner Sepp and Lester Embree (London and New York: Springer, 2010), 115.

(*Rak Ti Khon Kaen*, 2015). The reason behind these choices stems from the director's personal relation to the contents of the film, which are based on his childhood memories. Both films are set in hospitals, due to the fact that Apichatpong's parents were both doctors. Moreover, as the director states in an interview on the subject of *Syndromes and a Century*:

> [Memory] may well be the only impulse [behind my filmmaking]! Everything is stored in our memory, and it's in the nature of film to preserve things ... But I've never set out to recreate my memories exactly. The mind doesn't work like a camera. The pleasure for me is not in remembering exactly but in recapturing the *feeling* of the memory—and in blending that with the present.[16]

Therefore, the intention behind these personal accounts of Apichatpong's memories is to merge multiple temporalities within the film. This causes a sense of indiscernibility between the real and the imaginary, the actual and the virtual which, through slowness, is reflected on the phenomenological viewer's own perception of time.

Syndromes and a Century: Contradicting Memories

Syndromes belongs to a series of Apichatpong features that are structured in twofold, dichotomous narratives, creating what Brett Farmer describes as "a cinema of odd conjunctions that confounds and frustrates, as much as it dazzles and seduces".[17] Much like the director's previous *Blissfully Yours* (*Sud saneha*, 2002) and *Tropical Malady* (*Sud pralad*, 2004), *Syndromes and a Century* uses this structure to play with the boundary between the real and the imaginary. The narratives of *Blissfully Yours* and *Tropical Malady* are split by what Kim Jihoon calls an "*interstice*—an abrupt extradiegetic gap that interrupts the spatio-temporal continuity of a film's narrative in such a way that it is not

---

[16] Tony Rayns, "Memories, Mysteries: From an Interview with Apichatpong Weerasethakul", *Kick the Machine* (Bangkok, July 2006), accessed 29 January 2021, http://www.kickthemachine.com/page80/page24/page12/index.html.

[17] Brett Farmer, "Apichatpong Weerasethakul, Transnational Poet of the New Thai Cinema: Blissfully Yours/Sud Sanaeha", *Senses of Cinema* 38 (2006), accessed 29 January 2021, http://sensesofcinema.com/2006/cteq/blissfully_yours/.

chronologically or causally justified by its diegetic elements".[18] Thus, both films disrupt cause-and-effect narration, creating a spectatorial experience wherein the viewer is forced to find sensorial or experiential, rather than dramatic, links between the film's two halves in order to piece the picture together. Later, Kim adds: "the interstices achieve resonance between two types of duration: two interspersed durations of the director's memory in the diegetic space, and the duration of images on the screen space embodied by the viewer's phenomeno-logical perception and attentiveness".[19] This understanding of how Apichatpong's twofold structures operate resonates with the concepts expressed in this chapter's introduction about the durational qualities of Apichatpong's cinema. By interspersing different durations and enabling the viewer's perception of duration, Apichatpong actualizes the multiple, contradicting temporalities of memory and recollection.

Syndromes and a Century follows a similar pattern to the director's previous two films, although it lacks an interstice, cutting instead from the first half to the second with a seamless transition and no apparent break point. The twofold structure becomes evident when the spectator notices the film's repeating events despite a sudden change in location. The first half of the film is set in a small countryside hospital, whose atmosphere is distinguished by a friendliness among characters and a use of natural landscape shots that make the space feel particularly idyllic. The narrative focuses on the young Dr Toey as she engages in different activities, such as conducting a job interview with a former army medic, writing a prescription for a Buddhist monk, and engaging in a long flirtation with a florist who sells her a rare orchid to plant in the hospital courtyard. The film intercuts this with scenes involving other characters, such as a dentist who gives a free check-up to one of the monks visiting the hospital.

Many of these episodes repeat in the film's second half, although they operate with a stark change in tone. Now set in a large city hospital, the film replaces the open, naturally illuminated interiors of the first half with artificial, tungsten-lit rooms. There is almost a total absence of landscape shots, and the repeated scenes (the job interview, the prescription writing, and the dental check-up) now showcase a lack of friendliness an increased emotional detachment among the same

---

[18] Kim Jihoon, "Between Auditorium and Gallery: Perception in Apichatpong Weerasethakul's Films and Installations", in *Global Art Cinema: New Theories and Histories*, ed. Rosalind Galt and Karl Schoonover (Oxford: Oxford University Press, 2010), 132; emphasis mine.

[19] Kim, 2010, 134.

characters who coloured the film's first half. In light of the context around the film and its aim to recreate faint memories, it is evident that Apichatpong is trying to create ambiguity around which of the two diegeses is based in reality and which one is imagined or, alternatively, whether they are both real or both imagined.

Moreover, the film deliberately confounds causal and temporal boundaries within individual scenes. Right after the opening scene, as Dr Toey and her assistant Toa walk out of her office, the camera briefly frames their silhouettes leaving the room before tracking into a window behind them and focusing on an empty grass field, on top of which the film's opening credits are superimposed. Meanwhile, the voices of the two characters can be heard having a conversation, together with their reverberating footsteps mixed so that they still sound close to the viewer's ear, despite the characters having moved out of frame. The discrepancy between the optical and the sound in this sequence is picked up by Kim's chapter:

> The soft discrepancy between the visual and the audible interestingly mutually reinforces the qualities of each: the visual track acquires the phenomenological duration of its presence reinforced by the spatial disorientation from the deep diegetic soundscape of the audio track. This strategy does not simply impose on the stream of images a linear sense of time, but it combines the past that is recorded in them with the temporality of their presence, the projection time as the present.[20]

Here, Kim reconnects the audiovisual discrepancy of this sequence to certain practices found in Apichatpong's video installations at the time. In particular, the director employs an excessive shot duration that is more commonly found in video than in film, due to film's higher cost and video's capacity to store large amounts of footage within a single memory card. Obviously, the lengthy shot duration as well as the type of shot are to be considered exemplary of Apichatpong's slow cinema: after the initial track, the camera remains still for the entire sequence, framing nothing but the field of grass with a row of trees and a small cottage in the background, all standing perfectly still. This effectively grinds the film's visual rhythm to a halt.

Moreover, this sequence's disorientating effects are effectively an abandonment of sensorimotor schemas in favour of pure optics and sound. Apichatpong's camera briefly frames the two characters just

[20] Kim, 2010, 131.

Fig. 1: Landscape shot of the empty field of grass outside the rural hospital. From *Syndromes and a Century* (2006), dir. Apichatpong Weerasethakul.

enough for the viewer to identify them and spatialize them, but then fails to follow their movement. Nevertheless, their aural presence makes their movement perceptible, while the visual image negates it. Thus, the image is not subservient to action, freeing the film's duration from subordination to movement. In its first few minutes, *Syndromes* already achieves the objective of recreating the uncertainty of memories expressed by Apichatpong in the previously quoted interview, as we already entered a principle of indiscernibility between image and sound, perception and action, and, by extent, objective and subjective.

On top of that, there is an even more evident disruption of temporal linearity that occurs in the first half of *Syndromes and a Century*. After her assistant Toa declares his love to Dr Toey, she sits down with him by a stone table to have a conversation. There, she begins to tell the story of how she met a florist at a local market, seemingly with the intention of placating a visibly upset Toa who is afraid of rejection. This prompts a flashback to the day Toey met the florist, only interrupted by a brief interjection by Toa. Then, the film returns to the flashback, but the next cut back to the stone table after that shows the florist, rather than Toa, sit opposite Dr Toey in the same position. From here on, the film continues in this apparent flashback timeline, without ever returning to the conversation between the doctor and her assistant. A long series of vignettes shows Dr Toey become friendly, and eventually flirt with the florist while visiting his house. Not only does Toey's storytelling fail in its purpose of comforting the distressed Toa (or it would, if his reaction was shown), but it completely overtakes the main narrative to the point where it is impossible to tell whether this sequence is a flashback any longer. The same indiscernibility of different spaces in the film's first scene is now extended to different times. As mentioned earlier, the film extends this sensation to its overall structure. The two different "timelines" shown in the film's two halves directly contrast and contradict each other, thus casting doubt about either of them as an accurate portrayal of the director's past. The presumed objectivity of the events is contradicted by the subjectivity of memory, making it impossible to discern where one begins and the other ends.

The two halves also showcase different means of achieving cinematic slowness. If the earlier described sequences make use of static shots (such as the shot of the empty grass field) and mundane conversations, the second half of the film features several breaks from the character narrative that focus, instead, on the building surrounding them. A montage halfway through this section of the film features several shots of the camera panning around various statues adorning the hospital's courtyard, along with shots of people walking through its vast corridors and an extra-diegetic soundtrack composed of a long, low-frequency hum. The same soundtrack is repeated in a second montage at the end of the film, where the camera again pans around the courtyard statues before showing various characters leaving the building, lingering on its empty corridors, while others sit in their offices with a lost gaze. Glyn Davis describes this montage as "a durational portrait of a building" akin to Andy Warhol's *Empire* (1964).[21] The building itself being the centre of this sequence imbues the film with a certain stillness inherent in the hospital's sterile architecture.

As is the tendency in Apichatpong's cinema, none of this is divorced from the corporeal. While the medical setting itself is inextricably linked to the exploration of biological processes, Apichatpong also devolves several sequences to the observation of character's bodies: two young doctors passionately kiss by a window for an extended period of time; a group of people work out in an open-air aerobics class serving as a coda to the film. These stark appeals to sensation, paired with the embodied nature of the slow cinematic style, make for an experience that does not prioritize the mental over the physical. Rather, it hardly

---

[21] Glyn Davis, "Stills and Stillness in Apichatpong Weerasethakul's Cinema", in *Slow Cinema*, ed. Tiago de Luca and Nuno Barradas Jorge (Edinburgh: Edinburgh University Press, 2016), 99–111.

distinguishes between the two. Memory, as it is, is a physical process made of sensations and affections. The very *Syndromes* of the title are human, physical processes such as sickness or heartache, which then become intertwined with the passing of time: the *Century*, as it were. Apichatpong says as much in the previously cited Tony Rayns interview:

> The word "Syndromes" could apply equally to *Blissfully Yours* or *Tropical Malady*: it does refer to human behavior, such as the way we fall in love ... "Century" for me conveys the sense of moving forward. A century is more or less the same as a lifetime. I'm interested in the ways things change over time, and in the ways they *don't* change. It seems to me that human affairs remain fairly constant.[22]

Such contrast between the changing and unchanging also evokes a contrast between movement and stillness, a disruption of linearity. Again, the dividing lines between these contrasts remain indiscernible: even when portraying "constant" human affairs, Apichatpong manages to showcase a great degree of heterogeneity in the way that such affairs are informed by people's environments—i.e. the two hospitals.

In summary, *Syndromes and a Century* is a useful case study on how Apichatpong uses narrative structure and duration to confound boundaries between objective and subjective, past and present. However, while a holistic look at the film provides the viewer with a shifting and heterogeneous memory-image, the structure itself is still binary. Therefore, taken on their own, the two halves of the film could both operate as objective images, and it is only through the interplay between the two that the film blurs those lines. Fortunately, even within individual halves there are moments that disrupt linear temporality, as my analysis suggests. However, in order to properly collapse the objective and subjective, the real and imaginary, Apichatpong eventually abandoned twofold structures altogether: his two subsequent features—*Uncle Boonmee Who Can Recall His Past Lives* (*Lung Bunmi Raluek Chat*, 2010) and *Cemetery of Splendour*—do without interstices, opting instead for narratives that overlap a distinctly material reality with an apparently immaterial one.

---

[22] Rayns, 2006.

Cemetery of Splendour: Shared Memories

Cemetery more explicitly recalls Apichatpong's childhood through its setting in Khon Kaen, the director's hometown. Like *Syndromes*, the narrative centres around a hospital. Although its structure is not explicitly divided in two halves, the film still manages to create a dialogue between two different temporalities by overlapping the physical space of the hospital with a metaphysical, or supernatural one. As a review in *The Guardian* aptly points out, the film crafts "a spiritual realm which overlaps with our own: a realm from which ghosts and spirits will appear, and be just as ordinary as anyone else".[23] The film portrays this dichotomy through the narrative device of a group of soldiers, who enter in a supernaturally induced sleep state due to being possessed by the ghosts of ancient kings buried below the hospital ground. These ghosts are awoken by a digging expedition ran by the soldiers who, quite literally, unearth a buried past that rises back to haunt them. The majority of the film unfolds through the perspective of the protagonist Jen, a volunteer nurse who befriends one of the soldiers, Itt, but who is herself not affected by the sleeping sickness. Nevertheless, she is able to catch glimpses of the sleeping world through communications with Itt. Through this narrative, the film exercises Apichatpong's usual indiscernibility between real and imaginary, past and present, without the need of a twofold structure or an interstice.

The director's attention for the everyday also confers a traditionally realist aesthetic to the film's supernatural narrative. For instance, a scene that involves Jen having a conversation with two embodied goddesses is framed in a single medium shot showing the three characters having casual conversation at a table while Jen calmly eats langsat fruits. Similar sequences exemplify the film's merging of the ordinary with the extraordinary, where the latter is always sublimated into the former. There is, however, one sequence which stands out from the rest as it foregrounds the dream-like perspective of the sleeping soldiers over the physicality of the material world. It consists of an eight-shot montage, which opens on a shot of the ceiling fan in the hospital room where the soldiers sleep, followed by two medium-long shots of the soldiers in their beds. Besides the soldiers' beds there are tall, candy cane-shaped neon lamps whose colour gradually shifts as they illuminate the room.

---

[23] Peter Bradshaw, "Cemetery of Splendour Review: A Very Calm Sort of Hysteria", *The Guardian*, 18 May 2015, accessed 29 February 2020, https://www.theguardian.com/film/2015/may/18/cemetery-of-splendour-review-apichatpong-weerasethakul.

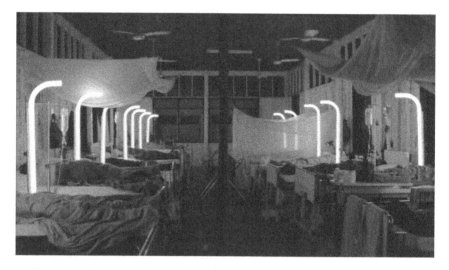

Fig. 2: The hospital room with the sleeping soldiers and neon lights. From *Cemetery of Splendour* (2015), dir. Apichatpong Weerasethakul.

Narratively, the hospital staff employs these lamps to soothe the soldiers in their troubled sleep. In an interview, Apichatpong comments on the inspiration for this imagery:

> There was an MIT professor who manipulated brain cells into re-enacting certain memories, via lights. He said that the findings sort of disproved Descartes' belief that the mind and the body are separate entities. This hypothesis aligned with my thinking that meditation is nothing more than a biological process. Sleep and memory can always be hacked into ... The lights in this film vaguely reflect this idea. They are not only for the soldiers but also for the audience as well.[24]

These words echo the phenomenological qualities of slow cinema. By using a slow rhythm paired with soft lights and a relaxing sound track, the director intends to directly alter the viewer's affective, bodily experience of the film. On top of that, his refusal of the Cartesian mind/body dichotomy is shared not only by phenomenology, but also by Deleuze, who refuted Descartes' transcendentalism in favour of "pure

---

[24] Apichatpong Weerasethakul, "Apichatpong's Cemetery", *Kick the Machine*, accessed 12 February 2021, http://www.kickthemachine.com/page80/page24/page26/index.html.

REPRESENTING MEMORY THROUGH SLOWNESS

immanence", a concept informed by Baruch Spinoza.[25] *Cemetery of Splendour* reflects such concept by merging the supernatural into the concrete and mundane, thus indicating that the supernatural does not lie in a transcendental dimension but, rather, one that is close to ours, with the ability to influence and being influenced by it.

This becomes more evident throughout the rest of the montage, as it continues with a shot showing a group of homeless people sleeping next to a sculpted wall, illuminated by a solitary street lamp. The hum of the hospital room's ceiling fan pervades the soundtrack, despite the stark change in location. This is followed by the shot of a canal, on the left side of which two young people are sitting and chatting, while a street cleaner picks up litter. Here and through the remainder of the montage, the same soundtrack persists, overlapping the hospital's soundscape with the outside world. This inscribes the shots of the montage in a continuum held together by a sound whose point of origin is now uncertain, rather than spatial, cause-and-effect links.

Other than sound, the film links together these shots with its use of light. In the canal shot, a green filter is gradually superimposed over the image. The filter carries over to the following shot, figuring a woman sleeping on a bus stop, where it slowly shifts to orange, then red. This filter matches the shifting neon lights previously shown inside the hospital room, thereby extending the sleeping soldiers' visual (on top of their aural) perspective to the space outside the hospital. Therefore, the rhythm of this montage is dictated by the soldiers' experience of duration while they dream. The film also juxtaposes this duration to images that lack or minimize diegetic action, acting as pure optical situations. Therefore, the montage creates an interplay of three durations: the duration felt by the spectator; the duration of the static, uneventful images; the duration of the soldiers' dreams, expressed by sound and light.

The montage concludes with two more shots, which stand out from the rest due to the fact that they are separated by a 40-second long dissolve. The first is a shot of a busy mall, where Jen and Itt previously went to visit the cinema. Jen walks towards an escalator, together with two mall guards who carry Itt's sleeping body. After the four leave the frame, the camera pans down to focus on a set of escalators, while the light filter keeps changing and the sound of the ceiling fan plays over the mall's diegetic soundscape. This shot dissolves into a wide shot of the hospital room with the sleeping soldiers, which brings back the sound

---

[25] See Gilles Deleuze, *Pure Immanence: Essays on a Life*, trans. Anne Boyman (New York: Zone Books, 2005).

and lights to their spatial point of origin. All in all, this montage disrupts spatiotemporal continuity and merges different durational perspectives to the point where the subjective and objective are no longer discernible. The coloured filters are not perceived by the Khon Kaen inhabitants featured in the montage's mundane tableaux. Moreover, it is unclear whether the tableaux themselves are seen by the sleeping soldiers, whose bodies are still inside the hospital. However, both realities are perceived by the spectator, whose visual and aural consciousness is at once inside and outside of the hospital.

Thus, *Cemetery of Splendour* foregrounds the possibility to experience multiple, subjective temporalities at once. Again, this reflects Apichatpong's aim of portraying memory-images, in a way similar to what he describes in the essay "Ghosts in the Darkness":

> I think this is one of the reasons I make films: my personal memories are always interwoven with those from various other sources, reading, listening and travelling (my own travels and those of others). It was hard then to remember the real past clearly, so I made films without knowing how true they really were. This was an important detail: it was like waking the dead and giving them a new soul, making them walk once more.[26]

By creating an interplay of subjectivities, *Cemetery of Splendour* visualizes how memories can be "shared" or interwoven with each other. The film's utmost magnification of this idea occurs near the end, when Itt falls into one of his regular sleeps and a psychic medium channels his dreaming spirit so that he may communicate with Jen. Through the medium's body, Itt describes to Jen the contents of his supernatural dream, although neither she nor the spectator can see it. Jen and the medium step into a forest area, which Itt describes as the kings' ancient palace, asking Jen to lower her head below an invisible doorframe and step over an invisible threshold while the two of them walk through the natural landscape. While Itt, through the medium's body, describes the palace interior, Jen comments on their contingent surroundings, such as an orchid that she has been growing on a tree. An example of the discrepancy between their two perspectives can be seen in a static shot, which opens with Jen pointing out the markings on a tree trunk caused by a past flooding. Seemingly ignoring her, Itt

---

[26] Apichatpong Weerasethakul, "Ghosts in the Darkness", in *Apichatpong Weerasethakul*, ed. James Quandt (Vienna: Synema, 2009), 104.

Fig. 3: Deep-focus shot that puts multiple temporalities in direct relation with each other. From *Cemetery of Splendour* (2015), dir. Apichatpong Weerasethakul.

steps into the background and traces the contours of an invisible mirror, where he claims that he can see Jen's reflection.

Using depth of field, Apichatpong separates the two characters between two different planes. The foreground is dominated by Jen, who curiously looks over at the invisible mirror, and the large tree trunk. Itt stands in the background facing away from the camera. This shot places multiple temporalities in relation with each other: the past of the ancient palace, relegated to Itt's dream; the past of the flooding, which left an indexical mark on the tree trunk; the present of Jen and the medium with their contingent, spatial surroundings. The use of depth of field to put multiple temporalities in relation to each other can be traced back to many of the mid-twentieth-century Euro-American films that Deleuze writes about. In particular, when analyzing the use of depth of field in the cinema of Orson Welles, the philosopher claims: "In this freeing of depth which now subordinates all other dimensions we should see not only the conquest of a continuum but the temporal nature of this continuum: it is a continuity of duration which means that the unbridled depth is of time and no longer of space", adding later that "most of the occasions where [it] appears wholly necessary are in connection with memory".[27] Creative uses of depth of field are

---

[27] Deleuze, 1985, 113–114.

common in many slow films, particularly those that make frequent use of static, tableaux-like shots. In the case of Apichatpong and *Cemetery of Splendour*, shots like the one earlier described further the director's aim to portray time and memory-images, by collapsing figures from different times and dimensions into the same shot.

The sequence and the film conclude by reaching pure indiscernibility between reality and dream. After Jen's long interaction with the medium/Itt, which concludes with the latter providing a long leg massage to the former, she suddenly wakes up next to Itt's bed. The shot of her waking up is repeated twice, immediately casting doubts about whether she has awoken at all. After both Jen and Itt have woken up, the two strike up another conversation, during which Jen says: "I can read your thoughts all of a sudden. I saw your dream", to which Itt replies: "And I saw yours", again opening the possibility of sharing dreams and consciousnesses, thereby further blurring the line between subjectivity and objectivity. In the film's final shot, Jen is framed staring at a distance with her eyes wide open, unblinking, a technique that was earlier taught to her by Itt as a means of forcibly waking up from a dream. Jen does can no longer know whether she is awake or asleep and, perhaps, neither can the viewer: the boundary between dream and wake has fully collapsed.

Again, as in the case of *Syndromes and a Century*, none of these experiences can be fully divorced from the corporeal. Once again, the medical setting provides ample room to explore the characters' biological processes. Among the bodily effects that the film shows are: Itt's mid-sleep erection, remarked upon with hilarity by the nurses; his urine, which must be collected in a catheter as he sleeps; Jen's surgery scar, which prompts the medium-Itt to administer the aforementioned leg massage. The fact that these characters are made of flesh is even more evident here than it is in *Syndromes and a Century*, and the flesh becomes the site for interpersonal encounters to the same degree as the sharing of dreams. As such, it would be futile to discuss whether one process is prioritized over the other: both inform Jen and Itt's experience and, by extension, the spectator's relation to them. The physical and metaphysical thus become inextricable and indiscernible.

Conclusion

Although the epithet "slow" carries with it a huge degree of subjectivity, making it a difficult descriptor to apply to any director's work, Apichatpong's adherence to the generic paradigms of slow cinema can offer us an interesting window into his approach to temporality.

By avoiding causal narrative, focusing on landscape and privileging wide shots over affective closeups, Apichatpong's films break the sensorimotor schema, opening up the image to a multiplicity of temporal interventions. The feeling of slowness, which has the potential to make the spectator frustrated, distracted or sleepy, also encourages them to actively engage with the present of the image, rather than build their cinematic experience around temporal anticipation or the search for linearized patterns. As such, Apichatpong's films directly confront the spectator with an experience of time as shifting and heterogeneous. In turn, this reflects the director's view of memories as indiscernible and often mixed with other sources, people or times. It is important for me to mention that, although this chapter has thus far discussed the director as the main, individual agent behind his films, Apichatpong himself refutes authorial signature on most of his credits, opting for the descriptor "conceived by" rather than "directed by". This signifies the fact that, although the main inspirations for films such as *Syndromes and a Century* and *Cemetery of Splendour* are the director's memories, these memories are always intertwined with others: those of his parents, his collaborators, and his cinematic subjects.

Albeit using different approaches, the two films analyzed in this chapter serve as excellent examples of this idea. While *Syndromes and a Century* confounds boundaries by placing two familiar but different narratives next to each other, *Cemetery of Splendour* overlaps two dimensions/temporalities/perceptual modes on top of each other. On top of that, both films also introduce elements of temporal disruption on a smaller scale by way of using uncanny flashbacks, disjoining sound and image, or blurring contingency with dreams. Rather than presenting them as purely abstract exercises, Apichatpong always brings these concepts back to corporeality: through alleged "slowness" in the case of the spectator, and through an attention for the everyday and the bodily in the case of his characters. As a matter of fact, most of Apichatpong's films, including the ones analyzed in this chapter, pay particular attention to the bodily functions of their characters from sleep, to copulation, to bowel movements. It is no coincidence that the final interaction between Jen and the medium in *Cemetery of Splendour* is an elongated leg massage during which the medium employs both her hands and mouth. Through all of these methods, Apichatpong's film break the Cartesian binary: they portray memory as an exercise of the mind *and* the body, because there is no stark separation between the two, as the director himself addresses in his remarks on *Cemetery of Splendour*. Thus, the embodied spectator can experience but also *feel* memories and dreams as direct images of time.

Bibliography

Bergson, Henri. *Time and Free Will: An Essay on the Immediate Data of Consciousness*. 1889. Trans. F.L. Pogson. Repr. 1910. Abingdon and New York. Routledge. 2013.

Bergson, Henri. *Creative Evolution*. 1907. Trans. Arthur Mitchell. Mineola. Dover Publications. 1998.

Bradshaw, Peter. "Cemetery of Splendour Review: A Very Calm Sort of Hysteria". *The Guardian*. 19 May 2015. Accessed 29 February 2020. https://www.theguardian.com/film/2015/may/18/cemetery-of-splendour-review-apichatpong-weerasethakul.

Çağlayan, Emre. *Poetics of Slow Cinema: Nostalgia, Absurdism, Boredom*. Cham. Palgrave Macmillan. 2018.

Ciment, Michel. "The State of Cinema". Speech at the 46th San Francisco International Film Festival. In *Unspoken Cinema*. Accessed 29 January 2021. https://unspokencinema.blogspot.com/2006/10/state-of-cinema-m-ciment.html.

Davis, Glyn. "Stills and Stillness in Apichatpong Weerasethakul's Cinema". In *Slow Cinema*. Ed. Tiago de Luca and Nuno Barradas Jorge. Edinburgh. Edinburgh University Press. 2016. 99–111.

Deleuze, Gilles. *Cinema 1: The Movement-Image*. 1983. Trans. Hugh Tomlinson and Barbara Habberjam. Minneapolis. University of Minnesota Press. 1997.

Deleuze, Gilles. *Cinema 2: The Time-Image*. 1985. Trans. Hugh Tomlinson and Robert Gaeta. London and New York. Bloomsbury Academic. 2013.

Deleuze, Gilles. *Pure Immanence: Essays on a Life*. Trans. Anne Boyman. New York. Zone Books. 2005.

Farmer, Brett. "Apichatpong Weerasethakul, Transnational Poet of the New Thai Cinema: *Blissfully Yours/Sud Sanaeha*". *Senses of Cinema* 38 (2006). Accessed 29 January 2021. http://sensesofcinema.com/2006/cteq/blissfully_yours/.

James, Nick. "Passive-Aggressive". *Sight & Sound* 20, no. 4 (2010): 5.

Kim, Jihoon. "Between Auditorium and Gallery: Perception in Apichatpong Weerasethakul's Films and Installations". In *Global Art Cinema: New Theories and Histories*. Ed. Rosalind Galt and Karl Schoonover. Oxford. Oxford University Press. 2010. 125–141.

Lim, Song Hwee. *Tsai Ming Liang and a Cinema of Slowness*. Honolulu. University of Hawai'i Press. 2016.

de Luca, Tiago. "Slow Time, Visible Cinema: Duration, Experience and Spectatorship". *Cinema Journal* 56, no. 1 (Fall 2016): 23–42.

de Luca, Tiago and Nuno Barradas Jorge. "Introduction". In *Slow Cinema*. Ed. Tiago de Luca and Nuno Barradas Jorge. Edinburgh. Edinburgh University Press. 2016. 1–24.

Quandt, James. "Resistant to Bliss: Describing Apichatpong". In *Apichatpong Weerasethakul*. Ed. James Quandt. Vienna. Synema. 2009. 13–30.

REPRESENTING MEMORY THROUGH SLOWNESS

Rayns, Tony. "Memories, Mysteries: From an Interview with Apichatpong Weerasethakul". *Kick the Machine*. July 2006. Accessed 29 January 2021. http://www.kickthemachine.com/page80/page24/page12/index.html.

del Rio, Elena. "Film". In *Handbook of Phenomenological Aesthetics*. Ed. Hans Reiner Sepp and Lester Embree. London and New York. Springer. 2010. 111–117.

Rodowick, D.N. *Gilles Deleuze's Time Machine*. Durham and London. Duke University Press. 1997. Repr. 2003. 81.

Sobchack, Vivian. *The Address of the Eye: A Phenomenology of Film Experience*. New Jersey. Princeton University Press. 1992.

Weerasethakul, Apichatpong. "Ghosts in the Darkness". In *Apichatpong Weerasethakul*. Ed. James Quandt. Vienna. Synema. 2009. 104–117.

Weerasethakul, Apichatpong. "Apichatpong's Cemetery". *Kick the Machine*. Accessed 29 January 2021. http://www.kickthemachine.com/page80/page24/page26/index.html.

Nonhuman

3

Stray Dogs and Strange Beasts
Apichatpong Weerasethakul's Queer Animal Ethics

Duncan Caillard

In the final scene of *Mysterious Object at Noon* (2000), Apichatpong Weerasethakul shows a dog being casually abused by two children. Split over nine shots, the encounter begins with a two shot of the children crouching in a garden playing with a toy car, before cutting to a closeup of their hands, and then panning over the shoulder of one of the children to a dog looking on from behind them. It cuts again, this time to a goat watching from the edge of the garden, then to a wide shot of the children grabbing the dog, followed by a close up of the dog as it struggles against the children tying a rope around its collar, then four cuts in quick succession: the dog runs away, the children chase after it, the shocked goat retreats behind a tree, and the dog flees in panic, dragging the toy car tied to its collar behind it. Coupled with the blur and unpredictability of the handheld camera, the unusually rapid editing of the four final shots (two seconds, two seconds, two seconds, four seconds) induces a state of alarm, a disorienting flourish to end a structurally disorienting film. Apichatpong refuses to show the children's faces, guiding our sympathies towards to the body of the suffering dog. We see the face of the dog—its expression a mixture of confusion and concern as the children tie it to the toy car—accompanied by the sound of the children's laughter. In this moment, Apichatpong distances us from his human subjects to instead invest us in the suffering of a non-human animal.

Stray dogs litter Apichatpong's cinema. They linger in train stations and guard posts, or approach characters looking for food. Jenjira Pongpas walks a pair of dogs through a garden in *Syndromes and a Century* (2006), feeds a stray dog fruit in *Uncle Boonmee Who Can Recall His Past Lives* (2010), and greets a stray dog who approaches her in the second act of *Cemetery of Splendour* (2015). Jessica Holland (Tilda Swinton) is followed through the streets of Bogata by a stray dog in *Memoria* (2021), whose unsettling presence recalls an earlier story from her sister (Agnes Brekke).

In *Memoria*, the uncanny body of the dog simultaneously trespasses social boundaries (as a stray animal) and spiritual boundaries between life and death (as a potential ghost). An entire page of his website is devoted to his pet dogs, who are named after famous movie monsters: King Kong, Dracula and Vampire.[1] Excluding *Tropical Malady* (2004) and *Memoria*, no dog returns to the narrative after its first appearance, and most occupy no more than two shots. Yet despite their recurrence throughout his work, dogs occupy a marginal position in Apichatpong's films, and more time is spent in cars, in doctors' surgeries, or among spirits and soldiers than with wandering dogs. Despite their marginal presence in each film, these dogs assume a collective importance when viewed as a metaphor of Apichatpong's broader filmmaking practice in which improvisation and nonhuman animals assume an elevated importance.

In this chapter, I trace the ethics of Apichatpong's filmmaking through the stray, a figure that allows us to reconcile the queer, migrant and animal subjectivities at the centre of his work. In her book *Stray: Human–Animal Ethics in the Anthropocene* (2017), Barbara Creed argues that the stray blurs categorical distinctions between humans and animals, as both are alienated from human society and are forced to survive tactically on its margins. By acknowledging what is shared by both human and animal strays—lost dogs, unhoused people, unregistered migrants, unaccepted queer people—all of whom populate Apichatpong's films. I begin by teasing out the concept of straying, placing Creed in conversation with French philosophers Emmanuel Levinas and Jacques Derrida to argue that the figure of the stray blurs categorical boundaries between animals, migrants and queers and can therefore serve as grounds for ethical relations between them. As straying crosses categorical boundaries between animals, migrants and queers, we can begin to understand their struggles and experiences in continuum with one another.

Building on this, I address the place of straying in Apichatpong's early filmmaking, examining his first three major films: *Mysterious Object at Noon* (2000), *Blissfully Yours* (2002) and *Tropical Malady* (2003). I first address how Apichatpong incorporates straying into his creative practice, describing how he prioritizes improvisation and collaboration over planning and narrative closure and, through this, argue that their unusual rhythms and production processes create inclusive spaces for human–animal intimacy and the reconciliation of queer, animal and migrant subjectivities in his films. I then consider the straying functions

---

[1] "Animals", *Kick the Machine,* accessed 18 December 2020, http://www.kickthemachine.com/page30/index.html.

as both a social practice and a relationship with time, functioning like queer temporality as a disengagement from the conventional rhythms and expectations of everyday life and a reinvestment in the moment-by-moment necessities of survival. Finally, I analyze how the categorical blurring of humans and animals facilitate intimate encounters between strays otherwise excluded by dominant society, allowing for the emergence of stray intimacies between them.

The Ethics of Straying

The figure of the "stray" resists stable definition. Creed resists defining "stray" as a single unifying concept, but broadly defines the stray as "an outsider, the other, an exile—the one who lives apart from the mainstream", a concept that applies to both humans and animals who "have drifted from their normal path, separated themselves from their kin, or been banished, rejected or abjected form their society because of their nature, situation, status or species".[2] As their homes are lost to the anthropocenic conditions of climate change, war, natural disaster and economic inequality, all beings can be uprooted and become strays, regardless of species. As such, a stray is not defined by its innate characteristics but rather by conditions of its exclusion. As Creed insists, "The concept of the stray helps civilised, settled societies define what it means to be civil and proper, obedient and law abiding. The stray is the 'other' of the symbolic order."[3] Humans, animals and things can all stray from established paths, places and ways of doing things, and in the process become strays: refugees stray when they escape across borders in pursuit of safety; dogs stray when they live without an owner; criminals and deviants stray when they trespass beyond the laws of the state. Our thoughts can stray—like Walter Benjamin's *flânerie*—diverging from our established tasks to creatively consider other objects of our attention.[4] On its most fundamental level, straying is characterized by abandonment and exclusion, both from communities and by the alienating conditions of anthropocenic modernity itself; as Creed writes, strays are united by their lack of "a place to belong, a sense of belonging and a sense of feeling cared for and/or loved".[5]

---

[2] Barbara Creed, *Stray: Human–Animal Ethics in the Anthropocene* (Sydney: Power Publications, 2017), 7–8.

[3] Creed, 2017, 8.

[4] Creed, 2017, 17.

[5] Creed, 2017, 10.

However, this very exclusion can serve as grounds for an emergent ethical relationship between strays who cohabitate at the margins of modern society. Strays transgress the socially imposed demarcations separating human and nonhuman animals, placing their suffering and marginalization in continuum with one another. "Straying", Creed writes, "is therefore not always an act of separation, but ... can potentially unite human and animal, particularly woman and animal, living on the fringes of society."[6] By recognizing that all strays—human and animal, migrant and queer—are alienated by intersecting social, economic and environmental marginalities, we can understand straying as an ethical act in itself.

This emphasis on otherness places Creed in contact with Emmanuel Levinas, whose philosophy—which he brands "ethics"—hinges on the obligations between Self and Other.[7] Levinas theorizes an ethical philosophy centring on the hospitable treatment of outsiders, and demands that "I" elevate the well-being of the Other over myself. For Levinas, the Other comes to me from a position of weakness—she is "the stranger, the widow, and the orphan" who arrives at my doorstep starving, cold and alone, whom I am obligated to assist.[8] For Levinas, this ethical demand hinges on the moment of a face-to-face encounter, an event which precedes identification or rational understanding. According to Levinas, when I come face-to-face with another person, I enter into a "primordial discourse" that obligates me to her, and places her well-being and right to existence above my own.[9] To see the face of the Other is to recognize the precarity of her life and to acknowledge the reality of her suffering.

Levinas insists that my obligation to the Other is not contingent on similarities between us, as to do so would reduce otherness to sameness. The Other is wholly other; she is unfamiliar to me and comes from a place outside of my immediate community of social obligations. By

---

[6] Creed, 2017, 9.

[7] Levinas' use of the term "ethics" differs substantially from its conventional definition. Across his writing, Levinas is less concerned with specific moral questions of right or wrong than with interrogating the very conditions by which human beings can behave ethically at all. For further discussion, see Jacques Derrida, "Violence and Metaphysics", in *Writing and Difference*, trans. Alan Bass (Chicago: Chicago University Press, 1980), 111.

[8] Emmanuel Levinas, *Totality and Infinity: An Essay on Exteriority*, trans. Alphonso Lingis (The Hague, Boston and London: MartinusNijhoff Publishers, 1979), 215.

[9] Levinas, 1979, 201.

STRAY DOGS AND STRANGE BEASTS 73

situating the Other from a place outside of my home or tribe, Levinas ruptures nationalistic logics that demand ethical obligation only to those *like me*, as the Other is *nothing like me*. Therefore, the Levinasian encounter with otherness is not concerned with reducing the Other to a comfortable sameness, but rather operates by leaving the alterity of the Other intact, without collapsing it into conditions that are familiar to me.[10] As Judith Butler argues in her own reading of Levinas:

> To respond to the face, to understand its meaning, means to be awake to what is precarious in another life or, rather, the precariousness of life itself. This cannot be an awakeness, to use his word, to my own life, and then an extrapolation from an understanding of my own precariousness to an understanding of another's precarious life. It has to be an understanding of the precariousness of the Other.[11]

A stray is by its very nature Other, and it approaches me from outside my immediate community of obligations. Rather than reject the stray on the basis of this difference, Levinas calls for the stray to be accepted on the basis of its alterity, for me to recognize its needs and treat it hospitably accordingly.

However, unlike Creed, Levinas ultimately excludes animals from his ethics, and denies that an animal can make ethical demands in the same way as human beings. Echoing Martin Heidegger, Levinas maintains an ontological distinction between humans and all other beings, refusing to accept the evolutionary assertion that "the human is only the last state of the evolution of the animal", and insists instead that "the human is a new phenomenon".[12] As Jacques Derrida argues in his essay "The Animal That Therefore I Am", Western philosophy has historically operated under the belief that animals are deprived of language, without which they are deprived of the capacity to transcend their imminent circumstances and find their own recognisable place in the world.[13] As Derrida argues, this

---

[10] Brian Bergen-Aurand, "Regarding Anna: Levinas, Antonioni and the Ethics of Film Absence", *New Review of Film and Television Studies* 4, no. 2 (2006): 109.

[11] Judith Butler, *Precarious Life: The Powers of Mourning and Violence* (London and New York: Verso Books, 2004), 134.

[12] Cited in David L. Clark, "On Being 'The Last Kantian in Nazi Germany': Dwelling with Animals after Levinas", in *Postmodernism and the Ethical Subject*, ed. Barbara Gabriel and Suzan Ilcan (Montreal: McGill-Queen's University Press, 2004), 56.

[13] Jacques Derrida, "The Animal that Therefore I Am (More to Follow)", in

animal lack of language strips them of "the power to name, to name oneself, and indeed to answer for one's name", and instead, the word "animal" is used by humans "to corral a large number of living things within a single concept" in order to designate, as a single homogeneous group "all the living things that man does not recognise as his fellows, his neighbours, or his brothers".[14] Following this tradition, Levinas argues that an animal's lack of language precludes it from rationality and subjectivity, (supposedly) preventing humans from participating in ethical discourse with it. He writes, "the [human] face speaks to me and thereby invites me to a relation incommensurate with a power exercised".[15] The linguistic silence of animals and their inability to name themselves excludes them from the human neighbourhood and marks them as inhuman and subject to violence. Comparably, this imposed silence also serves as grounds for violence against migrants and queer people who, much like animals, are marginalized to the point where they are unable to speak for themselves and are thereby exposed to social exclusion and violence.

Apichatpong, however, rejects this categorical distinction between humans and animals. Subscribing to a Buddhist logic of reincarnation, his films understand human and animal existence in continuum with one another; humans become animals and animals become humans in an ongoing chain of death and rebirth.[16] In a director's statement for *Uncle Boonmee*, Apichatpong reinforces his belief in continuity between human and animal, stating that "I believe in the transmigration of souls between humans, plants, animals, and ghosts. Uncle Boonmee's story shows the relationship between man and animal and at the same time destroys the line dividing them."[17]On these terms, Apichatpong not only places humans and animals in ontological continuum with one another but understands the medium of cinema as uniquely suited to express this relationship. Many of his animals—from magical catfish to monkey spirits—speak, while many of his human characters only do so sparingly. Even without speaking to us directly, the dog at the end of *Mysterious Object at Noon* calls us to consider its treatment ethically,

---

The Animal That Therefore I Am, trans. David Willis (New York: Fordham University Press, 2008), 32.

[14] Derrida, 2008, 19, 32, 34.

[15] Levinas, 1979, 198.

[16] Bronwyn Finnigan, "Buddhism and Animal Ethics", *Philosophy Compass* 12, no. 7 (2017): 9.

[17] Cited in Anders Bergstrom, "Cinematic Past Lives: Memory, Modernity, and Cinematic Reincarnation in Apichatpong Weerasethakul's *Uncle Boonmee Who Can Recall His Past Lives*", *Mosaic* 48, no. 4 (2015): 11.

and to recognize its needs as valid and meaningful. Apichatpong refuses to show the children's faces, and we instead see the face of the dog—its expression a mixture of confusion and concern as the children tie it to the toy car—accompanied by the sound of the children's laughter. Here, Apichatpong frames the children as impersonal tormenters, cutting off their upper bodies to instead centre the scene on the body of the suffering dog. Yet rather than simply being a question of representation, Apichatpong incorporates the act of straying into the filmmaking process itself, using it as a means of maintaining ethical relation to his subjects—both human and animal.

Stray Practice: *Mysterious Object at Noon* (2000)

A curious feature of Apichatpong's filmmaking is the common recurrence of animals wandering in and out of shots, with little or no apparent purpose to their actions. In *Cemetery of Splendour*, Apichatpong includes not one but two shots of a family of chickens wandering past an open door, with no narrative motivation to drive their presence. In one long take of *Tropical Malady*, four characters converse over Pepsi in an older woman's shopfront with a group of stray dogs congregating in the background of the frame. The movements of the dogs are undirected, and they are allowed to move about freely within the shot without regard for their impact on continuity. In each of these cases, Apichatpong's camera finds pleasure in watching their unrehearsed movements, prioritizing their unpredictable bodies over narrative progress and resolution. Here, we see straying function as an approach to filming itself, a comfort with improvisation and unexpected outcomes that grounds Apichatpong's method of filmmaking.

Given the (historically) high costs of film production, straying has occupied a marginal place in studio filmmaking, instead finding greater resonance with independent filmmakers. Characters stray frequently in the post-war films of Vittorio De Sica and Michelangelo Antonioni, but also manifest in contemporary works of slow cinema, such as the films of Tsai Ming-liang (one of Apichatpong's major influences). In his own analysis of Apichatpong's films, David Teh situates his work within both a history of itinerant cinema in Thailand and the practice of Surrealist ethnography, an approach to filmmaking that prioritizes uncertainty and chance within the production process.[18]

---

[18] David Teh, "Itinerant Cinema: The Social Surrealism of Apichatpong Weerasethakul", *Third Text* 25, no. 5 (2011): 595–609.

Like bodies, our thoughts and observations can themselves stray, we can become bored or distracted and, through this, challenge established orders of business. As Creed writes, "An unexpected word, a stray thought and outside point of view, all have the power to inspire and challenge the dominant and controlling point of view .... Perhaps the most precious things we have are those stray thoughts that shift the ground from under us."[19] On these grounds, I identify three key characteristics of stray practice: first, an openness to improvisation and comfort with unplanned or unintended outcomes; second, an emphasis on process over outcome, with a disinterest in resolution; and, finally, a focus on communality over hierarchy, taking an inclusive approach to creative practice that allow for the contributions of different voices and subjectivities.

Stray practice manifests in Apichatpong's filmmaking as early as *Mysterious Object at Noon,* his first and most unusual feature film. Apichatpong took an improvisational approach to the film's construction, famously structuring the film as an *exquisite corpse,* a Surrealist parlour game in which collaborators contribute to a single work by adding new details to a piece without seeing the work as a whole, through which images and texts emerge as chimeras of juxtaposed details. Using the method, Apichatpong filmed a series of interviews across Thailand in which he invited his subjects to improvise new additions to an evolving story that centred on a disabled boy and his carer, a woman named Dogfahr. These interviews are interspersed with scripted recreations by actors, although Apichatpong makes little effort to stylistically differentiate between them. The story only ends when a group of children decide to have Dogfahr killed and eaten by a tiger and, even then, Apichatpong kept shooting until he ran out of funding and film stock, providing a natural limit to the filming process. Through this approach, Apichatpong abdicated narrative control—exchanging his director credit for "conceived and edited by"—thereby allowing the film's narrative to evolve over time without his direct interference. Through this production strategy, Apichatpong refuses to orient his narrative towards a predetermined destination, and instead prioritizes the moment-by-moment decisions of his collaborators.

This comfort with improvisational straying allows for a more inclusive approach to creative practice, permitting both greater diversity among human collaborators and leaving room for the unexpected actions of animals. As already discussed, Apichatpong's long take, deep focus coverage method allows for characters and objects to move more freely

---

[19] Creed, 2017, 18.

within the frame, allowing both humans and animals to improvise without disrupting continuity. At one point in *Mysterious Object at Noon*, one of his child actors breaks character and asks when the catering will arrive. In response, Apichatpong calls cut but keeps the camera rolling, stepping into the frame himself to converse with his actors. The rest of the scene shows actors rehearsing, Apichatpong conversing with his crew, and children playing on-set, further blurring the distinction between the film's scripted narrative and a documentary about the film production process itself. Allowing these otherwise unimportant activities to continue but actually centralizing their presence within the body of the work itself, embodies the act of straying itself, leaving room for the improvisations and unexpected actions of his collaborators.

As Apichatpong's career has progressed and the political controversies surrounding his work have intensified at home, his straying has become an act of political necessity. Following the 2014 coup d'état that brought General Prayuth Chan-ocha's junta to power, censorship in Thailand has intensified, exacerbating the already undemocratic tendencies of the state's military government. Citing the increased risk to himself and his crew, Apichatpong stated that *Cemetery of Splendour* would be his last feature film shot in Thailand under the current regime; his forthcoming film *Memoria* instead would be shot in Columbia—his first feature filmed outside of Thailand. Apichatpong describes this creative migration as an alienating process, a fundamental separation from spatial and cultural memories that he can count as his own. Describing the new setting of his film, he states that "I cannot represent a genuine memory there. As an outsider, you just feel like you cannot and will not understand certain things. You're really on the outside."[20] Forced into a position of political vulnerability, Apichatpong strays from the familiar conditions of Thailand to a place in which he is an unsettled outsider. Yet by accepting his status as an outsider and continuing to produce work despite pressures at home, Apichatpong demonstrates that the act of straying serves as both a means of personal survival and of political resistance, a method of exceeding and evading the authoritarian structures of present reality.

Straying therefore functions as a rhythmic feature of Apichatpong's filmmaking, partly explaining the unique temporalities of his films. Through long take, deep focus cinematography and a freeform approach

---

[20] Cited in James Wham, "News to Me: Apichatpong Weerasethakul, Lisandro Alonso, RIP Roeg and Bertolucci", *Film Comment*, 27 November 2018, https://www.filmcomment.com/blog/news-apichatpong-weerasethakul-lisandro-alonso-rip-roeg-bertolucci/.

to narrative, Apichatpong allows himself to stray with his collaborators, open to their contributions without reducing them to prewritten expectations. By doing this, he creates an inclusive space for artistic collaboration in which the diverse needs of others—such as untrained actors, people with disabilities, and animals—can meaningfully contribute.

Stray Temporality: *Blissfully Yours* (2002)

Across his films, Apichatpong's characters display unconventional relationships with time, characterized by an emphasis on playfulness and unproductivity. His multichannel installation *Primitive* follows a group of young men in the small Isan town of Nabua, and responds to the generational trauma that reverberates through the region from the anti-communist purges that took place decades earlier. Rather than restage this trauma directly, Apichatpong instead passes time with his subjects, dressing up, playing games and building a mock spaceship out of wood in a field.[21] One channel of *Primitive*, titled *Phantoms of Nabua*, shows the group playing soccer with a flaming soccer ball on a field surrounded by projector screens. When a screen catches fire, the men watch on as the fabric disintegrates and collapses with little regard for the consequences of their actions. *I'm Still Breathing*, another channel of *Primitive*, was shot as a music video and shows the men running through the dirt roads of the town with no clear direction or purpose; they simply keep running. Living under the shadow of possible military conscription, the actions of the young men reject the militarization of Thai society (the very government responsible for purges decades earlier), as they do not lead them anywhere, produce anything or serve a discernible purpose, and steadfastly refuse to be regimentalized. In the act of straying, the young men reject the structures and strictures of conventional life and offer an alternative way of living in the world.

Such stray temporality emerges from the tactical exigencies of survival, a focus shift from social priorities of futurity and progress to moment-by-moment conditions of life. Defined by precarity, stray existence demands strategies for survival, and therefore unites human and animal strays in the tactical demands of the here and now.[22] Stray

---

[21] Ryan Inouye, "Apichatpong Weerasethakul: In Time", interview with Apichatpong Weerasethakul, in *Apichatpong Weerasethakul: Primitive* (New York: New Museum, 2011), 12.

[22] Creed, 2017, 64.

temporality is characterized by a jarring alternation between moments of frantic activity and long periods of comparative inaction, comingling desperate acts of survival with extended periods of listlessness. To stray entails periods of languished wandering, of generalized disinterest in ordinary tasks or objects, and a fluid relation to time.

Given its alienation from conventional forms of social productivity, stray temporality exists in continuum with the similarly non-normative structures of time. In his theorization of queer temporality, Jack Halberstam argues that, following the AIDS crisis, the "constantly diminishing future" of queer existence places "a new emphasis on the here, the present, the now, and while the threat of no future hovers overhead like a storm cloud, the urgency of being also expands the potential of the moment and ... squeezes new possibilities out of the time at hand".[23] Similarly, in her work on queer phenomenology, Sara Ahmed argues that queerness is a fundamentally disorienting state of being, as conventional landmarks of family, progress and normative embodiment slip away, and queerness becomes "a way to inhabit the world at the point at which things fleet".[24] Rather than pulling back from this uncanny disorientation, Ahmed suggests that one "might even find joy and excitement in the horror", to relish this disappearance of organised purpose and productivity that can be found in a new relationship to time.[25]

Acts of temporal rebellion manifest across all of Apichatpong's films, but are most overt in *Blissfully Yours*. The film follows three marginalized individuals living in a Thai border town: Min, an illegal Burmese immigrant with a painful skin condition, Roong, a young female factory worker, and Orn, her middle-aged landlady. As May Adadol Ingawanij and Richard MacDonald argue, the border town is represented "as a space of alienation and repressive authority", within which different characters are restrained by overlapping social forces of work, family and nation.[26] The film's plot is divided into two acts, separated by a title sequence that starts 40 minutes into the film. The first shows the stifling

---

[23] Jack Halberstam, *In a Queer Time and Place* (New York and London: New York University Press, 2005), 2.

[24] Sara Ahmed, "Orientations: Toward a Queer Phenomenology", *GLQ: A Journal of Lesbian and Gay Studies* 12, no. 4 (2006): 566.

[25] Ahmed, 2006, 544.

[26] May Adadol Ingawanij and Richard Lowell MacDonald, "Blissfully Whose? Jungle Pleasures, Ultra-modernist Cinema and the Cosmopolitan Thai Auteur", in *The Ambiguous Allure of the West: Traces of the Colonial in Thailand* (Hong Kong: Hong Kong University Press, 2010), 128–129.

conditions of their everyday existence, and the second their escape to a nearby forest for a day of relaxation.

In the film's opening scene, the two women take Min to a doctor to medicate his skin condition, but he is unable to speak without exposing his identity as a Burmese immigrant. Unable to speak for himself, Min is reduced to a position of helplessness and leaves unmedicated. After leaving the clinic, Orn takes Min to visit her husband at work, where she expresses her desire to have another child, but her husband is disinterested and instead blames her for the unexpected death of their first. Roong works in an antiseptic, windowless factory where she paints dozens of identical porcelain *Looney Tunes* figurines (a curious juxtaposition of American escapism with the stifled conditions of her own life), and must feign illness to escape work with her friends. As their lives interweave with each other over the course of a morning, we witness the subtle overlapping forms of institutional repression: Min is marginalized and silenced as an undocumented Burmese migrant; Roong struggles with the stifling conditions of her low-status work as an industrial worker; Orn is frustrated as a married woman dependent upon a disinterested husband and lives a life devoid of emotional intimacy. These repressive conditions push the three characters to escape the boundaries of the town to nearby jungle—and by extension stray beyond the social confines of their everyday lives—where they spend the remainder of the film walking, eating and sleeping together by the side of a river.

In this act of socio-temporal straying, all three characters adjust their relation to time, productivity and progress. As an "illegal" migrant, Min has strayed from his legally defined home country, and survives precariously through the support of Orn and Roong. For the first half of the film, Min exists as an accessory to the women of his life, carrying shopping bags and waiting for them to finish their errands, with limited control over his own life schedule. In a voiceover later in the film, Min notes how Roong compared teaching him Thai to training a dog, further associating his social marginalization with a state of animality. Despite this, Apichatpong conditions the wilderness as a space devoid of external authorities and the imposition of conventional time, and the two lovers are given time to drift between places and activities. Rather than follow a strict path through the forest, Min guides them by memory, crossing cliffs and ravines until they find a rocky outcrop looking out onto a valley where the two prepare a picnic lunch. By showing Roong leave work earlier in the day, Apichatpong places this liberated temporality in direct contrast to expectations of work and productivity; their actions in the forest do not serve a material purpose—or even work towards narrative conclusion—but rather offer a form of existence detached from those expectations of progress. As viewers, we are given no indication of where the narrative will progress and must instead (like characters on screen) experience the film world haptically, intimately engaged with the immediate conditions of existence.

Understood on these terms, *Blissfully Yours* intersects two forms of stray temporality: one diegetic, one formal. Diegetically, Apichatpong's characters stray from the restrictive structures of everyday life in the border town to the moral and temporal freedoms of the wilderness. In opposition to the restrictive social circumstances an unregistered migrant, a female factory worker and a middle-aged housewife found in the town, their experiences in the wilderness present an alternative temporal logic that prioritizes immediacy over conventional expectations of productivity and progress, enmeshed in the elemental pleasures of life in the wilderness. Yet this temporal straying also permeates the film form itself. Like its diegetic strays, *Blissfully Yours* prioritizes momentary and immediate pleasure over narrative progress and resolution. Instead of motivating spectatorship through the promise of narrative payoff, Apichatpong invests our attention in the moment-by-moment unfolding of its action, avoiding conventional mandates of pacing and developmental progress. As spectatorial strays, we follow the film's temporal unfolding with our "nose to the ground", confronted only by what is immediately and sensorially present.

Stray Intimacy: *Tropical Malady* (2004)

This focus on immediate existence and entailed forms of non-normative temporality can also serve as grounds for divergent forms of intimacy, linking back to a Levinasian ethics. Intimacy entails physical, emotional or social closeness between beings, a comfortable familiarity shared between intimate partners, within families or close-knit communities. To be intimate (sexually or otherwise) is to be exposed to someone else and is therefore characterized by a condition of shared vulnerability. Intimacy is also temporal. It can last for years or just moments, but entails a shared sense of time, spending time together, 'stepping into' someone else's time rather than an imposition of my own. Given its social and emotional significance in human life, intimacy is regulated by society and culture, setting strict parameters on how, when, why we can be intimate, and with whom. For these reasons, intimacy strays, forming improvised and unexpected relationships between people, places and things.

Issues of intimacy recur across Apichatpong's films, but are felt most acutely in *Tropical Malady*. A queer love story in two acts, *Tropical Malady* engages with questions of human–animal intimacy, which are established through the film's opening quote from Japanese novelist Ton Nakajima: "All of us are wild beasts. Our duty as human beings is to become like trainers who keep their animals in check and even teach them to perform tasks alien to their bestiality." This engagement with animality is reinforced by *Tropical Malady*'s original title—*Satpralat* (สัตว์ประหลาด)—which translates into English as "monster", but is the compound of the Thai words "sat" (animal) and "pralat" (unusual). Within the film, this "monster" refers to the shape-shifting tiger of Thai folklore of the film's second act, but subtextually refers to its use in early-1980s queer magazines as gay speak for male homosexuals.[27] This threefold meaning—unusual creature, monster, homosexual—highlights the permeability of these categories and the social monstrosity of queerness, and lays groundwork for *Tropical Malady*'s dramatic conflict between civilization and animality.

The film's first act centres on a gay romance between Tong (a young man from the country, or *chao baan*) and Keng (a soldier visiting his family home), and follows the pair as their relationship blossoms across a series of dates in town. Whereas the town of *Blissfully Yours* is explicitly repressive, the city of *Tropical Malady* is far more ambivalent. As moral strays deviating from conventional expectations of their sexuality, the public spaces of the city allow Keng and Tong to be freed from the expectations of home, spending time together in music lounges, movie theatres and night markets, where their intimacy is permitted. In one of the film's utopian scenes, Tong is invited on stage at a music performance, where he publicly performs a ballad to Keng sitting in the audience. As Anika Fuhrman notes, this "seemingly unopposed public homoeroticism" runs counter to the usually conservative representations of queer sexuality in Thailand, and that by situating their relationship in moments of leisure rather than narratives of overcoming adversity challenges the conventional representation of its working-class protagonists.[28]

Nevertheless, the utopian dimension of *Tropical Malady* is stifled by the conditions of its protagonists' everyday lives. Born into a poor rural

---

[27] Benedict Anderson, "The Strange Story of a Strange Beast: Receptions in Thailand of Apichatpong Weerasethakul's *Sat pralaat*", in *Glimpses of Freedom: Independent Cinema in Southeast Asia* (New York: Cornell Southeast Asia Program Publications, 2012), 149.

[28] Anika Fuhrmann, "Ghostly Desires: Sexual Subjectivity in Thai Cinema and Politics after 1997", Ph.D. diss., University of Chicago, 2008, 183–184.

family, Tong cannot read, write or drive a car. He works at a factory processing large cubes of ice—loud, uncomfortable and dangerous work that runs counter to the pleasurable conditions of his leisure time with Keng. Apichatpong establishes this dissatisfying rhythm of Tong's everyday life through repetition, placing two near-identical sequences at the ice factory less than two minutes apart near the beginning of the film, interspersed with games of volleyball and a bus trip, and in the next scene he struggles drive a military truck under Keng's instruction, and stalls next to a lake. The rhythms of these everyday failures, placed in dissatisfying succession, emphasize the depressing pace of Tong's everyday life along with his crushing sense of inadequacy in comparison to Keng, to the point where Tong puts on a military uniform to search for better work in town. Later in the film, as the pair sit in a gazebo on the edge of the forest, Keng notices a series of cuts along Tong's arm, who quickly turns away and changes the topic. At each moment, Tong is marginalized: he is illiterate, unhappily employed and implicitly at odds with his family over his sexuality, undermining the socio-sexual freedoms of his life with Keng.

Just as Min's powerlessness in *Blissfully Yours* is linked to his inability to speak, Tong's illiteracy demonstrates his incapacity to articulate his sexuality. By contrast, Keng is comfortable enough to express his sexuality publicly (he chats amicably with another gay man in a restroom and shares knowing smiles with an aerobics instructor), whereas Tong remains silent with his family, diverting attention from a love letter his mother finds while washing his pants. Like an animal, Tong has lost the power to name, to name himself, or indeed to answer for his own name, and is reduced to a state of deprivation and helplessness.[29] He is, in the Derridean sense, poor-in-the-world twice over: first due to his social marginalization as a queer *chao baan*, and second due to his illiteracy and corresponding incapacity to articulate his sexuality.[30] In this position of vulnerability, Tong is animalized. Due to this barrier, there is an irreconcilable difference between the two men, where differences in social status prevent them from being fully intimate with one another. Socially alienated, Tong retreats into the darkness of the jungle at the film's midpoint, abruptly ending the relationship with Keng, and beginning the film's transition to its second act.

At this point, *Tropical Malady* shifts genre from realist romantic drama to supernatural horror film, its second act framed as the journey

[29] Derrida, 2008, 19.
[30] Derrida, 2008, 38.

84 DUNCAN CAILLARD

of a soldier (played by Keng) into the heart of the jungle in pursuit of a malevolent shape-shifting tiger spirit, the *satpralat* (played by Tong). In contrast to the bright, open spaces of *Blissfully Yours*, the jungle of *Tropical Malady* is dense, claustrophobic and impossible to navigate. Creed notes that the tropical jungle operates as an uncanny space in which categorical distinctions between human and animal are blurred and conventional orientations are lost.[31] Unlike the differentiated social spaces of the first act, the jungle of the second is a homogeneous space devoid of landmarks, treated through a mixture of shallow focus and dense foliage to confuse our spatial orientation. As Keng moves through the jungle, he is observed by the *satpralat*—taking the form of Tong's naked human body—through the tree line, eventually fighting one another on the verge of the forest where Tong steals Keng's equipment and irreparably damages his radio (the last vestiges of modern civilization in the wilderness). This act is almost entirely devoid of spoken dialogue, but instead focuses on the gestures and physicalities of its characters, which become increasingly animalistic as the film progresses. Understood on these terms, the second act of *Tropical Malady*—like *Blissfully Yours*—inverts the social dynamic of the first; whereas the city (as a domain of language) represents a space of cultivated social hierarchy, the jungle collapses those differences into animal horizontality. As an animal space without language and civilization, Tong and Keng exist on equal footing for the first time in the film.

This equality is realized in the film's final scene, when Keng and the *satpralat*—which has transformed into the shape of a magnificent tiger—finally come face-to-face. In this moment of cathartic intimacy, the social distinctions that previously separated its human and animal characters dissolve. This reconciliation is stated to Keng by the film's final lines of dialogue from the *satpralat*, who through Tong's voice speaks: "Once I've devoured your soul, we are neither animal nor human. ... I give you my flesh, my spirit, and my memories. Every drop of my blood sings our song. A song of happiness. There, can you hear it?" In this moment of face-to-face contact, Keng and Tong not only reconcile with each other but also resolve the seemingly oppositional states of humanity and animality. As a space inhabited by talking monkeys and speechless humans, the jungle of *Tropical Malady* collapses the distinction between human and animal, allowing Tong to communicate intimately with Keng in ways they could not when they were both "fully" human. Consequently, Apichatpong presents the act of straying

[31] Creed, 2017, 133.

as a condition of intimacy between humans and animals, between humans-as-animals and animals-as-humans capable of making ethical demands of one another.

Conclusion

Apichatpong incorporates straying as an ethical principle into all levels of his practice: in the diegetic lives of his characters, as a temporal feature of his film form, and as an approach to film production. His characters are temporal rebels, diverging from conventional expectations of productivity and progress to focus on the immediate (often pleasurable) conditions of everyday life. He attempts to liberate his creative practice from expectations of progress, structure and resolution, concentrating instead on moments of chance and improvisation, and rather than trying to limit the movements of his subjects (human or animal) to predetermined schemas. Apichatpong instead allows them to roam freely within the frame, challenging the conventional expectations of blocking and dramatic storytelling. Through this, Apichatpong creates space for intimate interpersonal encounters, collapsing socially imposed distinctions and allowing moments of face-to-face contact between humans and animals sharing the subaltern status of the stray.

Acknowledgement

An earlier draft of this paper was presented at the 13th Asian Cinema Studies Society Conference at LASALLE College of the Arts, Singapore in 2019. I express my thanks to my friends, colleagues and supervisors at the University of Melbourne for their feedback on early drafts.

Bibliography

Ahmed, Sara. "Orientations: Toward a Queer Phenomenology". *GLQ: A Journal of Lesbian and Gay Studies* 12, no. 4 (2006): 543–574.

Anderson, Benedict. "The Strange Story of a Strange Beast: Receptions in Thailand of Apichatpong Weerasethakul's *Sat pralaat*". In *Glimpses of Freedom: Independent Cinema in Southeast Asia*. Ed. Adadol Ingawanij and Benjamin McKay. Ithaca. Cornell Southeast Asia Program Publications. 2012.

Bergen-Aurand, Brian. "Regarding Anna: Levinas, Antonioni and the Ethics of Film Absence". *New Review of Film and Television Studies* 4, no. 2 (2006): 107–129.

Bergstrom, Anders. "Cinematic Past Lives: Memory, Modernity, and Cinematic Reincarnation in Apichatpong Weerasethakul's Uncle Boonmee Who Can Recall His Past Lives". *Mosaic: A Journal for the Interdisciplinary Study of Literature* 48, no. 4 (2015): 1–16.

Butler, Judith. *Precarious Life: The Powers of Mourning and Violence.* London and New York. Verso Books. 2004.

Clark, David L. "On Being 'the Last Kantian in Nazi Germany': Dwelling with Animals after Levinas". In *Postmodernism and the Ethical Subject.* Ed. Barbara Gabriel and Suzan Ilcan. Montreal. McGill-Queen's University Press. 2004.

Creed, Barbara. *Stray: Human–Animal Ethics in the Anthropocene.* Sydney. Power Publications. 2017.

Derrida, Jacques. *Writing and Difference.* Trans. Alan Bass. Chicago. Chicago University Press. 1980.

Derrida, Jacques. "The Animal That Therefore I Am (More to Follow)". In *The Animal That Therefore I Am.* Ed. Marie-Louise Mallet. New York. Fordham University Press. 2008.

Finnigan, Bronwyn. "Buddhism and Animal Ethics". *Philosophy Compass* 12, no. 7 (2017): 9.

Fuhrmann, Arnika. "Ghostly Desires: Sexual Subjectivity in Thai Cinema and Politics after 1997". D.Phil. South Asian Languages and Civilisations. University of Chicago. 2008.

Halberstam, Jack. *In a Queer Time and Place.* New York and London. New York University Press. 2005.

Ingawanij, May Adadol and Richard Lowell MacDonald. "Blissfully Whose? Jungle Pleasures, Ultra-modernist Cinema and the Cosmopolitan Thai Auteur". In *The Ambiguous Allure of the West: Traces of the Colonial in Thailand.* Ed. Rachel V. Harrison and Peter A. Jackson. Hong Kong. Hong Kong University Press. 2010. 119–134.

Inouye, Ryan. "Apichatpong Weerasethakul: In Time". In *Apichatpong Weerasethakul: Primitive.* Ed. Gary Carrion-Murayari. New York. New Museum. 2011. 18–27.

Levinas, Emmanuel. *Totality and Infinity: An Essay on Exteriority.* Trans. Alphonso Lingis. The Hague, Boston and London. Martinus Nijhoff Publishers. 1979.

Teh, David. "Itinerant Cinema: The Social Surrealism of Apichatpong Weerasethakul". *Third Text* 25, no. 5 (2011): 595–609.

Wham, James. "News to Me: Apichatpong Weerasethakul, Lisandro Alonso, RIP Roeg and Bertolucci". *Film Comment.* 27 November 2018.

STRAY DOGS AND STRANGE BEASTS

Filmography

Blissfully Yours [*Sud Sanaeha*]. Dir. Apichatpong Weerasethakul. Thailand. Kick the Machine. 2002.

Cemetery of Splendour [*Rak Ti Khon Kaen*]. Dir. Apichatpong Weerasethakul. Thailand. Kick the Machine. 2015.

Memoria. Dir. Apichatpong Weerasethakul. Thailand and Columbia. Kick the Machine. 2021.

Mysterious Object at Noon [*Dogfahr Nai Meu Marn*]. Dir. Apichatpong Weerasethakul. Thailand. 9/6 Cinema Factory. 2000.

Syndromes and a Century [*Sang Sattawat*]. Dir. Apichatpong Weerasethakul. Thailand. 9/6 Cinema Factory & Firecracker Films. 2006.

Tropical Malady [*Sud Pralad*]. Dir. Apichatpong Weerasethakul. Thailand. Kick the Machine. 2004.

Uncle Boonmee Who Can Recall His Past Lives [*Lung Boonmee Raluek Chat*]. Dir. Apichatpong Weerasethakul. Thailand. Kick the Machine. 2010.

4

Imagining the Nonhuman in the Cinema of Apichatpong Weerasethakul

Çağatay Emre Doğan

Introduction

Towards the end of Apichatpong Weerasethakul's *Syndromes and a Century* (2006), in an approximately eight-minute sequence, the camera shows a corridor in the hospital's basement, seats to the right and a striped tarp to the left hiding an unsightly view behind. As the camera tracks left ever so slightly as if catching the wave of the billowing tarp, we find ourselves looking at the construction work, the source of the industrial sounds of grinding and hammering. A non-diegetic electronic ambient noise joins the industrial sounds. The camera moves through the doors, corridors, and offices, showing Dr Wan, waking up from a nap, Dr Toey, staring right ahead with a blank expression, Dr Nohng sneaking out with his lover and Jen (Jenjira Pongpas) leaving the all-white sterile corridor limping. In this sequence, the people appear as descriptive components of the atmosphere rather than centers of a narrative. With a slow pan, we discover the parts of the prosthetics workshop covered with a mist: first, we see the ceiling with the pipes, insulated air ducts, the lights, and below a power lathe and other machinery, pieces used to make prostheses and a few wheelchairs. The camera slowly follows the mist in a weightless featherlike movement and stops right in front of a funnel-like ventilation pipe that sucks in the air. The camera wanders in an artificial landscape of pipes, machinery and smoke. The long takes of these nonhuman beings almost create a separate plane of existence. Looking at a funnel where the smoke slowly disappears for more than a minute makes us, the spectator, lose the linear sense of cinematic time and the anthropocentric habit of a continuous space where we are asked to partake in an experience that, as I will argue, pushes us towards the nonhuman.

Nevertheless, discussing a director such as Apichatpong in terms of nonhuman can be seen as a fruitless attempt. First, as an *auteur*,

89

Apichatpong uses his personal memories, political histories of people and places to create a unique cinematic style. So we have a strong presence of the author that focuses on human stories across centuries, past, present, personal or collective. In one sense, if we consider the cinematic apparatus itself in "essence" designed to mimic the human vision, or when we think of the conventions of expression that are created for human perception and phenomenological experience of images, a post-humanist cinema may be meaningless. So the question is, what can be the nonhuman of cinema, and in what ways Apichatpong's films can be viewed through the lens of post-humanism? In this chapter, I am examining Apichatpong's cinema in its manifestation of the nonhuman turn by specifically concentrating on scenes from *Syndromes and a Century* (2006), *Uncle Boonmee Who Can Recall His Past Lives* (2010), *Mekong Hotel* (2012), *Sakda (Rousseau)* (2012), *Cactus River* (2012) and *Cemetery of Splendor* (2015).

In the following section I will review the theoretical discussions of the nonhuman in cinema. After that, I will examine how Apichatpong's cinema gives power to the objects, spaces and relationality to challenge the authority of the camera and anthropocentric imagination of the viewer. I will start with the landscape in Mekong Hotel and move on to the question of genius loci to demonstrate how nonhuman and physical spaces in particular play an essential role in Apichatpong's cinema.

Posthumanism/Nonhuman Turn

In media and film studies, post-humanism is commonly equated with post-humanity, a temporal and ontological marker often exemplified with the cinema of extinction; in other cases, the post-human thought takes a teleological move towards a new form of existence, embodied as cyborgs, and other hybrid life forms, but most notably the post-human question revolves around the transformative power of technology, and what comes after the Anthropocene.[1] The widespread confusion between the transhuman and post-human is a consequence of this future-oriented understanding, despite the attempts to clear the definitions of post-humanism from the teleological aspect.[2] For the

---

[1] Michael Hauskeller, Thomas D. Philbeck and Curtis D. Carbonell, eds., *The Palgrave Handbook of Posthumanism in Film and Television* (London: Palgrave Macmillan UK, 2015). Articles collected in the book will give an idea of the preoccupation with what comes after humans.

[2] Cary Wolfe, *What Is Posthumanism?* (Michigan: University of Minnesota Press, 2010), xi–xiii.

majority of the thinkers, such as Eva Horn, Katherine Hayles and Rosi Braidotti, post-humanism is a novel and opportune historical moment of rethinking humanity's place in the world and the displacement of human exceptionalism.[3] A similar trend on the displacement of the human, as William Brown observes, can be found in what he calls cinema of extinction and dystopian sci-fi cinema that imagines what comes after the human.[4]

Against the utopian/dystopian visions of the future after the human, Richard Grusin uses the term nonhuman that relies on the idea that "the human has always co-evolved, coexisted, or collaborated with the nonhuman—and that the human is characterized precisely by this indistinction from the nonhuman".[5] Grusin names several theoretical developments that are under this umbrella term, nonhuman turn: actor-network theory, affect theory, animal studies, assemblage theory, new brain sciences, new materialism(s), new media theory, systems theory, varieties of speculative realism, object-oriented philosophy, neo-vitalism, panpsychism.[6] Rethinking the ontological primacy of the human and its limits, these theories often question the relation between what is putatively designated as a human agency—hence dethroning its privileged position—and its others, be it objects, things, or other species. Nevertheless, not all these theories found a resonance in the domain of

---

[3] Eva Horn, *The Future as Catastrophe: Imagining Disaster in the Modern Age*, trans. Valentine Pakis (New York: Columbia University Press, 2018); Braidotti, *The Posthuman* (Oxford: Polity Press, 2012); N. Katherine Hayles, *How We Became Posthuman: Virtual Bodies in Cybernetics, Literature, and Informatics* (Chicago: University of Chicago Press, 1999).

[4] William Brown, "Man without a Movie Camera—Movies without Men: Towards a Posthumanist Cinema?", in *Film Theory and Contemporary Hollywood Movies*, ed. Warren Buckland (New York, London: Routledge, 2009), 66–85.

[5] Richard Grusin, "Introduction", in *The Nonhuman Turn*, ed. Richard Grusin (Minneapolis, London: University of Minnesota Press, 2015), ix–x. Grusin refers to Brian Massumi's reading of Simondon as a source for the term nonhuman. Massumi writes: "For me, a Simondonian ethics of becoming is best to befound not in a next 'posthuman' phase, but in the nonhuman at the 'dephased' heart of every individuation, human and otherwise." Brian Massumi, "'Technical Mentality' Revisited: Brian Massumi on Gilbert Simondon", in *Gilbert Simondon: Being and Technology*, ed. Arne De Boever, Alex Murray and Jon Roffe (Edinburgh: Edinburgh University Press, 2012), 36.

[6] Grusin, 2015, viii–ix.

film theory.[7] This was perhaps because cinema has always been anthropocentric, not only by featuring, "human figures carrying out heroic deeds" but also by producing images specifically for the human eye.[8]

However, cinema has always had the potential to open new perspectives and show us worlds that are not our own. In this sense, cinema would be the best place to experiment with the return to the nonhuman things themselves. Thomas Elsaesser points out such an ontological turn in late twentieth and twenty-first century world cinema, prioritizing "the presence and agency of things".[9] Against a realism rooted in correspondence, this new ontological realism is against the groundlessness of representation and cinema's epistemological reliance on the visible evidence. Elsaesser further argues that this new realism "responds to the unknowability of 'other minds'" and respects this otherness.[10] It is precisely in this relation to the otherness that we can think of the nonhuman. The skepticism of the post-epistemological cinema does not necessarily remove the central role of human perspective from the films. Yet it is possible to find parallels with this new international realist cinema and the nonhuman turn in theory and philosophy of the last three decades.

Apichatpong's work creates a perfect opportunity to observe this new cinema, the cinema of art-house and international film festivals rather than the mainstream cinema or the popular media dominated by online streaming channels today. From the jungle in *Tropical Malady* to the cave in *Uncle Boonmee*, whether he is showing a landscape or an interior with ambient noises, Apichatpong's cinema seems to question the limits of human-centered cinematic narrative. Instead, his cinema pushes the classical protagonists to the margins and offers us a gateway

---

[7] Luka Arsenjuk, "On the Impossibility of Object-Oriented Film Theory", *Discourse* 38, no. 2 (2016): 197–214. For example, object-oriented philosophy despite its popularity in the museum and gallery spaces, is not well received in cinema studies. Arsenjuk argues that the real and the sensuous object distinction in Graham Harman's work—the sharp separation of appearance from being is opposed to what cinema is.

[8] William Brown, "From DelGuat to ScarJo", in *The Palgrave Handbook of Posthumanism in Film and Television*, ed. Michael Hauskeller, Thomas D. Philbeck and Curtis D. Carbonell (London: Palgrave Macmillan UK, 2015), 11–18.

[9] Thomas Elsaesser, "World Cinema: Realism, Evidence, Presence", in *Realism and the Audiovisual Media*, ed. L. Nagib and C. Mello (London: Palgrave Macmillan UK, 2009), 5.

[10] Elsaesser, 2009, 19.

IMAGING THE NONHUMAN

to the multiple plains of existence, of animals, ghosts, buildings, forests and rivers.

The traditional markers of his cinema are the use of the long take, static long shots, deep focus, and little to no action. Therefore, it is not a surprise that Apichatpong's name often appears in the discussions of slow cinema, among names such as Béla Tarr, Tsai Ming-Liang, and Abbas Kiarostami, who invite the viewer to experience the temporality as duration rather than action.[11] Indeed, static shots of landscapes, such as the eight-minute long final scene of *Mekong Hotel*, which is the image of the Mekong river with a few jet skis making circular maneuvers in front of the bridge that connects Thailand to Laos; or the use of still images in *Syndromes and a Century* and *Uncle Boonmee Who Can Recall His Past Lives* are the most obvious examples that bring Apichatpong's cinema one step closer to slow cinema.[12] Gilles Deleuze's formative concept of time-image, a post-World War II phenomenon in cinema, that replaces the cinema of movement-image, which relies on the sensorimotor images created primarily through montage, is an important starting point for discussing slowness. "Time ceases to be derived from the movement, it appears in itself", writes Deleuze to describe the salience of time in cinema.[13] The absence of diegetic "action, motion and emotion" inspires discussions of "contemplative" in slow cinema and directs our attention to the phenomenological experience of the audience.[14] According to Jihoon Kim, Apichatpong carries the "excessive duration" of video art into "the visionary and tactile long-takes of his feature films accompanying the ambient sounds

---

[11] Tiago De Luca and Nuno Barradas Jorge, eds., *Slow Cinema* (Edinburgh: Edinburgh University Press, 2016); Ira Jaffe, *Slow Movies: Countering the Cinema of Action* (London, New York: Wallflower Press, 2014); Lutz Koepnick, *On Slowness: Toward an Aesthetic of the Contemporary* (New York: Columbia University Press, 2014); Song Hwee Lim, *Tsai Ming-Liang and a Cinema of Slowness*, Illustrated edition (Honolulu: University of Hawaii Press, 2014).

[12] Glyn Davis, "Stills and Stillness in Apichatpong Weerasethakul's Cinema", in *Slow Cinema*, ed. Tiago De Luca and Nuno Barradas Jorge (Edinburgh: Edinburgh University Press, 2016), 99–111.

[13] Gilles Deleuze, *Cinema II: Time Image (1985)* (London, New York: Continuum, 2005), xi.

[14] Ira Jaffe for instance refers to Raymond Bellour's article "The Pensive Spectator" (1984), and writes, "The physical stillness, emptiness and silence in slow movies may instigate, for instance, pensiveness about the non-existence that precedes and follows life, or about metaphysical emptiness in the human soul, a void at the root of human consciousness." Jaffe, 2014, 4.

of diegetic surroundings".[15] In other words, for Kim the slowness is a consequence of a happy exchange between cinema and video art, the duration of the diegetic space on the screen, and the duration of the viewer's "phenomenological perception".[16]

Yet there is more to Apichatpong's cinema than the absence of movement or action image or the emphasis on the viewer's phenomenological experience identified as self-reflection or meditative inquiry into the interior of one's own consciousness. The observational aspect of his cinema is not necessarily centripetal, refocusing on the human aspect, replacing the action, the human agency on the screen with that of the audience. The empty landscapes where nothing happens or the prominence of characters who engage in relaxing everyday conversations and float in the relaxing rhythms of nature bring a different meditative state that is not necessarily an inward movement. The quasi-documentary vision of realistic environmental details is rather an experience of immersion within the nonhuman world. While Apichatpong moves between fiction, documentary and experimental films, his cinema must not be confused with nature documentaries, or the search for scientific or technical images, or the materiality of the recording apparatuses. In other words, it is a question of neither reproducing the ocularcentric observational epistemes nor defining an apparatus completely "decoupled from human agency".[17] Indeed, Apichatpong's cinema demonstrates what Karen Barad names as the human, nonhuman intra-action, where the elements of this intra-action come to being through their relationality without one being ontologically privileged than the other.[18] Instead, Apichatpong's cinema reposits

---

[15] Jihoon Kim, "Between Auditorium and Gallery: Perception in Apichatpong Weerasethakul's Films and Installations", in *Global Art Cinema: New Theories and Histories*, ed. Rosalind Galt and Karl Schoonover (New York: Oxford University Press, 2010), 131.

[16] Kim, 2010, 134.

[17] Joanna Zylinska, for example, investigates the imaging practices "from which the human is absent—as its subject, agent, or addressee". Moving images that are never received by a human eye certainly is a very exciting topic, yet not a subject matter for this paper. Joanna Zylinska, *Nonhuman Photography* (Cambridge MA: MIT Press, 2017).

[18] Karen Barad, in contrast to the "interaction" which assumes that there are separate individual agencies that precede their interaction, defines "the notion of intra-action". Intra-action recognizes that "distinct agencies do not precede, but rather emerge through, their intra-action". Karen Barad, *Meeting the Universe Halfway: Quantum Physics and the Entanglement of Matter and Meaning* (North Carolina: Duke University Press, 2007), 33.

the relation between humans and the nonhuman in a way that calls into question the privileged position from which the anthropocentric perception experiences the world.

Within film theory, Adrian Ivakhiv's ecocritical cinema poses a similar question by following a process-relational ontology and affect theory to include not only the subject matter (what is being filmed) but also the process of semiosis, cinematic apparatus as materiality more than a representation: "The perceptual or mental realm is not the realm of ideas or meanings as distinct from matter. It is the interactive dimension among living things, which are material bodies perceived, or 'imaged,' and responded to by other material bodies."[19] This Deleuzean definition of the cinematic image allows a materialist thinking that overcomes mind–body duality but not necessarily the ethical question of anthropocentrism.

I argue, Gilbert Simondon's relational ontology of becoming offers an entry point, a source of inspiration toward a nonhuman cinema. I propose to look at Apichatpong Weerasethakul's cinema from a post-epistemological and post-anthropocentric lens, against the violent reduction of the complexity of matter to representations elaborated by human thinking. Simondon's primary theoretical move that makes his thought unique at the time is to replace the "unquestioned ontological privilege granted to the individual"[20] with relationality, particularly "as the relation of milieu and individual".[21] In this modality, the individual is not defined by a self-contained system of difference, but instead it is in a constant process of becoming within and through a milieu. This idea of constant becoming can be used to criticize the narrative center of cinema, which often takes the form of a system of signification surrounding a protagonist where the natural world is seen as separate *res extensa*. In contradistinction, an understanding of becoming with the milieu opens up a system of relationships and potentialities, which goes beyond a merely spatial understanding of the environment. Here, the subject–object dichotomy and epistemological centering of the human is abandoned, as for Simondon exteriority does not exist outside the individual. Even if the difference in space exists in Simondon,

[19] Adrian J. Ivakhiv, *Ecologies of the Moving Image: Cinema, Affect, Nature* (Waterloo: Wilfrid Laurier University Press, 2013), 36.
[20] Jacques Garelli, "Foreword: Introduction to the Problematic of Gilbert Simondon", in *Individuation in Light of Notions of Form and Information*, Vol. 1, by Gilbert Simondon (Minneapolis: Minnesota Press, 2020), xviii.
[21] David Scott, *Gilbert Simondon's Psychic and Collective Individuation: A Critical Introduction and Guide* (Edinburgh: Edinburgh University Press, 2014), 35.

this difference is not the Hegelian dialectical difference that puts objects/subjects against one another or a Cartesian difference that demarcates borders in their stability. Instead, the difference appears as disparation.[22] The term disparation, which Simondon borrows from the psychophysiology of perception, can be useful to think with. This term designates the production of depth in binocular vision and addresses the asymmetry of retinal images that create an irreducible disparity, which problematically produces a stable image through the resolution of their difference: each retina receives a different image, and these two images are integrated into a new axiom of tridimensionality and depth.[23] This is how Simondon defines transduction as a primary model for an ontology of becoming, and how disparities work in individuation:

> A discovery of dimensions whose system makes the dimensions of each of the terms communicate, such that the complete reality of each of the terms of the domain can become organized into newly discovered structures without loss or reduction [...] there is no impoverishment of information contained in the terms; [...] the result of this operation is a concrete fabric including all the initial terms.[24]

In other words, the disparity of different realms of existence lets them keep their own singularity. This, I argue, is how Apichatpong uses the background music and sounds, parallel timelines, and storylines, personal and impersonal memories. In each instance singularity of the disparate elements is preserved without reduction or loss of information. Instead of focusing on the characters as static entities, Apichatpong's cinema seeks the creative potential of disparities coming together while keeping their singularities, which is particularly significant for a non-anthropocentric vision in cinema.[25]

---

[22] Anne Sauvagnargues, *Artmachines: Deleuze, Guattari, Simondon*, trans. Suzanne Verderber and Eugene W. Holland (Edinburgh: Edinburgh University Press, 2016), 61–84.

[23] Gilbert Simondon, *Individuation in Light of Notions of Form and Information*, Vol. 1 (Minneapolis: Minnesota Press, 2020), 229.

[24] Gilbert Simondon, 2020, 15.

[25] Duncan Caillard and Graiwoot Chulphongsathorn, observe a similar concern for the nonhumans respectively for animals and for the planet in Apichatpong's cinema. Graiwoot Chulphongsathorn, "Apichatpong Weerasethakul's Planetary Cinema", *Screen* 62, no. 4 (2021): 541–548; Duncan Caillard, "Stray Dogs and Strange Beasts: Queer-Animal Ethics in the Early Films of Apichatpong Weerasethakul" in the same volume.

Mekong Hotel or the River as the Witness

In what follows, I will be specifically examining Mekong Hotel as a site of this nonhuman encounter in the way it displaces the spectator and invites for this different relation that undoes and question the privileged human-centered perspectives.

Mekong Hotel (2012) is Apichatpong's experimental documentary set in a hotel overlooking the Mekong river, the border separating Thailand from Laos. Concomitantly, the film itself remains at the border between documentary and fiction. In fact, the film's synopsis reads: "The film shuffles different realms, fact and fiction."[26] In other words, the fictional story of a film project and the story of making a film (documentary) merges and shift from one to another. Apichatpong explains this multilateral movement between fiction and reality:

> I think I am pretending to mean reality when I say "fact." But in movies, reality doesn't exist. One is just trying to capture moments and reconstruct them to simulate your view, your understanding. This film is conscious of these layers and levels of distortion. So I think that it can be called a "documentary" in a classical sense. It is a contemplation on making a fiction.[27]

Here, Apichatpong explains not only his interest in the transitions between genres, but also how these factual and fictional coexist in cinema, defining two separate realms that overlap with each other.

The scripted scenes of the fiction allow the spectators to follow the main storyline. However, it is not easy to separate these rehearsal scenes from the casual conversations among the crew members. In the reenactment of the original story, Ecstasy Garden, Apichatpong wrote in 2002, the daughter (Maiyatan Techaparn) falls in love with a young man (Sakda Kaewbuadee) the son of the owner of the nearby banana plantation. The girl's mother (Jenijira Pongpas) is a pob ghost (*phi pop*), who eats animal and human flesh.[28] She eventually kills and eats her

---

[26] Apichatpong Weerasethakul, "Mekong Hotel", accessed 2 January 2021, http://www.kickthemachine.com/page80/page1/page20/index.html.

[27] Apichatpong Weerasethakul, "Mekong Hotel Press Kit", *The Match Factory*, 2012, https://www.the-match-factory.com/catalogue/films/mekong-hotel.html.

[28] Weerasethakul describes this as a vampire-like alien species in the original Ecstasy Garden story. In Mekong Hotel, we see strong references to the Thai horror films where pob ghost, which is a genderless spiritual entity unique to the region's folklore, is presented as a female ghost

Fig. 1: Apichatpong Weerasethakul, *Mekong Hotel* (Illuminations Films, 2012).

own daughter. However, the mother, imprisoned in a magic pot at the river's bottom, remains connected to her daughter's spirit, who follows her lover through numerous reincarnations.

The opening of the Mekong Hotel is the black screen that follows the credits and the audio of the brief conversation between Apichatpong and the guitarist Chai Bhatana (the director's old friend). The guitar solo which continues all through the film starts shortly after the scene cuts into the view of the river from the terrace of the hotel. The architecture of the hotel (the balustrades, steel staircase and the roof structure above, parts of the canopy frame, the glossy flooring tiles and the sculptures on ionic pedestals, miniature palm trees, and another roof structure at the ground level) frames the river and the Laotian shores across the river (see Fig. 1). This cut from the recital scene to the long shot of the Mekong river provides us with an idea of how central the river is.

This incessant music replaces the sounds of the continuously flowing Mekong river, the unifying thread of the whole film. In an interview, Apichatpong states that the guitar reminded him of the flow of water. Indeed, he emphasizes continuity and movement: "I imagined music

---

with insatiable hunger and taste for human and animal flesh. Natalie Boehler, "Staging the Spectral: The Border, Haunting and Politics in Mekong Hotel", *Horror Studies* 5, no. 2 (2014): 198, https://doi.org/10.1386/host.5.2.197_1.

that flows like water. It is eternal and always transforming, with minute variations."[29] Although the use of music here feels like non-diegetic sound, it is possible to imagine the film through the opening guitar scene, the real-time recording of the music, and the stories that share the same space with the guitar's sound. The music remains at the same volume all through the film, hence, the meditative (or/and monotonous) guitar gives the feeling of a recording near a flowing water, a background noise. The music and the river concurrently play and interact through the visual, sonic and affective scenes. Just like the river itself, which overpowers the flood barriers, the music at points overpowers the conversations of the figures in the foreground; the music floods the film dialogues. Moreover, the music does not seem to follow the film's structure or editing, it does not contribute to the creation of mood, tempo or tension. On the contrary, the music almost has its own autonomous presence throughout the film. The sound of the guitar, despite its strong presence, is not fully supported by the visual cues; visual and acoustic do not necessarily create a unity.[30] This, as Selmin Kara observes with respect to digital documentaries, creates a "self-contained acoustic ecology" which is comparable to what Michel Chion describes as "anempathetic" sounds in cinema that "exhibit a conspicuous indifference to the action or emotion depicted in a scene".[31]

The guitar in the Mekong Hotel plays a very similar role vis-à-vis the diegetic sounds. Lovatt argues that in Apichatpong's films "the sound of the environment is often so dominant that it dismantles our reliance on the verbal or the linguistic to ground our understanding of what is happening in the narrative, and instead encourages (or rather insists upon) an embodied, phenomenological, engagement with the scene".[32] The sound design in classical cinema privileges the human

---

[29] Weerasethakul, "Mekong Hotel Press Kit", 2012.

[30] A similar observation is made by Selmin Kara and Justin Remes about Abbas Kiarostami's Five: Dedicated to Ozu. See Justin Remes, "The Sleeping Spectator: Non-Human Aesthetics in Abbas Kiarostami's Five: Dedicated to Ozu", in Slow Cinema, ed. Tiago De Luca and Nuno Barradas Jorge (Edinburgh: Edinburgh University Press, 2016), 231–242; Selmin Kara, "The Sonic Summons: Meditations on Nature and Anempathetic Sound in Digital Documentaries", in The Oxford Handbook of Sound and Image in Digital Media, ed. Carol Vernallis, Amy Herzog and John Richardson, Reprint edition (New York, Auckland, Cape Town: Oxford University Press, 2015), 582–597.

[31] Michel Chion, Audio-Vision: Sound on Screen, trans. Claudia Gorbman, 2nd edition (New York: Columbia University Press, 2019), 211, cited by Kara, 2015, 593.

[32] Philippa Lovatt, "'Every Drop of My Blood Sings Our Song. There Can

voice and lowers the ambient sound; thus the name "talking pictures" rather than sound cinema, became the first to mark the transition from silent films. The human voice brings the characters to the center of each scene, enhancing the hierarchical order between the protagonists and their environment, which exists only to support the main character's actions. Perhaps something he brings from his exhibition pieces and video installations, Apichatpong, on the other hand, creates his soundscapes, so that sonic spectatorship becomes as important as the visual experience.[33] What is most interesting is his use of ambient sound to create a non-hierarchical, flat surface, to use Laura Marks's definition of haptic hearing: "all sounds present themselves to us undifferentiated, before we make the choice of which sounds are most important to attend to".[34] This experience is continuous in Mekong Hotel, which creates a flatness, where speech and sound distinction becomes less essential and the way audio connects with the visual. In other words, the material presence of the nonhuman world, in the form of a separate acoustic universe, enters the scene as strong as if not stronger than the human narrative.

Similar layers of music and background noise appear in two of Apichatpong's short films of the same year. In *Sakda (Rousseau)* (2012), under the dim light of a stage, the monologue of the reincarnated Rousseau (Sakda Kaewbuadee), is accompanied by the same guitar melody as Mekong Hotel. We can see Chai Bhatana playing the guitar with short intervals of inaudible conversations. The monologue and the guitar performance seem to be two disparate yet overlapping events just like the lives of the actor (Sakda) and the reincarnated soul of Rousseau. The effect is the rawness of a rehearsal, elevated by the vitality, and the spontaneity of the actor. However, the second time Sakda's voice is heard from a recording machine on the terrace by the Mekong river, with slight differences from the original. Sakda asks "Will I remember the freedom? Will I remember the rubber tree stories?" as if questioning the traces of memory on the recording device, now a new plane of existence that is free of the human form.[35] In *Cactus*

You Hear It?': Haptic Sound and Embodied Memory in the Films of Apichatpong Weerasethakul", *The New Soundtrack* 3, no. 1 (2013): 62, https://doi.org/10.3366/sound.2013.0036.

[33] Lovatt, 2013.

[34] Laura U. Marks, *The Skin of the Film: Intercultural Cinema, Embodiment, and the Senses* (Durham: Duke University Press, 2000), 183.

[35] *Sakda (Rousseau)*, in *La Faute à Rousseau: une collection de films courts*, DVD (Genève: HEAD, 2012). The whole script reads: "I used to be a man named Rousseau. But today my name is Sakda. I have a boyfriend

IMAGINING THE NONHUMAN

River (Khong Lang Nam) (2012) Apichatpong uses the rumbling noise of the wind hitting a microphone as a continuous thread throughout the film. Apichatpong describes the film as "a diary of the time I visited the couple [Jenjira Pongpas who changed her name to Nach and her husband Frank Widner]—of the various temperaments of the water and the wind".[36] Indeed, the sound of the wind is the constant flow of time in fast forward, which allows measured time to enter the scene as the timecode indicator of a video camera. But it also slows down and allows the tactile sounds such as crinkling plastic sheets from the knitting yarn basket, the splash of water, or the cutting of a watermelon in the kitchen to appear as disconnected pieces of human memory. In both short films, just as in Mekong Hotel, human and nonhuman memories and multiple flows of time are juxtaposed.

The presence of the Mekong river is felt all throughout Mekong Hotel, not just through the flow of the guitar music. The river is visible in most scenes. The river is always on the scene, formally and as the central topic in the dialogues, such as the floods, government measures against the flood, and subsidized boats, which businesses would remain open. Since Apichatpong juxtaposes multiple stories without letting any narrative dominate the film, he allows the river to become more manifest than any other component.

Like one would expect from a more conventional filmic language, the Mekong river first appears as a landscape, a background, a decor defined by the characters it supports and the actions they perform. However, the river ceases to be the backdrop for the events, especially in the rehearsal scenes and in one scene through a unique spatial play. Right after the daughter, Phon (Maiyatan Techaparn), who was possibly possessed by her mother (pob ghost played by Jenjira Pongpas), consumes a piece of flesh in a rather beastly manner, we see her wearing the same clothes, on the terrace, staring and smiling at the camera. Yet we never truly know whether she is the actor Maiyatan Techaparn or Phon. In one of the rare moments when the director uses continuity editing to define a continuous perception of space, Phon walks into the next scene where she meets Thong (Sakda Kaewbuadee), the boy in the love story. This is the first time the young couple sees each other, and they discuss the

---

named Laurent. He is a rubber tree specialist. But today I will no longer be Sakda. Because my body belongs to no one nor myself. But I will remember the freedom ... He's a rubber tree specialist. I will no longer be Sakda. Because my body belongs to no one nor myself. Will I remember the freedom? Will I remember the rubber tree stories?"

[36] *Cactus River (Khong Lang Nam)* (Walker Art Center, 2012), https://youtu. be/H5vToT_ionU.

Fig. 2: Apichatpong Weerasethakul, *Mekong Hotel* (Illuminations Films, 2012).

remains of an imaginary dog eaten by a "pob ghost". Throughout the whole conversation, the actors turn their backs to the camera and face the Mekong river. The actors are placed within the context of their relationship with the river and each other more than the camera.

The long shot from behind does not create a distance between the audience and the actors. Instead, this small architectural unit of reinforced concrete frame creates an interior, an intimate space, and a backstage where the camera is located. The crew lives and shoots the film in the same location. Here, the hotel's terrace turns into a stage, but the camera is not where the audience would be. The documentary reenactment of acting faces the opposite direction, as if the audience of the stage is on the other side, where the landscape, Mekong river, and the Laotian shores are. It is a spatial marker: the hotel turns into a stage. The real question is which side of the stage the audience is on. At the end of the conversation, Phon and Thong turn and stare at the camera. This interaction with the camera is not exactly a Brechtian gesture of distancing because we, the audience, never, at any point, are fully immersed in the rehearsed story. The ambiguity of the fictional and factual does not allow that. On the contrary, this gesture is a subtle transition from fictional to factual and a marker that shows how Apichatpong articulates human and nonhuman relations.

This ambiguity brings his cinema closer to what Levi Bryant (after De Landa) calls the flat ontology, according to which humans are not at the center of being but are among other beings. Objects exist on their own regardless of whether any human being relates to them or not.[37] Apichatpong's camera captures what is out there—things that exist independent of us, human knowledge and human vision. This flatness exemplified here in acoustic terms is also pertinent to how we experience the figure-ground relationship in *Mekong Hotel*. The river ceases to be a background and a landscape and becomes something else, perhaps a witness, audience or spectator. This possibility of the sentient matter is something inaccessible to human knowledge, but the river and the indeterminacy of action displace the humanist center and blur the line between human and nonhuman, the environment and the subject.

Just like the sound and speech, and the sound and image relations, figure and ground appear as intra-acting where even if they are distinct, they can only become possible with the existence and relation to the other as equal participants of a relational space where their existence does not "precede their intra-action".[38] The river becomes something else than the body of water that we use for something, and it is no longer an object or a natural thing that is simply out there. The point is that we do not know what it is exactly. The river takes away its episte-mologically objective character; it is not knowable by us; it can only be experienced as such.

The way Apichatpong approaches the questions of place and space, whether it is landscape, architecture, natural or manmade environments, occupies a significant place among the scholars who study his films, particularly around the issues of memory, overlapping spaces and timelines. Boehler, who explores haunting in *Mekong Hotel*, argues that the ghosts in the film are carriers of the region's memory.[39] The cinematic presence of the river, the hotel, and, finally, the Laotian border

[37] Levi R. Bryant, "The Democracy of Objects", *New Metaphysics* (2011): 249, https://doi.org/10.3998/ohp.9750134.0001.001. De Landa wrote: "One philosophical consequence of this new conception of species must be emphasized: while an ontology based on relations between general types and particular instances is hierarchical, each level representing a different ontological category (organism, species, genera), an approach in terms of interacting parts and emergent wholes leads to a flat ontology, one made exclusively of unique, singular individuals, differing in spatio-temporal scale but not in ontological status." Manuel DeLanda, *Intensive Science and Virtual Philosophy*, Revised edition (London, New York: Bloomsbury Academic, 2013), 47.

[38] Barad, 2007, 33.

[39] The choice of in-between spaces certainly is essential for the spectrality and creating a ground for the return of the repressed traumas. Boehler, 2014, 204.

at a larger scale is as strong as the ghostly or supernatural beings. The nonhuman landscape, without being personified, joins the ghosts to create a non-anthropocentric cinematic world, where we encounter different layers of personal and collective memories, traumas, human and nonhuman, living and non-living beings on a flat plane cinematic mise-en-scene.

Genius Loci, Spatiality and Temporal Layering

Apichatpong's other films can be analyzed in similar terms. Ingawanij observes the layers of memory as a palimpsest, where "creatures and ghosts remain but are suspended in a state of silent waiting: they cannot haunt as yet but neither have they become permanently erased".[40] Nonhuman memories are not limited to mythical creatures or historical events; what is at stake, as Chulphongsathorn argues, is "an archive of world memories wherein the history of humanity intertwines with the history of Earth, or even of the universe itself".[41] In *Cemetery of Splendour* (2015), which revolves around the spirit of a place, Jen (Jenjira Pongpas) volunteers at a makeshift hospital that houses soldiers plagued with an unknown disease that makes them sleep. Jen befriends one of the soldiers Itt (Banlop Lomnoi), who does not have any family visitors and Keng (Jarinpattra Rueangram) a young psychic who helps the families communicate with the comatose men. Jen visiting Itt every day discovers the connection between the ancient site beneath the clinic and the mysterious sleeping sickness. We must add that the English title of the film is different from *Thai Rak Ti Khon Kaen,* which translates as *Love in Khon Kaen.* Khon Kaen is where the director spent his childhood. So, as in his other works, personal and collective memories overlap, and the landscape becomes an essential component of the film. The English title of the film directly refers to the cemetery underneath the school/hospital building. The film's opening and closing scenes show the excavation of a field near the hospital which refers to an "archaeological imagination" that looks at the landscape through the lens of layers of memory that can be recovered from the surface.[42] The whole landscape

[40] May AdadolIngawanij, "Animism and the Performative Realist Cinema of Apichatpong Weerasethakul", in *Screening Nature: Cinema Beyond the Human,* ed. Anat Pick and Guinevere Narraway (New York: Berghahn Books, 2013), 97.

[41] Chulphongsathorn, 2021, 543.

[42] Archaeological imagination is a term I borrow from Hauser's work on landscape photography. Kitty Hauser, *Shadow Sites: Photography,*

turns into an excavation as the kids play football on the mounds created by the construction crew. Also, during the imaginary tour Itt (in Keng's body) gives Jen of the hidden palace, broken pieces of statues in the park, unused signs, and dilapidated park furniture are similar to the archaeological objects found in an excavation. Yet the smooth transition from one archaeological layer to another is striking in this scene. Jen pointing to a small stem of figs grown on the giant trunk of a fig tree recognizes a line created by a flood she had witnessed: "Here during the great flood, some years ago, the water rose up to here." Itt responds, "come look. It's the princess's wardrobe. There are mirrors everywhere." The dialogue seems completely disconnected from each other. But, actually, it shows the copresence of multiple modes of existence, not necessarily tied to a central figure. Within the same dialogue, we witness multiple realities in three timelines: the present park Jen and Itt are walking in, the recent past Jen had experienced (Laotian war, great flood) the mythical ancient past of a Khmer palace, which Itt fully experiences.

In one of his interviews, Apichatpong Weerasethakul explains this sequence and states that, apart from the layers of memory and traces of the past, there is an influence of animist culture, in the creation of the scene where "the trees and every object have other spirits".[43] Apichatpong's cinema offers a unique spatiality, a strong sense of place, almost comparable to *genius loci*, the Latin term which translates as spirit of place, popularized by Norberg Schultz's 1979 work on the phenomenology of architecture against the homogenizing effects of modernist architecture.[44] Classical meaning of the term involves "a guardian spirit" or deities that create the specific character of a place; and are recognized and respected by the visitors of the place.[45] The

---

Archaeology, and the British Landscape 1927–1955 (Oxford: Oxford University Press, 2007), 30–57.

[43] Apichatpong Weerasethakul, Interview: Apichatpong Weerasethakul, interview by Nicolas Rapold, 1 June 2015, https://www.filmcomment.com/blog/cannes-interview-apichatpong-weerasethakul/.

[44] Christian Norberg-Schulz, *Genius Loci: Towards a Phenomenology of Architecture* (New York: Rizzoli International Publications, 1980). Norberg-Schultz follows a Heideggerian terminology to achieve a truthful experience of place, which is a guiding principle for architectural and urban design. Jorge Otero-Pailos, "Photo[Historio]Graphy: Christian Norberg-Schulz's Demotion of Textual History", *Journal of the Society of Architectural Historians* 66, no. 2 (2007): 231, https://doi.org/10.1525/jsah.2007.66.2.220.

[45] John Dixon Hunt writes: "The classical tradition of genius loci has [...] three aspects: that a place was sacred because it was peopled by deities; that these deities represented the specific character of a place; and

modern meaning is "the essential character or atmosphere of a place".[46] The key to understanding the unique character or the identity of a place is to shift our perspective from viewing space as an abstract geometric concept and a passive container of events into an active agent. However, *genius loci* as a concept implies a static vision of identity which is not the case in Apichatpong's cinematic places. Instead, layers of memory, traces of past lives fill the otherwise ordinary leftover spaces.

The spirits and ghosts do not make these films closer to the examples of the horror genre (haunted house). On the contrary, they almost declare their independence from the anthropic space and survive on their own as ghosts and spirits, sometimes in suspense, sometimes actively interacting with the other beings. It is possible to call this wandering and mobile presentation an animist, even a panpsychist spatiality.[47] As May Adadol Ingawanij observes, these allusions to animism, namely the metamorphosis into animals, reincarnation, ghosts and spirits in Apichatpong's films are not only the references to the Thai culture or the markers of the fantasy or horror genres; it allows to render the borders between human and nonhuman permeable.[48]

In *Syndromes and a Century*, Jen tells Dr Toey a parable about the evils of greed, of the two men who were given an opportunity to get rich during an eclipse, but one of them brought a disaster upon himself because of his greed. The camera shows a grassy land which it is said used to be a lake. And the scene is cut into the image of a total solar eclipse; as we observe the end of the eclipse when the darkened sky slowly changes back to blue Jen says: "This is a powerful place. No matter what people do, no matter what we do, something always

> that it behooved visitors to recognize and respect the particular site so identified and protected by its guardian spirits. It comprised both a belief in spirits and divinities and an understanding that every place was unique and special." John Dixon Hunt, *Site, Sight, Insight: Essays on Landscape Architecture* (Philadelphia: University of Pennsylvania Press, 2016), 92.

[46] "Genius Loci, n.", in *OED Online* (Oxford University Press), accessed 12 September 2020, http://www.oed.com/view/Entry/370503.

[47] Steven Shaviro's discussion of panpsychism is very useful for connecting Apichatpong's work to nonhuman turn. He refers to Skribina's formal definition of panpsychism: "the view that all things have mind or a mind-like quality ... Mind is seen as fundamental to the nature of existence and being." Steven Shaviro, "Consequences of Panpsychism", in *The Nonhuman Turn*, ed. Richard Grusin (Minneapolis, London: University of Minnesota Press, 2015), 19; David Skrbina, *Panpsychism in the West*, Revised edition (Cambridge MA: MIT Press, 2017).

[48] Ingawanij, 2013.

IMAGINING THE NONHUMAN   107

watches us. Like you coming here. It knows all about you."[49] These words are an expression of what one might call the spirit of a place. The solar eclipse is an image from the parable that effortlessly enters the scene, a component of the landscape from the imaginary past, living in the present. However, the nonhuman landscape alludes to a plane of existence that is not necessarily accessible to the viewer, audience or protagonists. According to Seung-Yoon Jeong, the scene of "the gradual disappearance of the eclipse within the same shot" suggests that "the transcendental realm exists as the duration of immanence in the actual world".[50] But at the same time, this makes us question the interrelations between the protagonists and the landscape: how the agency of the humans, and subject position is shaped by that very interaction with that particular landscape. On the one hand, components outside the main narrative easily seep into the frame; on the other hand, these nonhuman elements do not necessarily serve a purpose in terms of human agency.

According to Ingwanij, the choice of "using ontologically indeterminate beings" such as human/beast/ghost (Keng's metamorphosis in *Tropical Malady* or the monkey ghost in *Uncle Boonmee*)—is a strategy to displace the secure and stable place of the viewer, observer and the protagonist in the cinematic narrative.[51] The way these beings enter the cinematic frame is also unique. In *Uncle Boonmee*, for example, first, Boonmee's long-dead wife Huay appears at the dinner table, followed by his long-lost presumed dead son in the form of a monkey spirit. Then, after brief confusion, the family starts a conversation, and they show their love and hospitality by offering water and food. This gentle acceptance of these beings brings these different planes of existence to the two-dimensional cinematic frame.

The merging with the nonhuman is not only in the tranquilizing actions of the protagonists. Indeed, the director's long and medium-long

---

[49] Apichatpong Weerasethakul, *Syndromes and a Century (Sang Sattawat)* (Anna Sanders Films, Backup Media, Centre National du Cinéma et de l'ImageAnimée, 2007).

[50] Jeong Seung-hoon, "Black Hole in the Sky, Total Eclipse under the Ground: Apichatpong Weerasethakul and the Ontological Turn of Cinema", in *Dekalog 4: On East Asian Filmmakers*, ed. Kate E. Taylor-Jones (London: WallFlower Press, 2011), 145–146. These eclipses according to Seng-hoon are of the "ontological ground of the world, resonating around the Buddhist Eternal Return, Lacanian Real or Deleuzian Virtual". We could add Simondon's pre-individual to the list, particularly because of the dynamics of becoming.

[51] Ingawanij, 2013, 100.

shots "invite us to see how humans are not set against but are embedded within nature/the world".[52] The universe does not revolve around the protagonists; they are equally subject to the influence of their surroundings. Despite the atmospheric stasis, these smooth transitions bring rhythm to the seemingly static shots and slow tempo of these scenes.

Conclusion

Apichatpong's articulation of the figure–ground relationship and how he brings together the disparate beings in a state of meditative calmness speak to the contemporary discussions of the limits of anthropocentrism. Gilbert Simondon's philosophy, the way he theorizes the relation between individuals and their surroundings, particularly resonates with Apichatpong's cinema. Simondon's ontology avoids dualistic approaches and anthropocentric viewpoints and the types of subjectivity it creates. His theory of individuation replaces a static understanding of being with becoming: individuation happens out of the pre-individual state. Human beings are both an agent and locus of individuation. And individuals do not appear as stable subjects with unified identities; instead, they appear as dynamically entangled with the nonhuman. Simondon writes: "instead of grasping individuation on the basis of the individuated being, the individuated being must be grasped on the basis of individuation and individuation on the basis of pre-individual being".[53] So in Simondon's thought, we cannot start with individuals, static entities or identities; instead, we are invited to perceive individuation as a process that we are often a part of. Individuals appear only as one phase in the process of individuation. In Elizabeth Grosz's words: "[T]he pre-individual cannot adequately distinguish between terms that only apply to what has an identity; it is supersaturated, always rife with potential ... This real is full of potential energy, the energy never able to be drained to form an exhausted or stable point, and always able to generate more becomings."[54] To clarify, elements, objects, in other words, those things that we often take as distinct and stable beings separate from an anthropocentric eye, are, in

---

[52] Brown, 2015, 15.

[53] Simondon, 2020, 12.

[54] Elizabeth Grosz, "Identity and Individuation: Some Feminist Reflections", in *Gilbert Simondon: Being and Technology*, ed. Arne De Boever, Alex Murray and Jon Roffe (Edinburgh: Edinburgh University Press, 2012), 40.

fact, in constant formation that transforms the very relation between the perceptive eye and the things. In this, the static position of the anthropocentric subject can no longer hold a static privileged position.

When we look back at the way Apichatpong presents the landscapes, the jungle, the river, the lake, the hospital and the sky, we notice that they never are merely the background of action, nor they can be completely separated from the main characters. Whether it is a metamorphosis of a beast in the jungle or a journey of self-discovery in a makeshift hospital, we can only individuate a set of relations rather than a simple figure–ground relationship. The long shots reduce the role of individual agency and draw a picture of coordination rather than subordination between the screen elements. The long takes allow us to rethink our relation to the environment that we ignore. Apichatpong's camera captures what is out there—things that exist independent of us, human knowledge and human vision. Welcoming of different life forms, or supernatural beings, smooth flow of objects, and landscapes into the figures, it forces us to rethink our apperception of the relation between human and nonhuman constantly asking us to leave our customs of seeing from a privileged perspective that centers human as the sole maker of meaning.

Bibliography

Arsenjuk, Luka. "On the Impossibility of Object-Oriented Film Theory". *Discourse* 38, no. 2 (2016): 197–214.

Barad, Karen. *Meeting the Universe Halfway: Quantum Physics and the Entanglement of Matter and Meaning*. North Carolina. Duke University Press. 2007.

Boehler, Natalie. "Staging the Spectral: The Border, Haunting and Politics in Mekong Hotel". *Horror Studies* 5, no. 2 (2014): 197–210. https://doi.org/10.1386/host.5.2.197_1.

Braidotti. *The Posthuman*. Oxford. Polity Press. 2012.

Brown, William. "Man without a Movie Camera—Movies without Men: Towards a Posthumanist Cinema?" In *Film Theory and Contemporary Hollywood Movies*. Ed. Warren Buckland. New York and London. Routledge. 2009. 66–85.

Brown, William. "From DelGuat to ScarJo". In *The Palgrave Handbook of Posthumanism in Film and Television*. Ed. Michael Hauskeller, Thomas D. Philbeck and Curtis D. Carbonell. London. Palgrave Macmillan UK. 2015. 11–18.

Bryant, Levi R. "The Democracy of Objects". *New Metaphysics* (2011). https://doi.org/10.3998/ohp.9750134.0001.001.

Chion, Michel. *Audio-Vision: Sound on Screen*. Trans. Claudia Gorbman. 2nd edition. New York. Columbia University Press. 2019.

Chulphongsathorn, Graiwoot. "Apichatpong Weerasethakul's Planetary Cinema". *Screen* 62, no. 4 (2021): 541–548. https://doi.org/10.1093/screen/hjab058.

Davis, Glyn. "Stills and Stillness in Apichatpong Weerasethakul's Cinema". In *Slow Cinema*. Ed. Tiago De Luca and Nuno Barradas Jorge. Edinburgh: Edinburgh University Press. 2016. 99–111.

DeLanda, Manuel. *Intensive Science and Virtual Philosophy*. Revised edition. London and New York. Bloomsbury Academic. 2013.

Deleuze, Gilles. *Cinema II: Time Image (1985)*. London and New York. Continuum. 2005.

Elsaesser, Thomas. "World Cinema: Realism, Evidence, Presence". In *Realism and the Audiovisual Media*. Ed. L. Nagib and C. Mello. London. Palgrave Macmillan UK. 2009. 3–19.

Garelli, Jacques. "Foreword: Introduction to the Problematic of Gilbert Simondon". In *Individuation in Light of Notions of Form and Information*, Vol. 1. By Gilbert Simondon. Minneapolis. Minnesota Press. 2020.

"Genius Loci, n". In *OED Online*. Oxford University Press. Accessed 12 September 2020. http://www.oed.com/view/Entry/370503.

Grosz, Elizabeth. "Identity and Individuation: Some Feminist Reflections". In *Gilbert Simondon: Being and Technology*. Ed. Arne De Boever, Alex Murray and Jon Roffe. Edinburgh. Edinburgh University Press. 2012. 37–56.

Grusin, Richard. "Introduction". In *The Nonhuman Turn*. Ed. Richard Grusin. Minneapolis and London. University of Minnesota Press. 2015. vii–xxix.

Hauser, Kitty. *Shadow Sites: Photography, Archaeology, and the British Landscape 1927–1955*. Oxford. Oxford University Press. 2007.

Hauskeller, Michael, Thomas D. Philbeck and Curtis D. Carbonell, eds. *The Palgrave Handbook of Posthumanism in Film and Television*. London. Palgrave Macmillan UK. 2015.

Hayles, N. Katherine. *How We Became Posthuman: Virtual Bodies in Cybernetics, Literature, and Informatics*. Chicago. University of Chicago Press. 1999.

Horn, Eva. *The Future as Catastrophe: Imagining Disaster in the Modern Age*. Trans. Valentine Pakis. New York. Columbia University Press. 2018.

Hunt, John Dixon. *Site, Sight, Insight: Essays on Landscape Architecture*. Philadelphia. University of Pennsylvania Press. 2016.

Ingawanij, May Adadol. "Animism and the Performative Realist Cinema of Apichatpong Weerasethakul". In *Screening Nature: Cinema Beyond the Human*. Ed. Anat Pick and Guinevere Narraway. New York. Berghahn Books. 2013.

Ivakhiv, Adrian J. *Ecologies of the Moving Image: Cinema, Affect, Nature.* Waterloo. Wilfrid Laurier University Press. 2013.

Jaffe, Ira. *Slow Movies: Countering the Cinema of Action.* London and New York. Wallflower Press. 2014.

Kara, Selmin. "The Sonic Summons: Meditations on Nature and Anempathetic Sound in Digital Documentaries". In *The Oxford Handbook of Sound and Image in Digital Media.* Ed. Carol Vernallis, Amy Herzog and John Richardson. Reprint edition. New York, Auckland and Cape Town. Oxford University Press. 2015. 582–597.

Kim, Jihoon. "Between Auditorium and Gallery: Perception in Apichatpong Weerasethakul's Films and Installations". In *Global Art Cinema: New Theories and Histories.* Ed. Rosalind Galt and Karl Schoonover. New York. Oxford University Press. 2010. 125–141.

Koepnick, Lutz. *On Slowness: Toward an Aesthetic of the Contemporary.* New York. Columbia University Press. 2014.

Lim, Song Hwee. *Tsai Ming-Liang and a Cinema of Slowness.* Illustrated edition. Honolulu. University of Hawaii Press. 2014.

Lovatt, Philippa. "'Every Drop of My Blood Sings Our Song. There Can You Hear It?': Haptic Sound and Embodied Memory in the Films of Apichatpong Weerasethakul". *The New Soundtrack* 3, no. 1 (2013): 61–79. https://doi.org/10.3366/sound.2013.0036.

de Luca, Tiago, and Nuno Barradas Jorge, eds. *Slow Cinema.* Edinburgh. Edinburgh University Press. 2016.

Marks, Laura U. *The Skin of the Film: Intercultural Cinema, Embodiment, and the Senses.* Durham. Duke University Press. 2000.

Massumi, Brian. "'Technical Mentality' Revisited: Brian Massumi on Gilbert Simondon". In *Gilbert Simondon: Being and Technology.* Ed. Arne De Boever, Alex Murray and Jon Roffe. Edinburgh. Edinburgh University Press. 2012. 36.

Norberg-Schulz, Christian. *Genius Loci: Towards a Phenomenology of Architecture.* New York. Rizzoli International Publications. 1980.

Otero-Pailos, Jorge. "Photo[Historio]Graphy: Christian Norberg-Schulz's Demotion of Textual History". *Journal of the Society of Architectural Historians* 66, no. 2 (2007): 220–241. https://doi.org/10.1525/jsah.2007.66.2.220.

Remes, Justin. "The Sleeping Spectator: Non-Human Aesthetics in Abbas Kiarostami's Five: Dedicated to Ozu". In *Slow Cinema.* Ed. Tiago De Luca and Nuno Barradas Jorge. Edinburgh. Edinburgh University Press. 2016. 231–242.

Sauvagnargues, Anne. *Artmachines: Deleuze, Guattari, Simondon.* Trans. Suzanne Verderber and Eugene W. Holland. Edinburgh. Edinburgh University Press. 2016.

Scott, David. *Gilbert Simondon's Psychic and Collective Individuation: A Critical Introduction and Guide.* Edinburgh. Edinburgh University Press. 2014.

Seung-hoon, Jeong. "Black Hole in the Sky, Total Eclipse under the Ground: Apichatpong Weerasethakul and the Ontological Turn of Cinema". In *Dekalog 4: On East Asian Filmmakers*. Ed. Kate E. Taylor-Jones. London. WallFlower Press. 2011.

Shaviro, Steven. "Consequences of Panpsychism". In *The Nonhuman Turn*. Ed. Richard Grusin. Minneapolis and London. University of Minnesota Press. 2015. 19–44.

Simondon, Gilbert. *Individuation in Light of Notions of Form and Information*. Trans. Taylor Adkins. Minneapolis. University of Minnesota Press. 2020.

Skrbina, David. *Panpsychism in the West*. Cambridge MA. MIT Press. 2017.

Weerasethakul, Apichatpong. *Syndromes and a Century* [*Sang Sattawat*]. Anna Sanders Films. Centre National du Cinéma et de l'ImageAnimée. 2007.

Weerasethakul, Apichatpong. *Uncle Boonmee Who Can Recall His Past Lives* [*Loong Boonmee Raleuk Chat*]. Kick the Machine. Illuminations Films, Anna Sanders Films. 2010.

Weerasethakul, Apichatpong. *Cactus River* [*Khong Lang Nam*]. Walker Art Center. 2012. https://youtu.be/H5vToT_ionU.

Weerasethakul, Apichatpong. *Mekong Hotel*. Illuminations Films. 2012.

Weerasethakul, Apichatpong. "Mekong Hotel Press Kit". *The Match. Factory* 2012. https://www.the-match-factory.com/catalogue/films/mekong-hotel.html.

Weerasethakul, Apichatpong. Sakda (Rousseau) in *La Faute à Rousseau: une collection de films courts*. DVD. Genève. HEAD. 2012.

Weerasethakul, Apichatpong. *Cemetery of Splendor* [*RakTiKhonKaen*]. Kick the Machine. Anna Sanders Films. Match Factory Productions. 2015.

Weerasethakul, Apichatpong. Interview: Apichatpong Weerasethakul. Interview by Nicolas Rapold, 1 June 2015. https://www.filmcomment.com/blog/cannes-interview-apichatpong-weerasethakul/.

Weerasethakul, Apichatpong. "Mekong Hotel". Accessed 2 January 2021. http://www.kickthemachine.com/page80/page1/page20/index.html.

Wolfe, Cary. *What Is Posthumanism?*. Minneapolis. University of Minnesota Press. 2010.

Zylinska, Joanna. *Nonhuman Photography*. Cambridge MA. MIT Press. 2017.

Mind

5

The Stillness Wandering Within
Notes on the Caesura of the Cinematic Image in Apichatpong Weerasethakul's *Primitive* Project

Elizabeth Sikes

I want to begin my thoughts here with a story, a ghost story, from Apichatpong Weerasethakul's film, *Uncle Boonmee Who Can Recall His Past Lives*, about the protagonist of this chapter, Boonsong, Boonmee's son.

The story takes place in northeastern Thailand, in a small village called Nabua, which lies close to where the mighty Mekong—or Khong, river separates Thailand from Laos and its nextdoor neighbor, Vietnam. There lived a young man named Boonsong who lost his mother when he was a teenager. After she died he found her Pentax camera and began taking pictures—everywhere he went he brought his camera. He tried to

Fig. 1: From *Uncle Boonmee Who Can Recall His Past Lives* (2010), dir. Apichatpong Weerasethakul. Produced by Illumination Films, London; Kick the Machine Films, Bangkok.

Fig. 2: Photo: Nontawat Numbenchapol, Courtesy of Kick the Machine Films.

understand that thing his mother had called "the art of photography". One evening, upon return after wandering and picture taking in the forest jungle, something strange and shadowy caught his attention, from the corner of his eye, on one of the negatives he processed from the day. He took his magnifying glass and examined the negative closely.

Boonsong never developed that image, but the creature obsessed him. He wandered in the jungle day after day, trying to capture it on camera again. He wanted to communicate with it. One day he mated with the Monkey Ghost. These were the ones they heard outside their window at night when he was a child. Boonsong grew hair everywhere and his eyes slowly dilated.

Soon there was too much light, even in the dark jungle, and it hurt his eyes. After dusk, his eyes burned a dark red in the night.

Photophobia

Most commonly, photophobia describes an abnormal sensitivity to or intolerance of light, an excessive pain in its presence. Most of us experience it on those occasions when bright light blinds the eye, like

THE STILLNESS WANDERING WITHIN

when we exit a movie theater on a sunny summer afternoon. Only secondarily is the term used to describe an unusual fear of light. Some plants and other organisms are photophobic, which means they thrive in low levels of light. Films, too, are a strange little photophobic, spectral species populating dark, cavernous theaters, their autochthonous home.

Photophobia is a term that Thai film director and video installation artist, Apichatpong Weerasethakul, identifies with, and has even used it to conceptualize one of his video and photo exhibitions.[1] Photophobia is at the root of his filmmaking. This seems fitting for an artist whose various media in film depend so thoroughly on playing with what allows light and its intensities to monstrate: the dark. And behind this light something traumatic, overdetermined in the images, flickers, like firecrackers fulgurating in the dark hollows of the mind.

Photophobia is also connected with the project of memory for Weerasethakul. Indeed, his work, he tells us, is about memory, about the ways in which photography, film, video, television and stories serve as protectors of memory. Here we might refer to Rancière's notion of the "theater of memory", which he sees as peculiar to the "metamorphic image", and identifies specifically with installation art: Rancière writes, "the device of installation can also be transformed into a theater of memory and make the artist a collector, archivist or window-dresser, placing before the visitor's eyes not so much a critical clash of heterogenous elements as a set of testimonies about a shared history and world".[2] Indeed, Weerasethakul describes his photophobia as a compulsion toward archiving and cataloging memory, and his work certainly stands as testimony to shared spatial and temporal zones, but in a way that radically interrupts and reconfigures the linear historical narrative and subjective sense of time. In Rancière's terms, this is metamorphic image as *interruption*. He writes, "Installation art thus brings into play the metamorphic, unstable nature of images ... They are interrupted, fragmented, reconstituted by a poetics of witticism that seeks to establish new differences of potentiality between these unstable elements."[3]

Weerasethakul's *Primitive* (2009) is a multiplatform installation that includes two short films and seven short, intersecting video pieces

---

[1] "Apichatpong Weerasethakul Solo Exhibition PHOTOPHOBIA, ART GALLERY@ KUCA", directed by Masashi Nagara, June 2014, https://www.youtube.com/watch?v=gEogkNnUN8c.

[2] Jacques Rancière, *The Future of the Image*, trans. Gregory Elliott (London: Verso, 2007), 24.

[3] Rancière, 2007, 26.

made as part of Weerasethakul's extensive pre-production work on the feature-length film portion of the project, *Uncle Boonmee Who Can Recall His Past Lives*, about a man's final days dying of kidney failure. What seems to breathe depth and spirit into this project is an immense compassion for the place, people and legends that form the matrix in which these images monstrate and morph. Indeed, his love of and attention to place sets Weerasethakul's work apart. As a student at the Chicago Art Institute, after studying architecture in his home country, Weerasethakul was greatly taken by the experimental style and form of film making in the works of Antonioni and directors associated with the French New Wave, like Godard and Chris Marker, all three of whom haunt *Uncle Boonmee*. And yet a purely experimental style, with its adherence to strict rules of form, underwent a transmutation in Thailand, the land of "ghosts and legends", Weerasethakul says. Narrative and place take priority for Weerasethakul, where every story is a ghost and thus a ghost story, and every narrative one that wanders, meanders, connecting place and people.

It is this aspect of the spectral—of the *revenant*, in Derrida's terms, or repetition in Deleuze's—and its relationship to time, especially the future, that Weerasethakul's *Primitive* awakens in thought. Weerasethakul's "theater of memory" is a construction of memory that cracks open the present.

Allow me to say a few more words about Weerasethakul's *Primitive* project and then something about ghosts, cinema and the theater of memory. After that, I will move on to the caesura in this theater and its relationship to time.

Primitive and *Uncle Boonmee Who Can Recall His Past Lives* were filmed in Nabua, which is not far from Khon Kaen where Weerasethakul grew up. Inspired by a book given to him by a monk at the local forest monastery about a man who could recall centuries of past lives lived in this region of northeastern Thailand, Weerasethakul and his crew went there in search of stories and those who might have known Boonmee.

There is a district in the northeast where the men are said to be few and were for a long time ill-advised to go. There men are abducted by a beautiful woman who takes them into an invisible land to join her other husbands. She is the "widow ghost" and her district nicknamed "widow town". In 1965, one of the towns in this district, Nabua, flickered into national consciousness, however briefly, when the first gun battle between farmer communists and the totalitarian government broke out in the rice fields.

The men left the women behind, fleeing into the jungle to hide. The night sky was illuminated by red military flares and the stark floodlights

THE STILLNESS WANDERING WITHIN 119

in the streets. In the darkness of this light atrocities occurred. Women were raped and many farmers never returned. The physical and psychological siege of the area continued for two decades till after the Cold War was over. The government circulated their own media propaganda telling a story about what happened, which made people forget. And ultimately what is left, even in the stories of the elders who remain today, is the trace of a non-memory on the verge of extinction. It is a land of extinction.[4] And then there is Uncle Boonmee, living life after life in this region he will not forsake. The *Primitive* project reimagines Nabua as a town of men, and of male teenagers freed from the Widow Ghost, and gives them various vehicles of transport—a spaceship being one of them, the cinematic image being another—into a future that is not yet, to imagine a past that never was, which opens a crack in the viewer's present. An exercise in the future perfect tense, this is Weerasethakul's art.

Weerasethakul thanked the ghosts and spirits of Thailand in his acceptance speech for the *Palme d'Or* prize at the Cannes Film Festival in 2010 for *Uncle Boonmee*. It is fair to say these ghosts are the stars in this film. On the one hand, this is one of the things that makes his work, and this one in particular, essentially Thai. The belief in ghosts and spirits is pervasive there, horror films with monsters of all sorts (many of them female) are one of the most popular genres, and in the Thai royal costume cinema of the past the animals encountered in the jungle or by a glittering waterfall have magical powers of speech (and, in the hands of Weerasethakul, other kinds of naughty erotic powers). Thus, on a literal level his ghosts appear on screen. On another level, these old cinematic styles are reincarnated in the film in a self-conscious way awakening the viewer to the experience of remembering the past—that is, of a reminiscence of a past that, at the moment of such recognition, is something that was never present, perhaps until that moment.

Thus, the viewer awakens to the idea of cinema as such: "the art of allowing ghosts to come back" as Derrida claims in the film *Ghost Dance*. To watch a film is to be in the presence of specters, the already-dead or the soon-to-be-dead, those whose presence simultaneously says "I'm not there". In *Ghost Dance* Derrida, playing himself, is asked by the main character Pascale if he believes in ghosts. He answers: "that's

---

[4] Apichatpong Weerasethakul, "The Memory of Nabua: A Note on the *Primitive* Project", in *Apichatpong Weerasethakul*, ed. James Quandt (Vienna: Synema, 2009), 192–206.

a difficult question" because "you are asking a ghost".[5] Further on, he returns her question; her answer: "Yes, now I do, yes". Two or three years later, watching the film in a very different place and time during which Pascale, the actress, has suddenly died, Derrida was struck by the strange, uncanny feeling when watching this scene. He writes: "I had the unnerving sense of the return of her specter, the specter of her specter, coming back to say to me—to me, here, now: 'Now... now... now, that is to say, in this dark room on another continent, in another world, here, now, yes, believe me, I believe in ghosts.'"[6] In so far as the cinematic or metamorphic image serves as a time capsule or perhaps a spaceship allowing the recreation of a past by way of what will have been in the future, this art of ghosts is the uncanny art of memory.

But something more is going on in this art of ghosts that Weerasethakul's *Uncle Boonmee* shows quite clearly in the oneiric quality of the film: at the heart of this spectral structure is desire—the desire aroused by the memory-image that can only capture the ghost on camera, the phantom of the object of desire, just as Boonsong, in the opening story, captures the ghost of the monkey on film. This desire, as the story also illustrates, is cast underway by trauma, the interpenetration of fatality and natality. It is in this sense that Derrida claims, "I believe that cinema plus psychoanalysis equals the science of ghosts".[7] I will return to this art and science of ghosts at the end of my thoughts here.

Next, I want to connect the figure of the phantom in the *Primitve* project with Weerasethakul's use there of the cinematic caesura, a cut that produces a counter-rhythmic interruption in the movement of the image. The caesura is originally a poetic concept, introduced by Friedrich Hölderlin in the "Notes" to his translations of Sophocles' *Oedipus the Tyrant* and *Antigone*. Not only did Hölderlin translate the Greek into a German for the modern age, but he translated the entire genre of Greek tragedy and its mechanics, laid out in Aristotle's *Poetics*, into the terms of modern German *Trauerspiel*. The caesura is a term that parallels *katharsis*—clarification, purification, clearing, cleansing. With the affective intensity of the scenes in tragic drama as they rush toward the ineluctable fatality of the Real, Hölderlin says it becomes necessary to counterbalance it with a cut or interruption, a caesura, what he calls the "pure word". As an interruption or cut, the caesura is paradoxically

---

[5] Quoted in Laurence Simmons, "Jacques Derrida's Ghostface", *Angelaki: Journal of the Theoretical Humanities* 16, no. 1 (2011): 129–140, at 135.

[6] Simmons, 2011, 135.

[7] Simmons, 2011, 136.

THE STILLNESS WANDERING WITHIN

connective; as a word, paradoxically silent. This is the point at which the play becomes a play, when the viewer finds themselves simultaneously intensely caught up in the flow and most removed, projected into a space anterior to and outside the frame, such that the frame itself comes into view.

Translated into the mechanics of film, this radical cut produces an excellent example of what Deleuze calls a "pure time image", an image uncoupled from its subordination to movement. The automatism of film—that it makes its own movement, untying itself from the mind or body for its motility—has been much theorized in film literature. For Deleuze, this has the power to generate in us a *spiritual automaton*, that is, *thought*, which reacts in turn on movement.[8] For this thought to be generated by movement that actually opens up the future as the very possibility of becoming-other, rather than a repetition locked mainly in the past of habitual recognition, time must be introduced into thinking; the movement-image must become a time-image.

The following are just two examples in the *Primitive* project of minor shocks to the sensorimotor unity of the image, shocks that induce a disjoint between movement of the narrative and thinking of the spiritual automaton.

(1) *Uncle Boonmee* is not shot in the style of one cinematic genre, which I have already briefly mentioned. Scenes in six different reels circulate among six different styles, which reincarnate genres as different as old Thai horror films, royal costume drama, documentary, and what Weerasethakul calls his "usual way of filmmaking", which uses long takes.[9] Yet this circulation among styles occurs as a series of unequal juxtapositions—among the six reels and in each reel's relationship to the overarching narrative of the film. This produces a jarring effect that exaggerates the outlines of each style, making the viewer see the film as a film, something whose images also have their own history and life. Thus, the cinematic caesura is contained within the relationship of the images distributed unequally and incommensurately that provoke a sense of the uncanny. This has the effect of breaking the spell of immanence in the sensorimotor unity of the film and of any possible mystification that it might induce in the viewer. Weerasethakul does not want to mystify us with these ghosts. He wants to make us responsible for them.

[8] Gilles Deleuze, *Cinema II, The Time Image*, trans. Hugh Tomlinson and Robert Galeta (Minneapolis: University of Minnesota Press, 1989), 156.

[9] Jihoon Kim, "Learning About Time: An Interview with Apichatpong Weerasethakul", *Film Quarterly* 64, no. 4 (2011): 48–52, at 52.

Fig. 3: From *Uncle Boonmee Who Can Recall His Past Lives* (2010), dir. Apichatpong Weerasethakul. Produced by Illumination Films, London; Kick the Machine Films, Bangkok.

Nowhere is this more poignantly seen than in the "dinner with ghosts" scene toward the beginning of *Uncle Boonmee*. The scene is set around the dinner table where Uncle Boonmee, Jen (his sister-in-law), and Tong (Boonmee's nephew) are sitting. If we are literate in the old style of television in Thailand, we recognize it in the cheap costumes and the bright light over the table. Boonmee's wife, long dead, slowly fades in at the table. Soon after, a thump off-screen is heard; red glowing eyes ascend the stairs to the dining room. It is Boonsong, who greets his mother first. From his slow, almost mechanical movement and speech, he appears as an undead King Kong come to dinner. Boonsong, Boonmee's son as monkey ghost, then tells his ghost mother how he died. We hear too the story I began with. On one level, we have a man in a monkey suit appearing on screen, reminding us of a different story altogether, that of Thai television and film. And this image is funny—somewhat, except that it sits, on another level, uneasily within the deeply poignant context of a man being accompanied into death by his loved ones, both living and dead.

(2) *Phantoms of Nabua*: Deeper cuts in the sensorimotor unity of cinematic consciousness and its world. *Phantoms of Nabua* is one of the two short films of the *Primitive* project. Here the burning red light of Boonsong's photophobic eyes (the red-eye effect of the camera flash) reappears as the play of different forms of light and dark on the bare

Fig. 4: *Phantoms of Nabua* (2009), dir. Apichatpong Weerasethakul.
Courtesy of Apichatpong Weerasethakul.

Fig. 5: *Phantoms of Nabua* (2009), dir. Apichatpong Weerasethakul.
Courtesy of Apichatpong Weerasethakul.

ground in the village, where a projection screen stands beneath the stark fluorescent light of a streetlamp, and teenage Nabua boys play soccer with a ball they light on fire.

Projected on the screen, we see the image of this village, and a house lit up by cracks of lightning. In front of this screen, a fiery soccer ball

Fig. 6: *Phantoms of Nabua* (2009), dir. Apichatpong Weerasethakul. Produced by Illumination Films, London; Kick the Machine Films, Bangkok.

flies through the air, the sound of flames brushing against the thick night air. The light of the soccer ball refers to the lightning cracks of the image on screen, the phantoms of Nabua. When the boys kick the soccer ball into the screen, consuming it in flames, we are left with the image of what is behind the screen on the field, the naked light of the projector, flickering on our screen. The recursive use of light ending with the blinding blinking light of the projector abandons us to the darkness at the center of light—the photophobia of cinematic memory. Thus, the caesura here functions in the recursive use of light, but more shockingly, at the moment when the screen is destroyed. The interruption of the unity of movement and image altogether, lays bare the unseen—the backside of things, or the tain of the cinematic mirror—that makes possible the monstration of the image itself.

In both of the examples I have just given, the caesura works its effects on the sensorimotor unity of the image by shocking the spiritual automaton with something disjointed within the image itself—whether it be the self-conscious play of styles or the recursive use of a particular image in order to decouple it from the movement of the play. In both cases we might argue that these qualify as examples of what Deleuze calls the "time-image" in cinema.

Fig. 7: *Phantoms of Nabua* (2009), dir. Apichatpong Weerasethakul. Produced by Illumination Films, London; Kick the Machine Films, Bangkok.

When time enters into the image, at its extremity, rational or measurable temporal links between shots, the staple of the movement-image, give way to "incommensurable", non-rational links. When time enters into the image, at its extremity, the spiritual automaton registers this as a "dissociative force"; it introduces a "figure of nothingness" and a "hole in appearances".[10] The spiritual automaton has become, Deleuze says, "the Mummy".[11] We are encrypted by one thought: "the fact that *we are not yet thinking*, the powerlessness to think the whole and to think oneself, thought which is always fossilized, dislocated, collapsed"; it is a "being of thought which is always to come".[12] The arrival of thought in fracture, like the arrival of Dionysus' fractured birth, the eternally repeated trauma that every tragedy encrypts. Here every fatality links to natality.

[10] Deleuze, 1989, 167.
[11] Deleuze, 1989, 166.
[12] Deleuze, 1989, 167.

Uncle Boonmee Dies

At the center of the scene is the memory of the past, a repetition of a past life that he does not recall. Uncle Boonmee is led down to the floor of a great cavern that opens up to the starry night. Jen and Tong are there, along with his dead wife, while the monkey ghosts gather outside this earthen womb. In this womb, the non-memory of the past life literally interrupts the movement with a set of still images that seem to be unleashed from some umbilical connection with the cave they all gather within. Deleuze's words describe this perfectly: "On the one hand the presence of an unthinkable in thought, which would be both its source and barrier; on the other hand the presence to infinity of another thinker in the thinker, who shatters every monologue of a thinking self."[13]

This "thinker in the thinker" is Apichatpong Weerasethakul. He transports us into the modern-day cave/crypt/womb: the movie theater. This is not so much a physical space as it is an archaic psychic one, a zone that Bracha Ettinger calls the *matrixial borderspace*. This describes the feminine field of the matrix, drawing on its etymological meaning of uterus or womb, as well as its current usage as "original register".[14] I want to borrow a few of her concepts (without, however, being able to do justice to her schizo-psychoanalytic project) to sketch out something like a conclusion—more like impressions about what I think Weerasethakul does in this scene, and indeed, with the entire *Primitive* project. Her thinking helps us loosely tie together some of the strands I have been unraveling in this essay: photophobia, the science of ghosts and how these both relate to the phantoms of the world's Nabua.

Photophobia is linked to the desire to return to the womb, of phantasies of the *Mutterleib complex*, or intrauterine existence. Bracha Ettinger goes back to Freud's *Uncanny* and its appearance in the aesthetic phenomenon to show that, along with the Oedipal complex, the other primal phantasy Freud mentions in this text is that of intrauterine existence, or womb phantasies.[15] If we follow Ettinger here and admit

---

[13] Deleuze, 1989, 168.

[14] Bracha Ettinger, *The Matrixial Borderspace* (Minneapolis: University of Minnesota Press, 2006), 64.

[15] While Freud seems later to subsume this phantasy within the castration phantasy as the prototype for all separation from the bodily and archaic-partial dimension, effectively excluding the feminine as the basis for subjectivization, Ettinger argues that the reason Freud mentioned the *Mutterleibcomplex* at all was to prevent this from happening (Ettinger, 2006, 47).

two primal phantasies, this second one, what she calls the matrixial phantasy and complex, opens up another subjacent (not anterior) path for subjectivization based on a different logic of desire, one based for both sexes in an original feminine sex-difference.[16] The matrix and the matrixial borderspace it engenders is modeled on the feminine/ prenatal meeting; this meeting is a model for "relations and processes of change and exchange in which the *non-I* is unknown to the *I* (or rather uncognized: known by noncognitive process), but not an intruder. Rather, the *non-I* is a *partner-in-difference* of the I...". It "serve[s] as a model for a *shareable dimension of subjectivity*"[17] (64–65), a space of *transubjectivity*.

For Weerasethakul, this phantasy pushes the limits of what we understand as the womb and primal desire for it. The images haunt us with *a phantasy of the Earth's womb in which transsubjectivity border links across species lines*, even perhaps distributing itself promiscuously across the machine/animal/mineral divide, in so far as the spiritual automaton itself has already taken a step toward this. At Boonmee's death, his memories become fused with those of the director's. Are they true memories or have they been dreamt for the impossible passage to death, like that of the girl for Chris Marker's character in *La Jetée*?[18]

The Earth's womb and wound affects us in a double-sense: first, as the specific abandoned land and space of Nabua in which teenagers play soccer with its fire, or play at being its monkey spirits, in chains or enlisted by the military police—or imagine themselves as Antonioni's fashion photographer, or board a spaceship to the future perfect tense— the subjectivities and historicities multiply and swerve. After Boonmee's funeral in the hotel his in-laws watch television, the screen splits in

---

[16] Cf. Ettinger, 2006, 47.

[17] Ettinger, 2006, 65.

[18] As Raymond Bellour comments: "For, the overly still image, the far too visible suspension of time, leads irremediably to loss and death. This is the lesson of *La Jetée*. If there are so many stilled images composing an entire film, even a short one, it is because they all come together around a single image, the image of the main character's death", 118. Undoubtedly the influence of Marker's film is felt in Weerasethakul's *Primitive* project and specifically in *Uncle Boonmee*. The stillness inside the movement of the Weerasethakul's film confronts us not only with death, but also with birth, with the proliferation of lives, past and future, imaginary and real. Raymond Bellour, "The Film Stilled", trans. Alison Rowe with Elisabeth Lyon, published with permission of the author, https://chrismarker.org/wp-content/uploads/2013/10/bellour-raymond-the-film-stilled.pdf.

Fig. 8: From *Uncle Boonmee Who Can Recall His Past Lives* (2010), dir. Apichatpong Weerasethakul. Produced by Illumination Films, London; Kick the Machine Films, Bangkok.

Fig. 9: From *Uncle Boonmee Who Can Recall His Past Lives* (2010), dir. Apichatpong Weerasethakul. Produced by Illumination Films, London; Kick the Machine Films, Bangkok.

two, and the camera follows Tong and Jen out the door as their doubles remain on the bed.

Finally, the Earth's womb affects us as a psychic time-space of the world itself. In the late twentieth and early twenty-first century if we do find that, as Ettinger suspects, "the world carries enormous

Fig. 10: From *Uncle Boonmee Who Can Recall His Past Lives* (2010), dir. Apichatpong Weerasethakul. Produced by Illumination Films, London; Kick the Machine Films, Bangkok.

traumatic weight", then "we are unknowingly living it through its massive transitive effects upon us".[19] In a time when we, mummies and zombies, are living the post-traumatic oblivion of political and historical memory and the mass extinction of species, the image of the crypt, "a lacuna that corresponds to an unsymbolized event belonging to someone else"[20] becomes relevant for the working-through of the art work and the artist. This image of the crypt is the caesural cut linking Boonmee's sepulchral cave to the movie theater and its spectral world of shadow and light. The privileged instant, this "pure word" in the movement paradoxically links to the whole by virtue of the gap— of what remains unthought and unremembered, but affectively and hauntingly undead. This crypt is not our own; it belongs to a transubjective memory, and Ettinger calls this transmission transcryptum. She writes that in the work of art:

> Transcryptum is the occasion for that memory, enfolded in amnesia, to come to light. It testifies to the world's imprints on the artist and to the artist's potential to transform the world's waves and hieroglyphs, but also to the viewer's capacity to join in

[19] Ettinger, 2006, 169.
[20] Ettinger, 2006, 166.

this process. When in art a memory emerges, it captures what has just been born into and from a co-spasming, and it opens a land of fragility. It creates both the scar and its wound, the amnesia and its memory, and it makes sense, as an impossibility, as the impossibility of not-sharing the memory of oblivion of the veiled Event.[21]

I will end with this image of the transcryptum: the spaceship the teenagers in Nabua helped build for the other short film in *Primitive*, "A Letter to Uncle Boonmee".
Afterward they began to hang out in this wooden spaceship, listen to music, and drink.
Or dream. Future thought resting at the edge of the Nabua of the world.

Fig. 11: Photo: Chaisiri Jiwarangson © Kick the Machine Films.

---

[21] Ettinger, 2006, 168.

Fig. 12: Photo: Chaisiri Jiwarangson © Kick the Machine Films.

Bibliography

Bellour, Raymond. "The Film Stilled". Trans. Alison Rowe with Elisabeth Lyon. Published with permission of the author. https://chrismarker.org/wp-content/uploads/2013/10/bellour-raymond-the-film-stilled.pdf.
Deleuze, Gilles. *Cinema II, The Time Image*. Trans. Hugh Tomlinson and Robert Galeta. Minneapolis. University of Minnesota Press. 1989.
Ettinger, Bracha. *The Matrixial Borderspace*. Minneapolis. University of Minnesota Press. 2006.
Kim, Jihoon. "Learning About Time: An Interview with Apichatpong Weerasethakul". *Film Quarterly* 64, no. 4 (2011): 48–52.
Rancière, Jacques. *The Future of the Image*. Trans. Gregory Elliott. London. Verso. 2007.
Simmons, Laurence. "Jacques Derrida's Ghostface". *Angelaki: Journal of the Theoretical Humanities* 16, no. 1 (2011): 129–140.
Weerasethakul, Apichatpong. "The Memory of Nabua: A Note on the *Primitive* Project". *Apichatpong Weerasethakul*. Ed. James Quandt. Vienna. Synema. 2009. 192–206.

6

Dreams, Abstractions and Spectatorship in Apichatpong Weerasethakul's Films and Videos

Alessandro Ferraro

I

You can sleep during my film.

—Apichatpong Weerasethakul[1]

The analogy between film and dream has often been the subject of analysis and speculation by critics, directors and the public. Since its first manifestations, the possibility of seeing one's subconscious dreams and desires translated through the medium that, more than any other, has taken on itself the honour and the burden of visually representing the imaginative power of modernity, has been a fertile field of scientific investigation and theoretical speculation.[2] However, a director's attention to the dream topic cannot be studied exclusively through content or biographical interpretations. It can be hypothesized that a history of dreams in cinema, or a history of oneiric cinema—a decidedly difficult category to define—can contribute to a better understanding of the link between dream and film. On the basis of some recent studies regarding the ways of making experience of a film—mainly Julian Hanich and Jean Ma's recent essays[3]—it is useful

---

[1] The quote is taken from an online interview to Apitchatpong Weerasethakul. The video can be found online: "You Can Sleep During My Film", posted by SPH Razor, 26 July 2013, video, 5:46, https://www.youtube.com/watch?v=DVNIvTqIMs4. This essay would not have been written without the help and advice from professors, artists and curators such as Zoe Beloff, Julian Hanich, Jean Ma and Edwin Carels.

[2] Stephen Sharot, "Dreams in Films and Films as Dreams: Surrealism and Popular American Cinema", *Canadian Journal of Film Studies* 24, no. 1 (2015): 66–70.

[3] I am also referring to Jacques Rancière's studies and the so-called

to consider this dialectic in terms of relational and receptive impact on the spectator, leaning towards a social meaning of the question and thus understanding the cinematographic show as a device capable of triggering an emotional reaction in the viewer.

From the end of the American dream to the unusual oneiric hyperactivity detected during the COVID-19 pandemic,[4] it is clear that dreams and their aesthetics have a huge pervasiveness in the everyday context. Today there are numerous centers for sleep and dreams aimed at representing the act of dreaming in a scientifically objective manner. It is not clear, however, whether there are objective paradigms for the description of a dream. Recent studies define what the time spent during the REM and non-REM phases means in a qualitative sense, what visual implications it has and how it relates to our collective imagination.[5] The involvement of scientific research in this field is therefore a further step towards the complex intertwining of academic interests in a "visual" description of a dream.

Cinema has always been connected, in addition to a peculiar idea of entertainment, to the evolution of our modes of attention. The reasons for, and the consequent needs of, an entertainment show that created consciously passive spectators, who at the same time were unaware of the mechanism of signification of moving-images—as happens in dreams—were the basis of the first technical expedients in the cinematographic field. As Tom Gunning recalls, the amazement at the first moving images constituted a significant historical problem, especially as regards the mixture of scientific representation of the film medium, the stringent narrative logics of the story, the tricks of scenographic magic, the needs of the industry, the spectacle and mass identification of the spectator in a cohesive audience or, in other words, as an indistinct desiring subject.[6]

---

experiential turn in spectatorship, which implies a deeper embodiment of the public in what is seen.

[4] Caity Weaver, "Why Am I Having Weird Dreams Lately?", *New York Times*, 13 April 2020, https://www.nytimes.com/2020/04/13/style/why-weird-dreams-coronavirus.html (accessed 10 January 2020).

[5] Tomoyasu Horikawa et al., "Neural Decoding of Visual Imagery During Sleep", *Science* 340, no. 6132 (2013): 639, https://doi.org/10.1126/science.1234330 (accessed 7 December 2020).

[6] Tom Gunning, "An Aesthetic of Astonishment: Early Film and the (In) Credulous Spectator", *Art&Text* 34 (1989): 31–45. In his essay, the professor used the well-known, and yet invented, reaction of the public to the screening of *L'arrivée d'un train à La Ciotat* as a methodological tool to reconsider the history of films and the importance of the audience.

The dream sequence in a film can be understood as a latent content of the director's subconscious or, as Francesco Casetti said, as an object to be investigated through psychoanalytic research capable of contributing to the understanding of the development and content of the film.[7] Since this is the most useful interpretation to understand this connection, the dream structure is by its very nature a symbolic metaphor that stands for something else. It is an open structure subjected to meanings and interpretations stratified in time that led to a growth of the discourse around the film and the director himself. It is no coincidence that the works that have most directly addressed this topic have had a critical history full of conflicting judgments—just think of *8½* (1963) by Federico Fellini, of *Mulholland Drive* (2001) by David Lynch, and of *Waking Life* (2001) by Richard Linklater. These examples are not only cult movies that contain dream sequences, but they can be conceived as dreams visually transposed through the film itself, thanks also to the critics that speculated on them as milestones in the history of cinema. Moreover, this aspect leads us to think that the linking between film and dream is an unavoidable aspect of the cinematic canon.

A director who intends to talk to us about dreams in his films, such as Apichatpong Weerasethakul, implicitly takes on a sometimes romantic, even nostalgic dimension thanks to a rich cinematic historiography. Representing the most ephemeral and fleeting thing that exists, becoming aware of the transience of memory but at the same time dealing with the atavistic nature that this exerts on our imagination is what, in short, animates the artistic research of the Thai director. If we consider one of the main paradoxes of cinema, and one of the tensions that most contribute to making it a truly human medium—that is, representing the invisible through a medium created to faithfully record reality—Weerasethakul's works testify precisely to the limits and contradictions against which cinema itself moves, confronts and collides. This fact leads us to a reflection on the boundaries between what is real and what cannot be concretely defined: at the very core of his films and videos there is an intimate encounter between us, our dreams and visual desires, that the Thai director wants us to be aware of and witness.

One of the peculiarities of Apichatpong Weerasethakul's work consists of the reproduction of reality and in the restitution of a

---

[7] Francesco Casetti, *Theories of Cinema 1945–1990* (Austin: University of Texas Press, 1999), 158–160. Useful considerations about this topic can be found in Laura Rascaroli, "Oneiric Metaphor in Film Theory", *Kinema: A Journal for Film and Audiovisual Media* (Fall 2002), https://doi.org/10.15353/kinema.vi.982 (accessed 8 December 2020).

symbolic dialectical process made by antithesis: a strongly dreamlike realism, in which the real and the abstract are intertwined to produce a reflection on the meaning of vision. Magic realism is the lowest common denominator of each of his works: a decidedly problematic realism that lives by its very nature of its opposing contradictions. The concept of abstraction has often been used to refer to the Thai director's works, in this case as something that is hidden, which is not immediately visible, but by its very nature opposes the concept of realism: an extremely dialectical procedure that opposes visible to the invisible, human to nonhuman and concrete to immaterial.[8] This dialectic of concreteness and abstraction, between characters suffering from mysterious disabling diseases—presented in the most corporeal and physical way possible—and fascinating visions of microorganisms floating in the sky—presented in the most disorienting and unreal way possible—is at the basis of the reflection on the concept of concrete abstraction.[9]

As the title suggests, this short essay is mainly focused on Apichatpong Weerasethakul's artistic and cinematographic reflections about dreams, sleep, "abstractions", and spectatorship, but it also highlights several specific case studies from different contexts and decades—such as Delmore Schwartz's short tale *In Dreams Begins Responsibilities* (1937) that are useful to understand the interplay between the visual meaning of dreams and their influences on contemporary approaches. In the following section I draw up several reflections concerning the interplay of text and image in the visual translation of the dream. In the third section I deepen the dialectic between real and abstraction, mainly referring to a scene from *Cemetery of Splendour* (2015). The fourth and the fifth sections are respectively dedicated to the responsibility of the viewer while seeing a film on screen—specific attention is dedicated to

---

[8] Erik Bordeleau, "In Dream You Can't Take Control: Le cinema comme rêve et medium de l'âme", *Hors-champ*, 1 February 2016, https://www.horschamp.qc.ca/spip.php?article612 (accessed 12 December 2020).

[9] In the next sections I am going to explain in detail the concept of concrete abstraction. The term is often related to Henry Lefebvre's theory of space and the contemporary debate around the meaning of abstraction in contemporary culture. In this context I am mainly referring to Sven Lütticken, "Concrete Abstraction: Our Common World", *open! Platform for Art, Culture & the Public Domain*, 6 January 2015, https://www.onlineopen.org/concrete-abstraction (accessed 12 December 2020) and the essays published in Gean Moreno, ed., *In the Mind but Not from There: Real Abstraction and Contemporary Art* (New York: Verso, 2019).

DREAMS, ABSTRACTIONS AND SPECTATORSHIP

Julian Hanich's critical paradigm of the *joint deep attention*—and about a broad reflection of the meaning of the sleep and dreams as a partial political paradigm of the spectatorship. As a conclusion, the last section is dedicated to Weerasethakul's art project *SLEEPCINEMAHOTEL* (2018) and its specific meanings regarding to the linking between attention, dreams and sleep.[10]

II

In 1925, the American newspaper *Oakland Tribune* announced a $25 weekly prize for the best dream to film.[11] For the autumn call of the same year, the winning story was by Miss L.L. Nicholson, in which she dreams of losing her son on a trip to Marin County near San Francisco Bay. In the short film we observe the woman, her husband and their baby in a swaddling blanket making their way by car, by boat and, finally, by train, to their pre-established destination. On the way, the child disappears from the crib, throwing the couple into the darkest despair, only to find the child in the seat of their car after some bizarre misadventures.

In this case, the problem of the quality of dream translation is significant; it highlights the transition from a descriptive-literary approach to a filmic approach based on a rudimentary montage. On the growing wave of dream studies in the United States during the 1910s and 1920s,[12] the publishers offered a prize to readers first of all for the best idea, secondly for the way the dream was described.

---

[10] Weerasethakul's last film *Memoria* (2021), despite having clear linking with the main topic of this article, is excluded from this analysis. A specific section is going to be dedicated through this edited volume.

[11] "Boy, 11 Months Drives Fast Car in Dream Movie", *Oakland Tribune*, 25 November 1925, 14.

[12] Sigmund Freud spent a short time in the United States in 1909. He was particularly interested in the Dreamland amusement park built by William H. Reynolds in 1904 on Coney Island; the German psychoanalyst described it as "the most interesting place in all of America". Further information about this topic can be found in Norman Klein, "Freud in Coney Island", in *The Coney Island Amateur Psychoanalytic Society and Its Circle*, ed. Zoe Beloff (New York: Christine Burgin, 2009), 19–43. Despite what one might think, Freud never liked the possibility of transposing psychoanalytic ideas through cinema: he refused offers from producer Samuel Goldwyn and those from Hans Neumann for his scientific collaboration on the screenplay of *Secrets of a Soul* (1926), directed by Georg Pabst.

Attempts to transpose and translate dreams abound in the history of cinema, both dreams that someone actually dreamt, and fictional dreams made up by a screenwriter. We do not want, here, to trace a historical profile of these attempts; however it is useful to remember how the popular approach to the theme also allows us to understand the birth of numerous conflicting positions regarding the relationship between movies and dreams.[13]

For the purposes of research, the relationship with the concept of realism in the filmic translation of a dream—or of the very idea of a dream itself—is significant. In this short film, Miss Nicholson's dream is filmed to make the narration as credible as possible: without antici-pation of the lines in the captions, one would reasonably believe that a short film is not a dream but a simple dramatic story.[14] Only later, thanks to the artistic experiments of Hans Richter, Maya Deren, Jonas Mekas or Stan Brakhage,[15] can we concretely define the dialectic between discursive and non-discursive, or dreamlike narratives. However, it remains to be clarified, in the light of the historiography on the subject, whether technology in the field of cinema has made it possible for more people to reinvent the visual imaginary of their dreams and, consequently, to relate to them in different ways than in the past. In other words, what does the unveiling of the dream structure involve by means of the filmic medium and the functioning of editing?[16] What

[13] It is useful to quote Zoe Beloff's *Dreamland: The Coney Island Amateur Psychoanalytic Society and Its Circle, 1926–1972*: in the project the artist analyzes the relation between dreams, desires and American society during the twentieth century.

[14] The last quote of the film says: "Send in your dream—it might win $25.00 and the privilege (sic!) of acting on the screen."

[15] I am referring to Stan Brakhage's *I ... Dreaming* (1988) and his ideas concerning dreams published in Stan Brakhage, *I ... Sleeping (Being a Dream Journal and Parenthetical Explication)* (New York: Visual Studies Workshop Press, 1988).

[16] As recalled in Sergei Eisenstein's famous essay *The Montage of Film Attractions* (1924), the lexicon of the first reflections on editing was pervaded with references to magic and the impressionability of the viewer. The concept of dialectical editing developed by the Russian director can be compared with what Walter Benjamin said ten years later about dreams, awareness and dialectical thinking: "The realisation of a dream element in the course of waking up is the paradigm of dialectical thinking." Walter Benjamin, *Arcades Project*, trans. Howard Eiland and Kevin McLaughlin (Cambridge: Belknap Press of Harvard University Press, 1999), 898.

DREAMS, ABSTRACTIONS AND SPECTATORSHIP

role does the translation from a static-literary to a cinematic-visual approach play in the field of dreams?

I chose the case of Miss Nicholson's dream—which also appears as the protagonist in the short film—to relate it to the dream transpositions in the works of Apichatpong Weerasethakul. Almost a hundred years pass between the two terms of comparison, but, if compared, it is possible to find a common matrix. Thanks to a strong continuity between dream and reality, in the films of the Thai director there is no clear differentiation, in terms of filmic narration, between real scenes and dream scenes, first of all due to a cultural fact: the director explicitly chooses to exhibit and narrate the mythology and fairy tales of southeast Asia in many of his works—just think of *Uncle Boonmee Who Can Recall His Past Lives* (2010)—understood as an intangible heritage and, despite everything, capable of influencing the present, problematizing the concept of mythical memory and historical time.

Simplifying, on the one hand, we have a discursive language organized through the editing process to appear to be a dramatic representation of normal waking life. On the other hand, we have a dream language that favours non-discursiveness and a lack of logical narrative structures—an aspect also linked to the authorial dimension of the film.[17]

Weerasethakul dedicated the video *Fiction* (2018) to the link between dreams, verbal transcription and film visualization. In this video, conceived as a complex installation, we observe the director intent on transcribing by hand, in a notebook, some reflections on dreams. In the foreground we observe the artist's writing hand, to highlight the act of translating-transcribing his thoughts, intent on writing some sentences and thoughts, despite the fact that flies and gnats constantly disturb his activity. He then changes the page, rewrites, deletes. The dialectical gap is highlighted between thought and its physical translation by means of writing. This element is further exacerbated by the difficulty of transcribing, as if it were a dream journal, one's own considerations on dreams which, in the mind, appear flat and fluid, while in writing, they appear disconnected and illogical. It is useful to refer directly to the words written by the director during the video:

> I read somewhere that the idea of constant time doesn't exist in dreams. In case you find a clock in your dream you'd see that its hands are moving erratically, or that the hands are not visible. [...]

---

[17] Robert W. Rieber and Robert J. Kelly, *Film, Television and the Psychology of the Social Dream* (New York: Springer, 2014), 13.

> I dreamt about a mixture of horror film and meditation. I was followed by an alien in an anonymous town. Even though it had big eyes, it didn't really "see" me. It sensed me. [...] It was about awareness, yet I wasn't aware that I was dreaming.[18]

Regardless of the symbolic content of the dream, the director emphasizes the dialectic of senses and perceptions between the subject and otherness, as well as the importance of awareness *of* and *in* the dream. In this work we can read the issues that run through the director's work which will be the subject of analysis in the following sections: the relationship between fiction and reality, between dream vision and verbal translation, the role of awareness and definition of the individual.

III

One of the constants of Apichatpong Weerasethakul's films is the lack of a traditionally defined narrative plot: in his works we find minimal narrative structures—a woman who cares for sick soldiers, a man who spends the last days of his life with his loved ones, a lady who cannot stop thinking about a recurring weird sound—studded with digressions aimed at a narrative growth that creates various stories, sometimes interrelated each others. All this produces a symbolic stratification of contents typical of dream language. This narrative reductionism can be understood as a facilitation for the presentation of dream contents.

It is necessary to reiterate the director's strongly antithetical narrative procedure: a discursive, relational part, which often takes on realistic characteristics with reference to everyday life, and a part in which this link with reality is altered, so as to make time and space subjective concepts.

These visual and linguistic dialectics, as well as the idea of an ever-present mythical Thai past, are clearly spelled out in *Cemetery of Splendour*. In this film we witness the sad fate of some soldiers infected with an unknown disease that makes them fall into a deep sleep: the protagonist, Jenjira, together with the young nurse-medium Keng, takes care of the soldiers, sometimes interacting with them, encouraging them to narrate what they see in the afterlife. Those fairy tales previously mentioned become real in the sleeping bodies of the soldiers who, through the intervention of Keng and Jenjira,

---

[18] The video *Fiction* was made available by Kurimanzutto gallery.

DREAMS, ABSTRACTIONS AND SPECTATORSHIP

speak by narrating their dream visions; soldiers are able to read the dreams of living people, an element that conditions their actions. The soldiers' sleep is softened by luminous tubular structures placed next to their beds, a technology capable of improving their dreams and their precarious condition; when they are activated, there is a sudden change of colour, the ghostly light of which invades the rooms where the bodies of the soldiers lie.

Numerous dialectics are observed in the director's work: the inert bodies of the servicemen and their ability to directly influence the present, the dilapidated structure in which they are temporarily allocated—a former school building—and the avant-garde tubular structures, an abandoned school that rises above a rich and ancient cemetery of Thai rulers.

In one of the last dialogues between the nurse and the protagonist, we learn that the souls of the sleeping soldiers live in a parallel dimension where they lend their energies to previous Thai rulers, weakened by eternal wars of succession to the throne. Keng then acts as a medium for Jenjira, who enquires about her relative named Itt, a conscript soldier afflicted by the illness.

In the film's finale there is a particularly significant scene: in a tropical forest—where the palace of the Thai royals once stood—located next to the school building where the sleeping bodies of the servicemen lie, Itt shows Jenjira, by means of Keng, the "other" world that he himself sees. The medium Keng, possessed by the spirit of Itt, walks through the forest together with Jenjira, showing ornaments, decorated rooms, mirrors, weapons and antique furniture; what we see, however, are only plants, shrubs, trunks and bushes. The viewer listens to Keng's words describing what is not seen: instead, we observe what Jenjira sees. In this case, a strong contradiction is evident, in perceptual terms, akin to the previously anticipated concept of concrete abstraction, that is, the description of something ephemeral and immaterial which, however, through the senses or a fideistic choice, finds an ontological concreteness. On the one hand, the evanescent, immaterial and impalpable words that come from Itt and come out of Keng's mouth and, on the other, the concrete reality of Jenjira, made up of shrubs, trunks and bushes. In the film, Jenjira symbolically takes on the role of witness to unreality: to be a witness to what she does not see, but perceives and, through an act of faith, chooses to believe.

The choice to believe regardless of what we see is the basis of the abstractive process and connotes much of the imaginative power of cinema—and dreams as well. In the case of Jenjira, the choice to believe in Keng's words is based on the certainty that what really is essential is often invisible to the eye and sometimes cannot be concretely defined; in this case the concept of abstraction is comparable to the idea of the invisible as a mental region and as an ideal space. The world of Itt, closed to Jenjira, is therefore abstract *because* it is invisible: it has no real features, it has no contours, it has no specific weight, but it is extremely influential in concrete reality, both in terms of film narration and in aesthetic performative terms—Keng mimics the profile of the invisible objects in the forest described by Itt as if she would replicate them in reality. In this way, the Thai director does not relegate the dialogic-filmic process to a recording, but develops it to its very contradiction, that is, making the invisible visible.

The process of abstraction triggered in the narration of the film therefore firstly pertains to the senses and their fallacy and, secondly, to the possibility of bridging the physical concreteness of a sensation with the imaginative faculty. Scholars and researchers such as Jean Ma recently have deepened an analysis on Jenjira and Iit as symbolical figures of Weerasethakul's cinematic world. Ma quotes the cases of the installations *Fever Room* (2015), *Invisibility* (2016), *Blue* (2018); indeed, they stand as "platform from which other works can be built or a 'satellite' within a larger universe, such that it all ends up being one piece; all together".[19]

Can we therefore speak of empathic compensation on the part of the viewer with respect to something that he does not see but which he *chooses* to believe? It is useful to highlight what Ma writes about *Cemetery of Splendour*:

> *Cemetery of Splendor* penetrates far into the realm of dreams, so far as to lead the audience to question the ontological stability of the reality they have left behind. [...] *Cemetery of Splendor* presents a physical world encircled, undergirded, and overwritten by another reality that is never visually represented but still affects the actions of the characters and the perceptions of the audience.[20]

The issue goes beyond the traditional pact of trust between author and reader defined by Wolfgang Iser and Umberto Eco: in this case there is an essential visual component aimed at highlighting the contradictions on which the relational and emotional process between viewer and film is based. The spectator is indeed directly called into question,

[19] Jean Ma, *At the Edges of Sleep: Moving Images and Somnolent Spectators* (Oakland: University of California Press, 2022), 53–58.
[20] Ma, 2022, 56.

DREAMS, ABSTRACTIONS AND SPECTATORSHIP   143

he participates in the unveiling of truths that cannot be experienced through the senses—"I know, but yet I see".[21] Trusting the dream-abstract discourse is therefore an act of responsibility on the part of the public, which *actively* chooses to lend eyes, ears and mind to the film itself because it decides to believe in Weerasethakul's authorial discourse.

IV

In 1937 the American novelist Delmore Schwartz published a collection of short stories entitled *In Dreams Begin Responsibilities*. In the story that gives the title to the collection, the American writer describes a dream in which he imagines being inside a cinema, seeing a movie and witnessing his parents' courtship with increasing anguish. He then starts shouting at the screen and at the actors, namely his parents, questioning their own responsibility on being adults. After being forced out of the cinema due to his shouts and screams, he then wakes up in his own bedroom, "into the bleak winter of my 21st birthday, the windowsill shining with its lip of snow, and the morning already begun".[22]

The story is characterized by various narrative registers and presents some elements useful for our reflections: in the sections in which he describes what the protagonist sees projected in the room, Schwartz uses a descriptive and flat narrative, referring to the film scripts. Filled with explicit references to psychoanalytic symbolisms, these elements are exploited as a narrative mechanism to reflect on the great importance that the link between dream and cinema had on the viewer's subconscious as in the model of the 1930s.[23]

If, as Delmore Schwartz recalls, it is true that "in dreams begin responsibilities", it is still a question of responsibilities linked to the receptive modalities of the film and the dream. Indeed, one can choose to no longer believe in what one sees or to bring it into doubt, as the

---

[21] Gunning, 1989, 117. For further readings see Tom Gunning, "To Scan a Ghost: The Ontology of Mediated Vision", in *The Spectralities Reader: Ghosts and Haunting in Contemporary Cultural Theory*, ed. Esther Peeren and Maria del Pilar Blanco (New York: Bloomsbury, 2013), 207–244; Murray Leeder, *The Modern Supernatural and the Beginnings of Cinema* (London: Palgrave Macmillan, 2017), 97–135.

[22] Delmore Schwartz, *In Dreams Begin Responsibilities and Other Tales*, ed. James Atlas (New York: New Directions, 1978), 9.

[23] Among Delmore Schwartz's short stories there is significantly one set in a cinema theatre, titled *Screeno*, unpublished until his death in 1977.

144 ALESSANDRO FERRARO

protagonist himself does, before being expelled prematurely from the cinema. The moment in which the protagonist intervenes screaming during the film in the hall is extremely metaphorical; the protagonist in fact turns to his own parents, who act in the film he is seeing:

> What are they doing? Don't they know what they are doing? Why doesn't my mother go after my father? If she does not do that, what will she do? Doesn't my father know what he is doing?"—But the usher has seized my arm and is dragging me away, and as he does so, he says: "What are *you* doing?[24]

The responsibilities of which Schwartz writes primarily concern dynamics and theories explored by the first wave of psychoanalysis, first of all the idea of transfer. Affirming that in dreams responsibilities begin, a maxim that Weerasethakul also seems to adhere to, concurs to associate attention and understanding of what is seen and, above all, of feeling part of the drama itself, in so far "the field of the dream embodies the dreamer in that the screen becomes an extension of the dreamer".[25] According to this definition, the spectator is akin to the dreamer, because his awareness is constantly changing during a movie. It is possible to fall asleep, as the Thai director advises, while watching *Cemetery of Splendour*: however, a sense of responsibility remains with respect to that type of vision as long as one remains *witness of the invisible* and since, quoting Simone Weil, "attention, taken to its highest degree, is the same thing as prayer. It presupposes faith and love".[26] Trust, responsibility, attention are therefore interconnected concepts and, on the basis of these links, it can be deduced that the viewer is invested with a metaphorical role as believer of the discourse of the author. On the one hand, because he is the custodian of a transcendent and invisible truth to the eye and, on the other, because the viewer identifies with the same narrative that the director suggests, placing trust in him and recognizing his institutional and personal voice.

Although there are many ways of seeing a film, all the more in films with dream connotations, there is no universally accepted fruition paradigm; in a recent contribution on the subject, Julian Hanich reiterated the importance of the shared context and the function of

---

[24] Schwartz, 1978, 8.

[25] Robert Eberwein, *Film and the Dream Screen: A Sleep and a Forgetting* (Princeton: Princeton University Press, 1984), 98.

[26] Simone Weil, *Gravity and Grace*, trans. Emma Crawford and Mario von der Ruhr (New York: Routledge, 2002), 117.

the public in order to develop what he defines as *joint deep attention*: a phenomenological characteristic triggered by effects of emotional and cognitive resonance among the public, understood as cohesive subject and participating in the signification of the film itself.[27] If, on the one hand, the adjective *deep* refers to the climate of concentration that is created in a context explicitly delegated to film viewing, *joint* emphasizes the possibility of mutual influence that occurs between spectators, who, in addition to personal reactions, share desires and expectations from the film itself. The setting in which the vision takes place is therefore relevant, which necessarily follows appropriate precautions and expedients—the darkness of the room, the silence—for this particular collective effect to occur.[28]

This happens because attention and distraction—and consequently the responsibility of viewing—are linked to the negotiation of the institutional meaning of the venue where the video or film is observed and, inevitably, to the degree of trust that is placed in the cinematographic context.[29] Logical objections can be made to this assumption, motivated in the first place by the progressive emancipation from traditional user contexts—just think of the great success that online streaming platforms such as MUBI are enjoying. However, the institutional value that the new contexts assume remains to be clarified and, above all, whether it is better that the films belonging to the so-called slow cinema are preferably viewable alone and in private contexts, or in the presence of an audience that shares expectations, attention and responsibility with respect to viewing—thus triggering the effect of joint deep attention.

---

[27] Julian Hanich, "Watching a Film with Others: Towards a Theory of Collective Spectatorship", *Screen* 55, no. 3 (2014): 338–344, https://doi.org/10.1093/screen/hju026 (accessed 16 December 2020); Julian Hanich, "An Invention with a Future: Collective Viewing, Joint Deep Attention and the Ongoing Value of Cinema", in *The Oxford Handbook of Film Theory*, ed. Kyle Stevens (Oxford: Oxford University Press, 2022).

[28] For example, the architecture of Peter Kubelka's *Invisible Cinema* is significantly related to this topic. Julian Hanich, "The Invisible Cinema", in *Exposing the Film Apparatus: The Film Archive as a Research Laboratory*, ed. Giovanna Fossati and Annie Van Den Oever (Amsterdam: Amsterdam University Press, 2016), 345–353.

[29] Volker Pantenburg, "Attention, Please: Negotiating Concentration and Distraction around 1970", *Aniki* 1, no. 2 (2014): 328–343, https://doi.org/10.14591/aniki.v1n2.83 (accessed 6 January 2020). Further information about this topic can be found in Volker Pantenburg, "Temporal Economy: Distraction and Attention in Cinema and Installation Art", *Millennium Film Journal* 59 (2014): 44–51.

Taking for granted the essential relationship between consciousness, dream, setting and spectatorship, in the case of Apichatpong Weerasethakul, these dialectics are evident because they are explicitly aimed at improving the spectator's participation and identification in what he sees, and this, as the director states, leads to consequent awakenings of consciousness.

V

The idea of an individual consciousness awakened by means of filmic-dreamlike suggestions is not an element of novelty, but of continuity with an imaginary linked to the concept of daydreaming and meditation, aspects present in many recent works by the Thai director and in the directors that he affirms to be inspired by: think for example of David Lynch and his interest in forms of transcendental meditation and their influence in *INLAND EMPIRE* (2006). In particular, in the aforementioned *Waking Life* this symbolic awakening is investigated on the basis of the distinction between reality and animation, where the latter is a particular speculative surrogate—in the film a special animation technique, the rotoscope is used—to reflect on the concept of awareness of reality and on the distinction between real and reality. A similar distinction can be found in the relationship between the documentary approach and the non-discursive approach in Weerasethakul's films; moreover, the idea of awakening by means of the dream is an integral part of Buddhist and meditative practices, of which the Thai director declared himself a follower.[30] As the critic Paul Ward recalls, on the basis of the suggestions provided by Wendy Doniger O'Flaherty, the awakening of consciousness, from the collective point of view, coincides with a social critique of the existing through the utopian—and unreal—potentialities inherent in the dream.[31]

The political paradigm, often allusive and metaphorical, present in many of the Thai director's works can be interpreted in a similar way.

---

[30] Jihoon Kim, "Learning About Time: An Interview with Apichatpong Weerasethakul", *Film Quarterly* 64, no. 4 (2011): 52, https://doi.org/10.1525/FQ.2011.64.4.48 (accessed 12 December 2020).

[31] Paul Ward, "I Was Dreaming, I Was Awake and then I Woke up and Found Myself Asleep: Dreaming, Spectacle, and Reality in Waking Life", in *The Spectacle of the Real: From Hollywood to Reality TV and Beyond*, ed. Geoff King (Bristol: Intellect Books, 2005), 161–171.

DREAMS, ABSTRACTIONS AND SPECTATORSHIP

The particular reception given to the director in his own country is also indicative of political problems related to censorship and arrests.[32]

It is worth reflecting on the final scene of *Cemetery of Splendour*, in which Jen looks at astonished and startled kids as they play football, amid mounds of earth moved by a bulldozer, as they raise dust, earth and screams all around. It is possible to read a symbolic dialectic composed of two superimposed levels: on the one hand, the "real" and concrete plan, made up of diseases, soldiers, construction sites in action, *realpolitik*, on the other the imaginative and abstract plan, linked to what it involves to move the same ground trodden centuries earlier by illustrious rulers whose memory remains imperishable, despite their physical absence. The director's criticism of the current state of affairs in Thailand is evident as it is proposed on the basis of his own historical memory filtered through local traditions, represented through the figure of Keng; historical memory, the director suggests, without an effective mythology behind it, is ineffective in imposing itself on the present unless you choose to dig up and dredge up, literally, uncomfortable historical memories. The contemporary war fought by slumbering Thai soldiers is symbolically undermined by its own reasons and motivations as the soldiers lend their vital energies to previous rulers, who live in a different and alternative historical present. The present that those same soldiers live is therefore drowsy, made up of moments of fleeting and transient lucidity, where the only agent capable of altering things is the simple "taking care" of the other—think of Keng and Jen—understood as a political act.[33]

It is necessary to underline the literal character of the metaphors present in Weerasethakul's films; soldiers are inactive physically, not mentally: it is an obvious contradiction if one conceives the army as the most representative emblem of physical activity. Furthermore, absolute inaction also insists on the veiled political paradigm in the background of the whole film: can inactivity, and specifically sleep, therefore be interpreted as a paradigm of political activity?

In his famous essay *24/7 Late Capitalism and the Ends of Sleep*, Jonathan Crary illustrates the persistent relationship between economies of exploitation, globalized development and techno-corporeality in

---

[32] Vivienne Chow, "A Prominent Thai Artists Says His Country Is Becoming a Hybrid of Singapore and North Korea", *Quartz*, 30 September 2016, https://qz.com/789448/thai-artist-apichatpong-weerasethakul-says-his-country-is-becoming-a-hybrid-of-singapore-and-north-korea/ (accessed 7 December 2020).

[33] Similar thoughts can be found in Ma, 2021.

the capitalist age. He contrasts these elements with eschatological solutions, such as the act of sleeping or dreaming, activities intended as the last free space and not conditioned by the logic of economic systems, by the principles of efficiency and work optimization.[34] What is jeopardized, the scholar insists, is the biological integrity of the individual, endangered by the progressive colonization of areas deemed virgin—sleep and dreams—by the contemporary work system. It follows that the possibility of sleeping and dreaming, in addition to reviving a romantic *topos*, becomes a concrete political act that opposes the efficiency and optimization of working time.[35]

I chose to quote Crary's essay because his theories have often found an important echo in artistic contexts and Weerasethakul's considerations, however metaphorical and cryptic, can be placed on the same level as Crary's thought. It is worth mentioning the important travelling exhibition *Sleeping with a Vengeance, Dreaming of a Life* (2018), curated by Ruth Noack, within which the act of sleeping is presented, through traditional performances and works, as a pretext for reflection on contemporary political consciousness.[36]

In the case of the Thai director, sleeping and the act of dreaming are not always charged with political values. For the making of *async— first light* (2017) the director sent some smartphones to colleagues and friends—recognizable are Tilda Swinton, David Sylvian and Hidetoshi Nishijima—to film themselves while they are sleeping or in the moments before they doze off. The intimate character of the work, enhanced by the music of Ryuicki Sakamoto, is linked both to the grainy quality of the film, almost as if he wanted to return a sense of participatory intimacy deriving from both the "amateur" filming, and the possibility of sharing the moment for a few seconds in which the consciousness of

---

[34] Jonathan Crary, *24/7 Late Capitalism and the End of Sleep* (London: Verso, 2013), 11–25. For further readings, Sharon Sliwinski, *Dreaming in Dark Times: Six Exercises in Political Thought* (Minneapolis: University of Minnesota Press, 2017).

[35] Concerning the politics of vision, it is useful to refer to Jonathan Crary, *Techniques of the Observer: On Vision and Modernity in the 19th Century* (Cambridge: The MIT Press, 1992), 30–52.

[36] Ruth Noack, "Outrage: Subversive Sleep", *The Architectural Review*, 9 April 2020, https://www.architectural-review.com/essays/outrage/ outrage-subversive-sleep (accessed 12 December 2020). *Sleeping with a Vengeance, Dreaming of a Life* has been displayed in several international museums and galleries: Yellow Bricks (Athens, July 2018), Lìtost gallery (Prague, September 2018), Institute for Provocation (Beijing, October 2018) Württembergischer Kunstverein Stuttgart (Stuttgart, October 2019– January 2020).

the filmmakers moves or migrates to other places. In a recent interview, the director clearly explained the link between sleep, dreams, intimacy and eschatological possibilities.[37]

VI

Fig. 1: *SLEEPCINEMAHOTEL*, exhibition view, 2018, 47th International Film Festival Rotterdam. Photo by Jan De Groen.

SLEEPCINEMAHOTEL is neither a film, an installation, nor an imaginary script. It is an actual, operational hotel where the

---

[37] "Well, my boyfriend likes to sleep, so I thought, 'Let's shoot this'. It's a game to see if the presence of the camera has some kind of energy to wake him up. [...] I think dreams are really important as a means of escape, and to discover a new reality. It's a way for us to process information. It's similar to the way we need movies—the need to be in the dark and to lose oneself." Paul Dallas, "Apichatpong Weerasethakul on Friendship, Sleep, Ghosts and Science Fiction", 9 *Extra Extra Magazine*, https://extraextramagazine.com/talk/apichatpong-weerasethakul-friendship-sleep-ghosts-science-fiction/ (accessed 11 December 2020). In the first part of the quote, Weerasethakul refers to the video *Teem*, where he filmed his boyfriend while he was sleeping.

guests who have booked a bed (single or double) all end up in the same screening room. This is a large hall with on the one side a constellation of open sleep modules, and on the other side an impressive circular projection screen. Guests who stay overnight and daytime visitors alike will be transported to Weerasethakul's preferred plane of existence: one where sleep and film, ghosts and imagination, the past and the present collide.[38]

From the statements of the curator Edwin Carels, we understand the particular exhibition context of *SLEEPCINEMAHOTEL*, created in collaboration with Apichatpong Weerasethakul, on the occasion of the 47th International Film Festival Rotterdam: a fully functioning hotel, with receptionists and bathrooms, able to host fans of the Thai director, who, for the occasion, chose to show some videos and archival films for his audience. We thus have a large circular screen, instead of seats a complicated tangle of beds, scaffolding and mattresses. The projections consisted of archival footage selected by the director himself from the EYE Film Institute in Amsterdam and the Netherlands Institute for Sound and Vision in Hilversum—in particular films that dealt with the sea, the flow of waves, tropical rivers, animals, pleasant natural environments—with an evocative soundtrack specially chosen by the director's troupe.

The entire programming was designed so that no video was repeated twice during the duration of the viewing, so as to offer the public a constant renewal of film sequences. From the aesthetic point of view in conceiving the entire work, according to the statements of the curator and the director, both *Strike* (1925) by Sergei Eisenstein, in particular for the play of shadows that was created between the projection and the audience itself, and the short film *The Unchanging Sea* (1910) by David Griffith were relevant. The following morning, after the viewing, hotel guests were invited to have breakfast in the exhibition spaces and to write down, at the invitation of the director himself, a collective dream book.

The project can be understood as a work of art or installation by Weerasethakul himself in which the public has an essential role as the recipient of an "act of care": as mentioned, falling asleep while watching a film may not necessarily be symptomatic of the lack of interest in what is seen, but, however paradoxical it may seem, it can be a conscious and felt reaction to the vision itself, understood here not as a transfer of content or information, but as experiential participation.[39]

---

[38] International Film Festival Rotterdam, *Catalogue 47th IFFR* (Rotterdam: 2018), Exhibition Catalogue, 150.

[39] Hanich, 2022.

DREAMS, ABSTRACTIONS AND SPECTATORSHIP

The experience of *SLEEPCINEMAHOTEL* is also indicative of the value of the setting in the so-called cinematic daydreaming;[40] in this context there is also a nostalgic feeling towards the very architecture of cinemas. *SLEEPCINEMAHOTEL* mainly highlights the Thai director's interest in themes such as dreams and sleep. Secondly, he combines the community of the public with the significance of the work itself: you can sleep and then wake up and find yourself in a different scene, fantasize about what happened in the period of time in which one was "absent", to then go back to sleep and be, in any case, spectator. The case of the *SLEEPCINEMAHOTEL* clarifies some extra-filmic potentials inherent in Weerasethakul's poetics, primarily the significance of the film institution as a form of mediation of attention, in a complex balance between understanding, vision and individual conscience. These are the considerations reported by Travis Jeppesen, correspondent of *Artforum*, who reviewed the event highlighting the strong subjective and emotional component, in addition to the empathic compensation required of the viewer, at the mercy of sleep and dreams:

> Hi, Apichatpong. Can I really sleep inside your art? [...] Always the sounds of waves, water. The soundscape flowing. Sound detached from image, coming to reform that image. Seagulls mowing down the horizon. Sailboats go by windmills. Am I asleep yet? [...] What if there was a way to inscribe this cinema into my veins. To keep writing until it, the entire world, disappears. Now two rats sleeping. Side by side, the rats make their own dreams. They don't need the cinema to do that for them.[41]

---

[40] Julian Hanich describes the cinematic daydreaming as "an act of consciousness in which a viewer—voluntarily or involuntarily—enters into a chain of sensory presentifications (*Vergegenwaertigungen)* of something that is either absent or non-existent, and which partly removes attention from the immediate perceptual surroundings of the viewer and thus draws attention, however slightly, away from the film". Julian Hanich, "When Viewers Drift Off: A Brief Phenomenology of Cinematic Daydreaming", in *The Structures of the Film Experience by Jean-Pierre Meunier,* ed. Julian Hanich and Daniel Fairfax (Amsterdam: Amsterdam University Press, 2019), 340. For further readings concerning cinema and audience: Julian Hanich, *The Audience Effect: On the Collective Cinema Experience* (Edinburgh: Edinburgh University Press, 2018).

[41] Travis Jeppesen, "Lazy Sunday", *Artforum*, 15 February 2018, https://www.artforum.com/film/travis-jeppesen-on-apichatpong-weerasethakul-s-sleepcinemahotel-74262 (accessed 12 December 2020).

Bibliography

Benjamin, Walter. *Arcades Project*. Trans. Howard Eiland and Kevin McLaughlin. Cambridge. Belknap Press of Harvard University Press. 1999.

Brakhage, Stan. *I ... Sleeping (Being a Dream Journal and Parenthetical Explication)*. New York. Visual Studies Workshop Press. 1988.

Bordeleau, Erik. "In Dream You Can't Take Control: le cinema comme rêve et medium de l'âme". *Hors-champ*. February 2016. https://www.horschamp.qc.ca/spip.php?article612.

Casetti, Francesco. *Theories of Cinema 1945–1990*. Austin. University of Texas Press. 1999.

Crary, Jonathan. *Techniques of the Observer: On Vision and Modernity in the 19th Century*. Cambridge. The MIT Press. 1992.

Crary, Jonathan. *24/7: Late Capitalism and the End of Sleep*. London. Verso. 2013.

Chow, Vivienne. "A Prominent Thai Artists Says His Country Is Becoming a Hybrid of Singapore and North Korea". *Quartz*. 30 September 2016. https://qz.com/789448/thai-artist-apichatpong-weera-sethakul-says-his-country-is-becoming-a-hybrid-of-singapore-and-north-korea/.

Dallas, Paul. "Apichatpong Weerasethakul on Friendship, Sleep, Ghosts and Science Fiction". *Extra Extra Magazine* 9. https://extraextramagazine.com/talk/apichatpong-weerasethakul-friendship-sleep-ghosts-science-fiction/.

Eberwein, Robert. *Film and the Dream Screen: A Sleep and a Forgetting*. Princeton. Princeton University Press. 1984.

Gunning, Tom. "An Aesthetic of Astonishment: Early Film and the (In)Credulous Spectator". *Art&Text* 34 (1989): 31–45.

Gunning, Tom. "To Scan a Ghost: The Ontology of Mediated Vision". In *The Spectralities Reader: Ghosts and Haunting in Contemporary Cultural Theory*. Ed. Esther Peeren and Maria del Pilar Blanco. New York. Bloomsbury. 2013. 207–244.

Hanich, Julian. "Watching a Film with Others: Towards a Theory of Collective Spectatorship". *Screen* 55, no. 3 (2014): 338–359. https://doi.org/10.1093/screen/hju026.

Hanich, Julian. *The Audience Effect: On the Collective Cinema Experience*. Edinburgh. Edinburgh University Press. 2018.

Hanich, Julian. "The Invisible Cinema". In *Exposing the Film Apparatus: The Film Archive as a Research Laboratory*. Ed. Giovanna Fossati and Annie Van Den Oever. Amsterdam. Amsterdam University Press. 2016. 345–353.

Hanich, Julian. "When Viewers Drift Off: A Brief Phenomenology of Cinematic Daydreaming". In *The Structures of the Film Experience by Jean-Pierre Meunier*. Ed. Julian Hanich and Daniel Fairfax. Amsterdam. Amsterdam University Press. 2019. 336–352.

DREAMS, ABSTRACTIONS AND SPECTATORSHIP

Hanich, Julian. "An Invention with a Future: Collective Viewing, Joint Deep Attention and the Ongoing Value of Cinema". In *The Oxford Handbook of Film Theory*. Ed. Kyle Stevens. Oxford. Oxford University Press. 2022.

Horikawa, Tomoyasu, Masako Tamaki, Yoichi Miyawaki and Yukiyasu Kamitani. "Neural Decoding of Visual Imagery During Sleep". *Science* 340, no. 6132 (2013): 639–642. https://doi.org/10.1126/science.1234330.

Jeppesen, Travis. "Lazy Sunday". *Artforum*. 15 February 2018. https://www.artforum.com/film/travis-jeppesen-on-apichatpong-weera-sethakul-s-sleepcinemahotel-74262.

Kim, Jihoon. "Learning About Time: An Interview with Apichatpong Weerasethakul". *Film Quarterly* 64, no. 4 (2011): 48–52. https://doi.org/10.1525/FQ.2011.64.4.48.

Klein, Norman. "Freud in Coney Island". In *The Coney Island Amateur Psychoanalytic Society and Its Circle*. Ed. Zoe Beloff. New York. Christine Burgin. 2009. 19–43.

Leeder, Murray. *The Modern Supernatural and the Beginnings of Cinema*. London. Palgrave Macmillan. 2017.

Lütticken, Erik. "Concrete Abstraction: Our Common World". *open! Platform for Art, Culture & the Public Domain*. 6 January 2015. https://www.onlineopen.org/concrete-abstraction.

Ma, Jean. "Sleeping in the Cinema". *October* (Spring 2021): 30–52.

Ma, Jean. *At the Edges of Sleep: Moving Images and Somnolent Spectators*. Oakland. University of California Press. 2022.

Moreno, Gean, ed. *In the Mind but Not from There: Real Abstraction and Contemporary Art*. New York. Verso. 2019.

Noack, Ruth. "Outrage: Subversive Sleep". *The Architectural Review*. 9 April 2020. https://www.architectural-review.com/essays/outrage/outrage-subversive-sleep.

Pantenburg, Volker. "Attention, Please: Negotiating Concentration and Distraction around 1970". *Aniki* 1, no. 2 (2014): 328–343. https://doi.org/10.14591/aniki.v1n2.83.

Pantenburg, Volker. "Temporal Economy: Distraction and Attention in Cinema and Installation Art". *Millennium Film Journal* 59 (2014): 44–51.

Rascaroli, Laura. "Oneiric Metaphor in Film Theory". *Kinema: A Journal for Film and Audiovisual Media* (Fall 2002). https://doi.org/10.15353/kinema.vi.982.

Rieber, Robert W. and Robert J. Kelly. *Film, Television and the Psychology of the Social Dream*. New York. Springer. 2014.

Schwartz, Delmore. *In Dreams Begin Responsibilities and Other Tales*. Ed. James Atlas. New York. New Directions. 1978.

Sharot, Stephen. "Dreams in Films and Films as Dreams: Surrealism and Popular American Cinema". *Canadian Journal of Film Studies* 24, no. 1 (2015): 66–89.

Sliwinski, Sharon. *Dreaming in Dark Times: Six Exercises in Political Thought*. Minneapolis. University of Minnesota Press. 2017.

Ward, Paul. "I Was Dreaming, I Was Awake and then I Woke up and Found Myself Asleep: Dreaming, Spectacle, and Reality in Waking Life". In *The Spectacle of the Real: From Hollywood to Reality TV and Beyond*. Ed. Geoff King. Bristol. Intellect Books. 2005. 161–173.

Weaver, Caity. "Why Am I Having Weird Dreams Lately?". *New York Times*. 13 April 2020. https://www.nytimes.com/2020/04/13/style/why-weird-dreams-coronavirus.html.

Weil, Simone. *Gravity and Grace*. Trans. Emma Crawford and Mario von der Ruhr. New York. Routledge. 2002.

"You Can Sleep During My Film". Posted by SPH Razor. 26 July 2013. video, 5:46. https://www.youtube.com/watch?v=DVNIvTqIMs4.

7

EFFULGENCES Particles in Motion
Cycling the Mindscapes of Apichatpong Weerasethakul

Jeffner Allen

Orbs of light, a momentary streak as light and desire meet between the strings of a singing guitar, a firefly, the beetle aglow, is discovered and Skyped by a young man to a loved one far away. A three minute and 11 second response to an undersea megathrust quake on 11 March 2011, the most powerful earthquake on record to have impacted Japan, followed by a tsunami with waves reaching 40 meters and the Fukushima Daiichi nuclear power plant disaster, *Monsoon,* recorded with phone cam and computer cam, is described by artist and filmmaker Apichatpong Weerasethakul as a "lullaby".[1]

The sonic luminosity of the eerie, personal offering, soothing, perhaps, for spirits of the dead and the living, recalls the UFO-firefly, a wandering soul and a chirping communication device that releases into the night jungle what it has heard during the day, of Apichatpong's *Tropical Malady/Sud Pralad,* which received the *Prix du Jury* at Cannes, 2004. Journeying steadily across the darkened screen toward a tree whose leaves and interior branches are ablaze with pulsating lights, tranquilly illuminating the face of a forest ranger who accidentally killed a cow while helping local villagers, a shimmering dot becomes one with the tree; the white ghost body of a cow, rising on all four legs, ambles further into the jungle.

No longer a solitary beam, swarms of bugs carried by fierce winds, waves of mosquitos by the thousands, arrive during dawn and dusk shootings of *Primitive,* a multiplatform project that includes *A Letter to Uncle Boonmee* and *Uncle Boonmee Who Can Recall His Past Lives/ Lung Boonmee Raluek Chat,* awarded the *Palme d'Or* at Cannes in 2010.

---

[1] Apichatpong Weerasethakul's website, kickthemachine.com, features productions of Kick the Machine studio. Among the videos, stills, and commentaries is his reference to *Monsoon* as a "lullaby", http://www.kickthemachine.com/page80/page1/page37/index.html.

Soaring to devour the lights, falling from electric nets, crackling sparks, the insects that haunt Boonmee, who at once expresses regret for crushing many insects in his lifetime and for shooting communists during the military engagement in northeast Thailand in 1965, are invited by Apichatpong to be part of the footage. "I think they are very beautiful", he observes, "like ghosts darting across the frame", noting that the "swift blurry object in the shot" gives birth to "a moment of wonder that makes the audience become conscious of the filmic focal plane, and of filmmaking".[2]

"We as insects that are drawn to lights",[3] an image of multiple valences that surfaces in an interview with Apichatpong, opens upon a plural "we" of humans who have been reborn as insects and of insects reincarnated as plants, humans, ghosts and other phantoms, the connections between which emerge prismatically in his art. In that transformation, what might appear a simple swapping of bodily forms becomes an engagement with light that transplants "our" organs of perception.

So remarkable are the interactions that transpire in the aerial diving and flashing of fireflies during twilight, the mimicking of a flash response as a predacious species tricks a firefly in search of a mate, then pounces upon, kills, and consumes its prey, or the attunement of that airborne being to the sunlight to determine the length of a day and the approach of winter. Oriented to receive light from different directions, the sometimes hundreds or thousands of individual eyes of a flying insect, which function independently, though usually not in isolation, generate an image that enables a wide angle of view and extraordinary acuity in detecting movement. Each individual lens-capped unit, with its own cornea and photoreceptor cells, records part of a neural picture.

A form of wave motion that travels at high speed, light is captured indirectly through various organs of vision. A human eye, for instance, does not observe directly the vibrations of the waves, but receives light energy that is reflected off objects. Yet the single lens structure of the human eye, which focuses light on the retina to form an image in the brain, is often referred to as a "camera eye", while the assumed simplicity of a compound eye and associated nervous system is termed "primitive". If "camera eye" echoes the priorities of viewers who expect to concentrate on in-focus objects in a frame or who might find the

---

[2] Apichatpong Weerasethakul, *A Letter to Uncle Boonmee*, http://www. animateprojects.org/films/by_date/2009/a_letter_to.

[3] Andrea Lissoni, "Apichatpong Weerasethakul, *Vampire, M Hotel*", VDRome, n.d., http://www.vdrome.org/ apichatpong-weerasethakul-vampiresud-vikal-m-hotel/.

EFFULGENCES PARTICLES IN MOTION

unclear rendering of objects by a "primitive" lens "not clean", a glance at the visual apparatus of grasshoppers, which combines three simple and two compound eyes, suggests that ways of seeing may be neither mutually exclusive nor so easily delimited.

Suspended above stamen and petals, a honeybee perceives the near-ultraviolet light reflecting off a plant. Most airborne insects, moreover, perceive wavelengths from 300 to 650 nanometers, in abiding communication with the ultraviolet spectrum of electromagnetic waves. The shorter wavelengths of 300 to 400 nanometers, a few billionths of a meter, may mark but a slight difference from the 400 to 700 nanometers that a human eye generally can grasp.[4] Nonetheless, were that interval, replete with its archives of images, to rouse us at this moment, such a happening might suffice to draw a reader's attention from the printed page to wander among screens of darkness, visible and invisible, flooded by pools, passageways, and rivers of light, and nearby, Apichatpong, painting light.

"The flashes of light were frozen and digitally painted, creating fictional topographies",[5] comments Apichatpong with regard to *Primates' Memories* and *Mr Electrico (for Ray Bradbury)*, lightbox photographs that are part of the video installation *Fireworks (Archives)*, first shown in 2014. Impossible figurations of the light that flows beyond the reach of human organs of sight, the works portend a retrieval and reactivation of the powers of our anatomical eyes, as well as the eyes of our mind and camera lens.

Red yellow reverberations of the red shirt yellow shirt conflicts in rural and urban communities in Thailand, but also red yellow blue reverberations, an allusion to recent studies of the relationship between memory and light conducted at MIT, are percussively tapped by Apichatpong's colloidal brush. A blue light, introduced by the MIT team into the cavernous vault of the cranium, artificially activates a memory. The research, which focuses on a cell group within the hippocampus, a seahorse-shaped portion of the brain pertaining to the connection of the emotions and senses to memories, as well as to the formation of new memories, finds that memories are not lost, but may be dormant.[6]

Palpably imploding, *Primates' Memories* awakens a rhythmic profusion of memories and reincarnations. In that tri-colored

---

[4] Randolf Menzel, "Spectral Sensitivity and Color Vision in Invertebrates", *Comparative Physiology and Evolution of Vision in Invertebrates*, ed. H. Autrum (Berlin: Springer Verlag, 1979).

[5] Apichatpong Weerasethakul, *Fireworks (Archives)*, http://www.kickthemachine.com/page80/page22/page33/index.html.

[6] T.J. Ryan et al., "Engram Cells Retain Memory Under Retrograde Amnesia", *Science* 348, no. 6238 (2015): 1007–1013, doi: 10.1126/science.aaa5542.

reactivation, the lives of the teens and elders of Nabua, near the Mekong river and the border of Thailand with Laos, those who leave the small community to find work and those who stay, maintaining daily life and living from the earth by farming.

Red blue yellow, a looping entanglement of cosmic forces and political powers, tapped, tapped sharply, and in the vibrations, release, fingertips of palms electric, eyes in palms not eyes that scan a track, but eyes that travel into dream.

Cavernous Time Machine Dreaming

No one tale, the loops of images that combine and recombine, the intervals of darkness and light, the collaborative logics that sustain the multiplatform projects and films of Apichatpong Weerasethakul. Inviting viewers to float and dream amid fireworks emitted by archives released into the flickering gleam of the time machine of the future, the productions, and Apichatpong's reflections on them, nevertheless might surprise: A filmmaker who believes that we do not need movies?

In *PRIMITIVE*, a tiny book to hold in the hand, though almost 500 pages, Apichatpong recounts a story told by the abbot at Wat Saeng Arun Forest Temple, near the city of Khon Kaen, where he grew up. Phra Sripariyattiwet kept extensive written records of the memories of people of northeast Thailand, including those he gathered in *A Man Who Can Recall His Past Life*, the recollections of Boonmee, who was capable of remembering several of his lives over the centuries, and who was always reborn and wandered in the northeast, Isan, region. During a visit by the filmmaker and Aunt Jen, actress Jenjira Pongpas, Apichatpong shares a ghostly moment:

> He then told us a story of two orbs of light that would float out from the temple chapel. They usually came out at eight in the evening or around ten at night. They would float around the Bodhi tree and move along the roof of the temple, lighting up the roof tiles. They would then return to the chapel and sometimes not come out again. At other times, the orbs of light would play with the young novices, who would try to pounce on them, but they were never fast enough. The orbs looked like glass balls, similar to a child's toy. But one day they broke and after that they couldn't move around. So the monks put the glass balls on top of the temple spire.[7]

[7] Apichatpong Weerasethakul, "17 August, 2008", in *PRIMITIVE*, CUJO 2:1 (Milan: Edizioni Zero, 2009), n.p.

A tale of transformations in which, appearing and disappearing, zigzag, circling, the moving lights-in-writing elicit a reader's awareness of the rhythms of light, which the novices were never quick enough to catch. The accent on the drift of vision amid a play of unseen forces beyond control brings to mind the reminiscence by Apichatpong, that cinema, for him, "is still foreign, is still a strange animal, and for each film is a different animal. I feel that it is a very magical being that I cannot tame."[8]

Bouncing off the thoughtful advice of the monk, who once told him "meditation was like filmmaking ... when one meditates, one doesn't need film",[9] Apichatpong offers his personal belief, "if you know how to operate your mind, you don't need movies. Because movies are in your mind." The filmmaker's mention, as if in a single breath, of "an opposite call", "some conflict between", and "somehow I try to bridge them",[10] with reference to the loss of self, hypnosis, or deep sleep, which is induced by cinema and the self-knowledge that arises through observation of one's mind in meditation, engenders a fertile impasse. It is, perhaps, in the dehiscent cohabitation of film and meditation that historically chiseled fissures of the mind begin to open, yielding an excess of shapes, surfaces and dimensions.

Phos, light, shine, glitter, the nature, *physis,* of cinema, coming out at night, floating around, moving along, lighting up, and returning to darkness, is its own source of motion, though dependent on *techne*, the mind, to which Apichatpong refers as "the most powerful tool".[11] "But better than cinema is the light itself", he notes, while adding, "our eyes, our brain, is the best projector that is constantly interplaying with light."[12]

The recombinant noun *jai,* ใจ, although not evoked directly by Apichatpong, the heart as mirror of the universe, a fusion of mind, heart, spirit, their feelingful inner eye, emerges in the artist's expression

---

[8] Felix von Boehm, "Apichatpong Weerasethakul, On Memories", *CINE-FILS, Online Interview Magazine*, September 2010, https://www.youtube.com/watch?v=SeDS612TQ8M.

[9] James Quandt, "Push and Pull: An Exchange with Apichatpong Weerasethakul", in *Apichatpong Weerasethakul*, ed. James Quandt (Vienna: Synema, 2009), 184.

[10] Giovanni Marchini Camia, "Interview with Apichatpong Weerasethakul", *Fireflies, A Film Zine* 1 (July 2014): 8–9.

[11] Camia, 2014.

[12] Guy Carrion-Murayari, "Interview with Apichatpong Weerasethakul", in *Apichatpong Weerasethakul: Primitive*, ed. Guy Carrion-Murayari and Massimiliano Gioni (New York: New Museum, 2011), 14.

that, rather than tell a story, "I care about moments, feelings, and experiences."[13] A central faculty of self-transformation, *jai* is the base of a multitude of phrases, *jai-kaep*, for instance, indicates a narrow, selfish heart, which concern the condition of the heart and the feelings of others. A palpable shimmer that darts about, that streaks playfully from the void of mind that is no longer full of expectations, *jai* illuminates the pleasure of filmmaking, which, for Apichatpong, lies in "recapturing", through a dream within a dream, "the feeling of the memory—and in blending that with the present".[14]

Photophobia, a very painful sensitivity to light: "I like the term", Apichatpong states in conversation, "it is the cause, the root, of my filmmaking".[15] Fear of light, a malady of heart, mind, spirit, as well as an acute physical condition, often galvanizes the collapse and rebound of animate image bundles of social, political and cinematographic histories, which infuse the cosmos of his films. Drawn to orbs of light that illuminate the, indeed, heart-shaped leaves of the Bodhi tree of enlightenment, we are haunted by fear that we might not see at all, and that we might see too much.

The need to try to remember species, languages and beliefs that are disappearing, a theme of Terry Glavin's *Waiting for the Macaws*, one of the books, along with *A Man Who Can Recall His Past Life*, that inspired *Uncle Boonmee Who Can Recall His Past Lives*, is transmitted by the figure of Boonmee, as he approaches death, through his full-hearted desire for sight. Descending into a forest cave in which the shadow play of thousands of bioluminescent sparks and flashlight beams cast by loved ones, including his long lost son in the form of a monkey ghost, illuminates the cavern's walls and a flowing spring, Boonmee's gaze turns upwards, or inward, toward a ball of light that appears in the darkness, above an opening between the craggy boulders. "What's wrong with my eyes? They are open, but I can't see a thing. Or are my eyes closed?" he asks, only to be calmed, and coached in mind training to see other lives, by the ghost of his wife Huay, who suggests, "Maybe you need time to adjust to the dark." "I only know", rejoins Boonmee

---

[13] Tony Rayns, "Interview with Apichatpong Weerasethakul, Memories, Mysteries", July 2006, http://www.kickthemachine.com/page80/page24/page12/index.html.

[14] Matt Mansfield, "Apichatpong Weerasethakul's Double Vision, an Interview", April 2014, removed from, http://www.dazeddigital.com/artsandculture/article/19508/1/apichatpong-weerasethakul-double-visions-interview.

[15] Masashi Nagara, "Photophobia, Art Gallery @KCUA", June 2014, https://www.youtube.com/watch?v=gEogkNnUN8c.

matter-of-factly, "that I was born here. I don't know if I was a human, or an animal, or a woman or a man." One day, Boonmee may also wonder about and try to remember his life as 35 millimeter blown up from Super 16 millimeter film medium, which makes possible qualities of light, color, and motion that may soon become extinct.

Sketches of plants overlay photos of military occupations and insurgencies in the northeastern plateau of Isan and in the south of Thailand, in *On Photophobia*, a vision recorded in writing, where we meet the unforgettable collector of the memories of the world's vegetation as he works in darkness, attempting to tap into how plants utilize light. "Trembling with fever", the document recounts, "he lay in the mud with leaves covering his eyes. In his delirium he saw lights and stories, scenes witnessed by the dead plants that have been piling up for centuries beneath the spot where he lay."[16] Through his encounter with the memory of the land, by absorbing the plants' memories, the sudden insight almost makes him lose his mind. Once recovered, he dons sunglasses and departs for the Arctic to study mosses and lichens.

An architect of beautiful images, Apichatpong's dream—"Until we can train our mind to see other lives, past and present, with our eyes closed. Until we have a new heart ... Until the movie screens sprout in the forest and the trees fill them with stories"[17]—breaks off, or might be felt opening up midstream. Until what time, one might ask, and how to arrive? Amid "never-ending cycles" in which Boonmee, the delirious botanist, animals, plants and ghosts "trade places along an infinite span of time", might "we" be tugged, pulled, lured, to dream our selves adrift in countless, cotemporaneous, spaces and times, the narrative of that wandering, Apichatpong emphasizes, "an open arena with the co-existent forms"?[18] "It is important", he notes, "to accentuate this drifting",[19] which might be thought as a cycling or change of state that, when drawn through its Sanskrit cognates, *chakram*, circle, wheel, and

---

[16] Apichatpong Weerasethakul and Chai Siri, "On Photophobia", in *Apichatpong Weerasethakul: Photophobia*, ed. Brynjar Bjerkem (Oslo: TrAP, 2011), 22.

[17] No longer on the homepage of kickthemachine, where it appeared 30 October 2013, the passage is archived, https://mubi.com/notebook/posts/the-noteworthy-kick-the-machine-redux-the-railrodder-soviet-era-cinemas.

[18] Apichatpong Weerasethakul and Brynjar Bjerkem, "On Photophobia", in *Apichatpong Weerasethakul: Photophobia*, ed. Brynjar Bjerkem (Oslo: TrAP, 2011), 10.

[19] Sergr van Duijnhoven, "Interview with the Winner of the Palme d'Or 2010, Apichatpong Weerasethakul", 8 June 2010,

carati, to move or to wander, runs, glides, flows among remembrances as the energy of heart and mind dies and awakens.

Being adrift may even manifest an "element of casualness and carelessness". "The beauty of living", Apichatpong indicates in myriad interviews and writings, is "that everything does not have to make sense, that you really interpret freely ... You just look at the colors, the brush stroke, and at what it evokes in your feelings ... Meaning is secondary." "I think I just do my films instinctively", he remarks, conveying belief in a process in which each film "has its own life ... you have to let the film tell you what to do." Out of respect for the audience's imagination, with confidence that, should viewers fall asleep, "they wake up and can patch things up in their own way", he urges humorously, "don't think, everything is wonder, just watch it like a kid".[20]

Cinema that "is not meant to be monumental, but weightless",[21] that casts no limits on the horizons of interpretation, a director, actors and crew, rather than aspiring stars, a meteor shower that streaks red blue green gold across the night sky, until vanishing, should we be startled to pass the figure of Apichatpong, photographed in *Photophobia*, at the moment of springing into a backbend?[22] Trunk bent backwards, hands and feet on the ground, a bridge, wheel, mountain, lightly poised at the base of serpentine stairs, a naga-shaped conduit by which water, held in the skies, might one day stream to earth, he is almost unnoticed. A dog pauses nearby. Seven vibrant green heads of the naga, edged by fruiting banana plants, radiate outwards in the sun-filled afternoon.

"I'm afraid not", Apichatpong's reply to a query interjected by an interviewer, "Do you see yourself in any way as a Thai cultural ambassador?"[23] foregrounds his view that Thai films "are all different ...

    http://sergevanduijnhoven.blogspot.com/2010/06/interview-with-winner-of-palme-dor-2010.html.

[20] Carrion-Murayari, 2011, 14; Apichatpong Weerasethakul, "Artist Talk in *Photophobia* Exhibition, Oslo, October 9, 2013", https://vimeo.com/76932283, and with TrAP, "Nasjonalgalleriet NRK ApichatpongWeerasethakul i Oslo", https://www.youtube.com/watch?v=w28QnZK3_n4. See also, Michael Koresky, "Transformers, More than Meets the Eye: A Conversation with Apichatpong Weerasethakul", 13 April 2005, http://reverseshot.org/interviews/entry/492/apichatpong-weerasethakul; Mark Peranson and Kong Rithdee, n.d., "Spotlight, Ghost in the Machine: Apichatpong Weerasethakul's Letter to Cinema", https://cinema-scope.com/spotlight/spotlight-ghost-in-the-machine-apichatpong-weerasethakul-letter-to-cinema/.

[21] Carrion-Murayari, 2011, 14.

[22] Bjerkem, 2013, 32, 33.

[23] Matthew Hunt, "Exclusive Interview with Apichatpong Weerasethakul",

a mixture of many influences", and that, in Thailand, "everything is mixed. We absorb everything ...", placing in relief that the cinema he directs and produces is "not just contained in Thailand".[24] Whether a quote by novelist Ton Nakajima that opens *Tropical Malady*, the reincarnations, foreseen in *Mekong Hotel*, of Masato as several kinds of insect and as a boy in Philippines, the Afro-Brazilian Middle Passage within *Photophobia*, the Isan and Lao histories of resistance that span the Mekong river or a presentation of *Fireworks (Archives)* that draws upon affinities of spirit between Isan and Mexico, the artist's need for "a personal connection with the story", an attempt "to express what I experience just living" so that his films "become like a diary",[25] impels narratives that imagine beyond the grasp of neo-colonial discourses of nation. When considering what, if anything, might distinguish independent southeast Asian cinema, he arrives at but a single, open-ended, element, namely, that many southeast Asian filmmakers "practice independence" in the midst of economic and political struggles, "partly out of necessity".[26]

Tilting the "I" that appears in Apichatpong's reflections, an "*i*" whose acrobatics of heart, mind, and limbs varies according to time of day, season, location, shadows, light and mood—"*i* start from sleep. *i* observe my dreams and *i* write down what *i* remember. *i* try to find the logic, even though it's never really logical"[27]—releases a continually shifting composition of innovations, mutations and strategies of adaptation, the composite lens of a veritable *iii you you ii* that manifests in his diaries and film treatments. Dreaming, storytelling, the director side by side with the actors and crew, who maintain jobs in convenience stores, telecommunications, construction, crocheting and clothing alterations, monastic life and mooncake sales, sometimes working with other filmmakers and musicians or establishing their own studios, accumulate

---

Encounter Thailand 2, no. 13 (2013): 38, https://www.google.com/url?esrc=s&q=&rct=j&sa=U&url=http://www.matthewhunt.com/portfolio/exclusiveinterviewwithapichatpongweerasethakul.pdf&ved=2ahUKEwiet9y8ofHvAhXITd8KHQTHBGsQFjAAegQIABAB&us-g=AOvVaw3l_7bocJBp18F6pptuMUPp.

24 Koresky, 2005.
25 Koresky, 2005.
26 Apichatpong Weerasethakul, cover endorsement for *Glimpses of Freedom: Independent Cinema in Southeast Asia*, ed. May Adadol Ingawanij and Benjamin McKay (Ithaca: Southeast Asia Program Publications, 2011).
27 Patrick Brzeski, "Cannes: 'Cemetery of Splendor' Director on his Obsession with the Surreal (Q&A)", 14 May 2015, https://www.hollywood-reporter.com/news/cannes-2015-cemetery-splendor-director-795576.

layers of shared memories forgotten, recalled, and reincarnated through oral accounts, sketches, and collaborative writings.

The marked impact on Apichatpong of Jane Goodall's statement "that she doesn't keep diaries, she just lives her life",[28] echoes throughout the uncannily plural "just living", which sustains the "journey" that Apichatpong articulates, with emphasis on *Mekong Hotel*, a Cannes Official Selection, 2012, Special Screening, "to be really relaxed", to concentrate less on scripting and advance preparations and more on "the moment of making" film.[29] "It's always about absorption", he exclaims with regard to that moment, "really, it's about collaboration ... to become like a sponge".[30] A minute opening, small interstice that admits passage, sponges, riotous mounds, odiferous, pungent, neither "simple" amorphous aggregates nor "primitive", though continually reclaiming that which is simple and primitive, exercise porosity through periods of extinction, cultivating survival practices for more than six million years.

Submerged in an overfull, streaming, river of lights, a guitar plays. From a recording device on a balcony that overlooks the rose sky of the Mekong river, a voice emerges. Today the singer, Sakda, he was a person named Rousseau, ruminates in the short film, *Sakda (Rousseau)*, 2012. Do body, self, mind, voice, memories ... memories of freedom, exist, whether in this world, a sound recording, or a film? Do they belong to oneself, or to anyone? A fleeting mention of Jean-Jacques Rousseau and rubber trees conjures an existential nexus that might be heeded as allusion to the dispossession and eviction of villagers in the Phu Phan forest of Isan, where thousands of rubber trees were cut down under mandate of the Thai National Council for Peace and Order Master Plan for environmental conservation and reforestation. The five minute and 32 second philosophical gem gives way to a quandary: Where are movies, if movies are in "our" mind?

A tracing of limbs and metal rods glows in the dark, enwrapping

---

[28] Sveinung Walengen, "En samtale mid film regissor og kunstner Apichatpong Weerasethakul", 16 October 2013, https://montages.no/2013/10/ en-samtale-med-filmregissor-og-kunstner-apichatpong-weerasethakul/.

[29] Adam Cook, "Five Questions with Apichatpong Weerasethakul", 9 August 2012, https://filmmakermagazine.com/49959-five-questions-with-apichatpong-weerasethakul/#.YHCJT4Xj6gp.

[30] Daniel Casman, "A Shared Memory: Talking to Apichatpong Weerasethakul", 26 May 2015, https://mubi.com/notebook/ posts/a-shared-memory-talking-to-apichatpong-weerasethakul-about-cemetery-of-splendour.

the cover of the exhibition book *For Tomorrow for Tonight*, itself a screen in an installation, first mounted in 2011, of looped short videos, LED speaker, sound and photographs, which creates what Apichatpong terms "a compressed reality of dreams".[31] Replete with colorful images between which hidden pages of sketches, text, and invisible forms of power are wrapped in the darkness of a binding that gives viewers the choice whether to cut open the folded leaves, *Photophobia*, produced in 2013 by TrAP, Oslo, elicits an experience distinct from the mood prompted by the saturated color backgrounds on which some of the same, as well as different, photographs are situated in *Photophobia*, published in 2014 by KCUA Gallery, Kyoto. The subtle and sometimes ghostly body of inscriptions that inhabits all three volumes performs a release of heart and mind to permeating flows of non-self, which Apichatpong's movies cyclically expel and absorb.

Receptive, porous, breathing, the filmmaker's characters, conduits of communication between infinite boundless worlds, enact virtually his observation that "Nothing is really solid ... everything is just a moving particle."[32] Plants, animals, ghosts, and the sun, which he describes, with reference to *Blissfully Yours/Sud Sanaeha*, *Prix Un Certain Regard*, Cannes 2002, as "the main character", the primary source of energy for life and of destruction, an "invisible oppressive force", are held sway by the jungle, the film's "second character", a power that confines the several protagonists.[33] The jungle, which is transformed in *Tropical Malady* as it reveals emotions, becomes "a kind of mindscape. Sometimes it is a character. It is also a stage".[34] Quite literally particles in motion that issue from previous cycles of birth and demise, the Mekong river, which harbors and affects so many lives, Apichatpong finds impossible to talk about except "as if it were a living creature".[35]

She who incarnates her beliefs about the imminent future, and who can recall some of her past lives, Jenjira Pongpas, a principal actor

---

[31] Kyle Mullin, "Brimming Waters: A Thai Director Presents his Latest Work in Beijing", 22 November 2011, http://www.bjreview.com.cn/Cover_Stories_Series_2013/2011-11/22/content_515200.htm.

[32] Peranson and Rithdee, n.d.

[33] Apichatpong Weerasethakul, "Apichatpong on *Blissfully Yours*", https://www.secondrundvd.com/release_moreby.html.

[34] James Quandt, "Exquisite Corps: An Interview with Apichatpong Weerasethakul", in *Apichatpong Weerasethakul*, ed. James Quandt (Vienna: Synema, 2009), 126.

[35] Anna Tatarska, "Under Water: Apichatpong Weerasethakul", 1 August 2012, https://www.fandor.com/keyframe/under-the-water-apichatpong-weerasethakul.

in Apichatpong's films, as well as a friend who has dreamed projects together with him for nearly 15 years, introducing him to the Mekong river and its history and sharing her diaries of growing up near the Thai–Lao border, he refers to as a flowing river. Convinced that a new name will bring her good luck, Jenjira becomes Nach, water. "She is certain", Apichatpong emphasizes, with allusion to the short video, *Cactus River/Khong Lang Nam*, 2012, "that soon there will be no water in the river, due to the upstream constructions of dams in China and Laos. I noticed, too, that Jenjira was no more".[36]

In the wheel of reincarnations of the two rivers, Nach and Mekong, the naga's tails twist and turn among the rivers' eddies as each becomes a habitation of an almost absent other.

The Naga's Tale

Touched by mist and moonlight, we glided effortlessly, riding through the waves. Smooth as a jet ski, its wake tracing patterns on the river's surface, Turbo, trusted bicycle, held steady in the current and by the time we neared the concrete bridge, it was dawn. Already, men were at work repairing the steel piles beneath Friendship Bridge. A glistening arc of colors, a giant water serpent reared its head from the Mekong's muddy flow to drink water from the sky, a no less probable approach to drought at the end of the rainy season than the Thai Bureau of Royal Rainmaking's plans for cloud seeding by air. Warmed by the early morning light, Turbo pulled ashore to the palm edged-path.

"I wanted to take a picture, but he disappeared. He floated up and disappeared ...": Coming and going, arriving and departing, the wooden longboat that conveys the local villagers, cast, and crew of Apichatpong's *Luminous People*, 2007, Super 8 to 35 millimeters, as they say farewells in the middle of the river, passes under the bridge before circling back to land. Carried by the currents of simulation and spirit voices of the wind, an extraordinary sound design by Akaritchalerm Kalayanamitr, the group's deep reverie, punctuated by playful humor and talk about local DJs and Laotian hip-hop, drifts between worlds of the past and present, Thailand and Laos, the living and the dead.

"Perhaps", comments Apichatpong, "this water was so muddy because it was mixed with so much ash from so many deaths. After life, people want to be one with nature, with water." The shifting rhythms, textures

---

[36] Apichatpong Weerasethakul, *Cactus River*, http://www.kickthemachine.com/page80/page1/page17/index.html.

and colors of the waterway, which yield a fourth-dimensional mirroring of the "millions of ancestors once cremated and now suspended in its currents",[37] reflect, as well, the granularity rendered by a film medium and process that maintain any perceived solidity, including that of the faces of the living, on the verge of dissolution. Voyaging nearby that which floats up and disappears are the expressions of longing by a young singer, overjoyed, who dreamt that his father had visited and that he could see his face; the utterance that slips from the lips of a man who, upon the release of ashes into the river, yellow, white, red flower petals scattering on the waves, is prompted by his dog to lean over the side of the boat, toward the churning whirlpools, "Wow! Naga serpent is here."

Full of "water things", "nathi khong" in Isan or Lao, the mother river "Mae Nam Khong", this Mekong river on which, Apichatpong suggests, "our ancestors live and take a voyage", ebbs and flows from glacial springs in the mountains of the Tibetan plateau, through China, Burma, Thailand, Laos, Cambodia and Vietnam, emptying into the South China Sea. Replete with the archives of long time, "each time the river floods", the filmmaker recounts, "it deposits these ancestors through the land, and we build ... from this mud, and then we illuminate these buildings with electric lights".[38] Such riverine inundations and droughts, which once affected settlements on the Khorat plateau during the Neolithic period, the Bronze Age village of Ban Chiang, c. 3600 BCE, known for its ceramics, though temporarily abandoned due to climate change in the first century CE, the Mon and Khmer migrations of the Metal Ages and the arrival of Tai from southern China, may stir up the "water things" of Apichatpong's films. The assimilation of animism, Brahmanism, Mahayana and Theravada Buddhism during the Khmer empire and the Lao kingdom of Lan Xang may surface in the indigenous and Vedic cosmologies that wend their way through his works. Nonetheless, recalling his insistence that "Films are a very personal means of expression. They can only represent individuals. They cannot represent countries or regions ...",[39] the archival ooze becomes a material for building film through dream illumination, which is at once intimate and symbiotic.

[37] Apichatpong Weerasethakul, "February 7, 2554", in *Apichatpong Weerasethakul: For Tomorrow for Tonight*, ed. Maeve Butler and Eimear O' Raw (Dublin: Irish Museum of Art, 2011), n.p.

[38] Apichatpong Weerasethakul, "February 7, 2554". See also http://www.ponybox.co.uk/pictures/projects/apichatpong/.

[39] Aimee Lin, "Apichatpong Weerasethakul: Darkness Visible", 23 March 2012, http://www.leapleapleap.com/2012/03/apichatpong-weerasethakul-darkness-visible/.

Not unlike the 1,047 forms of naga identified in Isan and Laos,[40] for millennia slithering through the caves and tunnels, humid terrain and cities of Muang Badan, a fabled region beneath the Tai-Lao arteries of the Mekong, the figures of Apichatpong's films pursue one another among layers of histories, memories, and the magnetic tug of the invisibles. While relating the past lives of two lovers who would follow each other across centuries, Phangkhi, the Naga prince, and Princess Aikham, daughter of the queen and king of the ancient Khmer empire, the *Phadaeng Nang Ai*, a tale of Isan, which took written form in the eleventh to thirteenth centuries CE, recounts the end of the war between Phangkhi's father, the great ruler Phaya Naga, and his friend, which began over suspicions of disloyalty, owing to the qualities of a shared serving of porcupine. Commanded by the god of thunder to remake the course of the river, the two nagas, accompanied by more than one decillion nagas, flowed along, altering the shapes of the riverbanks and shores, "Smacking their tails, they created various creeks and cascades. Falling from the boulders, the water flowed to flood the Mekong."[41] Awakening viewers to a river which, Apichatpong reminds us, "is living and communicating",[42] his cinema and art installations demolish one wall, and then another wall, of psychic separations, through fireworks and light activating a diluvial outpouring of the "creatures of the night that are disappearing".[43]

Tranquilly, Turbo rolled along the dirt road in the mid-morning sun as we scanned the balustrade for lingering traces of the red, blue, green, purple light-draped specter, "Power Boy", casually seated on the metal railing, gazing over the river. "Even if the shimmering 'Power Boy' isn't a sight we'll ever see promenading on the banks of the Mekong",[44] the voice of a cinema critic once cautioned. Yet, unmistakably, the

[40] Mayoury and Pheuiphanh Ngaosrivathana, *The Enduring Sacred Landscape of the Naga* (Chiang Mai: Mekong Press, 2009).

[41] Wajuppa Tossa, trans. and ed., *Phadaeng Nang Ai* (Lewisburg: Bucknell University Press, 1990), 53.

[42] Tony Rayns, "Mekong Hotel: Apichatpong Q&A", 2015, https://whatson.bfi.org.uk/lff/Online/default.asp?doWork::WScontent::loadArticle=Load&BOparam::WScontent::loadArticle::article_id=361BA69A-05E0-449F-BE84-4AB9553D218A.

[43] Lina Yoon, "'Uncle Boonmee' Maker Explores Art", 30 November 2011, http://blogs.wsj.com/scene/2011/11/30/uncle-boonmee-maker-explores-visual-art-in-beijing/.

[44] May Adadol Ingawanif, "Playing for Real", *Singapore: Future Perfect*, 2011, https://www.academia.edu/3365764/Playing_for_Real.

undulating golden discs of *For Tomorrow for Tonight* hover nearby; the beacons atop more distant power plants flash

Cradling the desire that Apichatpong describes as a yearning "to communicate with the invisibles in the darkness, or in memory, or in the future",[45] the light of darkness illuminates a spacetime of repose and dream in which "ghosts and strange creatures of the world come to life".[46] Night, a prolonged instant that the filmmaker gathers loosely in the phrase, "When you can't see and your mind takes over",[47] also manifests as an interval in which anthropocentric enframing of the 'real' recedes. "Jenjiraplasmaelectric", a particularly memorable moment of *For Tomorrow for Tonight*, shows the actress with metal rods extending from her injured leg. The tiny lights attached to the rods wire Jenjira's healing process to the electrical and magnetic energies of the nearby river and jungle. Resonantly sharing the relaxed fluidity and fullness of night, "Power Boy", a shadow that inhabits the banks of the Mekong river, takes on a second life as poster image for "Today is the Day, Exhibition for the 70th Bombing of Hiroshima", Gallery Miyauchi, Japan.

"I wanted to express my love for Jenjira, my actress, and her house by the river", states Apichatpong, acknowledging and inviting into his photography and film the yellow stains, "a specter of the Mekong river", deposited on the interior wall of the house by the floodwaters. Water, he imagines as the witness of past, present, and future happenings in the house, returning every few years to record new traces, to update the stories. The lines and long horizontal crack in the wall, Jenjira tells him, are the water's memory.[48] Amid a nightly sharing of stories while listening to the murmuring river, "this invisible river" by whose floodwaters he and Jenjira were "quarantined", Apichatpong beams a flashlight on Jenjira's leg as she massages a cramp. "Her hand was busy squeezing the flesh, making it roll in waves", he recounts. "You could see the bloodlines branching on her calf like a tree's fibrous roots, like thunderbolts." Afterwards, they see "floating retinal memory images of her limbs, guiding them through the dark".[49] Without a need for filmmaker, camera, or cinema screen, when illuminated, the

---

[45] Lissoni, n.d.

[46] Yoon, 2011.

[47] UCCA, "Apichatpong Weerasethakul, *For Tomorrow for Tonight*", November 2011, http://ucca.org.cn/en/exhibition/apichatpong-weerasethakul-tomorrow-tonight/.

[48] Mullin, 2011; Lin, 2012.

[49] Apichatpong Weerasethakul, *For Tomorrow for Tonight*, http://www.kickthemachine.com/page80/page22/page11/. See also, Weerasethakul, "March 11, 2553", n.p.

superimposed layers of corporeal and spiritual sedimentation, the river's living archive, cascade over the light-sensitive retinal tissue, performing an almost unspeakable dream.

Where sand islands appear in the middle of rice paddies and, in the rainy season, houses are submerged by water that rises above the river promenade ... where red and white flying squirrels, eyeless cave-dwelling spiders and giant flying frogs abide,[50] though kerosene lamps and fireflies, beacons for nocturnal navigation of the river's curves, have been displaced by neon light ... a chain of hydroelectric power plants, including Xayaburi dam, in Laos, nears completion. But, for tonight, naga fireballs, igniting as they reach the river's surface, will rise high in the sky. And, at the close of the season of rains, banana leaf boats lit by candles will convey offerings to the river. Paper lanterns, launched by friends, will fill with hot air to journey, glowing orange gold beneath the full moon, bobbling and dancing until beyond the stars.

As the river walkway widened into granite terraces, heralding the center of Nong Khai, a golden Ganesh resting in the back of a white pick-up truck brought two-wheeled Turbo to a halt. Neighbors milled about the elephant-headed god, who frightens demons and brings good fortune, exchanging morning greetings and local news. On a mound of bricks jutting from the muddy waters, a sinking fifteenth-century chedi that holds the Buddha's foot relics, water serpents bathed in the sun.

During the long years in which political forces in Bangkok wedged Isan apart from Laos, the Mekong that friends and families once freely crossed became a river of separations. From the ban on performances of Lao music, by the king of Siam, in 1865, which proclaimed, "it is apparent that whenever there is an increase in the playing of laokaen there is also less rain ...",[51] to the impact of Thaification and the national education system on the cultures, ethnicities, and languages of the northeast— Tai-Lao, North Khmer, Khorat, Phu Tai, and Thai-Chinese communities have been particularly impacted and Kuy, Yogun, and Bru languages face imminent demise[52]—the Mekong has been marked as a region of suppressive exclusions and extinctions, but also, as a site of resistance.

Literally pursued by the Mekong river's histories, yet, like Phra

---

[50] Damian Carrington, "Flying Squirrel and Eyeless Spider Discovered in Greater Mekong", *The Guardian*, 4 June 2014, https://www.theguardian.com/environment/2014/jun/04/ flying-squirrel-and-eyeless-spider-discovered-in-greater-mekong.

[51] Terry E. Miller, *Traditional Music of Lao: Kaen Playing and Mawlum Singing in Northeast Thailand* (Westport and London: Greenwood Press, 1985), 38–39.

[52] John Draper, "Draft Constitution Neglects Minority Rights of Millions",

EFFULGENCES PARTICLES IN MOTION

Phikanet or Ganesha, the bearer of a third eye and seeing in all five directions, Bunleua Sulitat, born in the province of Nong Khai, is reputed to have learned about the naga underworld through studies with a wise man, Keoku, whom he met upon falling into a cavern in a forest. Subsequently, he trained as a Hindu rishi in Vietnam and fled to Laos, where he started a sculpture garden. Perceived as unorthodox, he again fled, returning to Nong Khai in 1974 and founding Sala Keoku. Later, accused of being a communist, he was jailed for a period. For more than 20 years, people living nearby joined Bunleua in building the stone sculptures of fantastical hybrid beings that inhabit the jungle garden, which includes a naga that stretches upwards 25 meters, its seven heads protecting a meditating Buddha seated on its serpentine coils, and a unique area of succulents and cactuses. The spirited resistance and independence manifest in the sculptures and in Bunleua's life are commemorated in *Fireworks (Archives)*, which Apichatpong refers to as "a record of stone sculpture in a temple of northeastern Thailand".[53]

Alive with the sonic splatter of fireworks, explosives, birdcalls, and the voices of the departed, a blaze of pyrotechnics irradiates the night. So bright as to annihilate, light rises from the arid earth, surrounding the stone apparitions, a cavalcade of dogs on mopeds, the cavernous mouth of a lion, Ganesh's shrew draped with colorful garlands, a man flicking a whip. Leaping out in the darkness, illuminations and shadow projections of red aloe, the curled tail of a stone dog, a flowering shrub beside an inscription, tease and taunt those who catch a glimpse. Flickering, the explosive energies of *Fireworks (Archives)*, which, Apichatpong observes, "functions as a hallucinatory memory machine",[54] ignite a palpable neural net. Spiking the circuits of memory, tremors of spirit and mind ripple across the fleeting dream, the endless, unrepeatable flow of a six minute and 40 second video loop.

Wandering the wheel of life and death, actor Banlop Lomnoi, his hand shielding his eyes from the light, emerges from a dark cave and pauses to take a snapshot. Wearing large glasses, Jenjira calmly passes before a row of potted plants. She turns to focus her small camera on something special and, with a click and flash that spawns a cascade of images, circles into the night. A suspended instant, she and he meet, assume a sitting

---

The Isaan Record, 23 April 2015, https://theisaanrecord.co/2015/04/23/draft-constitution-neglects-minority-rights-of-millions/.

[53] SCAI, "Apichatpong Weerasethakul, *Fireworks (Archives)*", September 2014, https://www.scaithebathhouse.com/en/exhibitions/2014/09/fireworks_archives/.

[54] Weerasethakul, *Fireworks (Archives)*.

pose and, leaning into each other, embrace. Two stone skeletons, seated on a bench, hold hands while lightning plays on their ribs and hollow eye sockets. In an intermittent flame of light, there is the statue of a couple, a handclasp. Although no longer frequently used, *Pann nam pen tua*, ปั้นน้ำเป็นตัว, a saying that expresses the risk of attempting to mold water into a shape, speaks nearby *Fireworks (Archives)*. Impossible to dam the river of memory in a frame, Apichatpong's archives, and this writing, of the "Naga's Tale" may be, but lines on water.

If Suttho, king of the Naga, encountered many "water things" flourishing in the Mekong, Apichatpong's *Cactus River*, too, might be said to come upon "water things", especially, as his phrasing suggests, "the various temperaments of the water and wind".[55] A conversation of light with the crackling, hissing, percussive signifiers of the waves and winds, the personal diary conjoins histories of aridity with the hot, harsh climate of Isan. Utilizing editing that resists constructing tall tales of a river's smooth, "natural" flow, through storms and stillness, time stretches and shrinks, times run at different speeds, the rate of image flow falls. Camera shake, fast forward, choppy film rate, dropped frames, a static frame, Nach chops vegetables, a road map appears of the Lao side of the Mekong, saguaro cacti flicker on a screen. Images nearly dam up, then release. Insects swarm from a heap of dry grasses; a skateboarder streams down the riverside colonnade and pivots, as a bicycle passes by; Nach, her face unforgettable, looks toward the river of Isan, and closes her eyes.

Cinema, Apichatpong notes, is "like an extension of our soul that manifests itself".[56] Not just the telling of a story, "the film itself becomes the manifestation of the medium" and, he stresses, "Concerning new technology, the soul is changing".[57] The experiencing apparatus may take different forms, becoming more subtle or ghostly, such that, in *Cactus River*, a ready-to-hand "very small camera that records low resolution film and sound"[58] and that impacts how the filmmaker moves, strikes a relationship with the temperaments of the water and wind. The final image a single color frame, standing on the promenade, Nach beckons out over the river.

The evocative moods of Apichatpong's Mekong river series, akin to those of the river, are conveyed through endless variations. A love story

---

[55] Weerasethakul, *Cactus River*.
[56] Jihoon Kim, "Learning About Time: An Interview with Apichatpong Weerasethakul", *Film Quarterly* 64, no. 4 (2011): 52.
[57] Walengen, 2013; Kim, 2011, 52.
[58] Walengen, 2013.

and "a contemplation on making a fiction", Apichatpong also describes *Mekong Hotel* as "a drifting dream of the future".[59] The digital (HD) short feature, which he terms an "instinctive version"[60] of an abandoned film treatment, was created by friends and actors in his films while sharing a temporary home, at once a hotel that overlooks the Mekong and the Mekong river. Reorienting a popular legend in which the *phi pob* ghost migrates into a person's body, slowly devouring the entrails, Jen's soul, condemned to stay under the water for 600 years, breaks out of the cold, dark chamber to which it was confined and winds around Phon, her daughter, and Tong, twinned lovers who follow each other through time. Impossible to return, the clay pot of the spirits of the dead shattered, the melancholia and fear that pervade the cine-poem's intimate tales of military conscription, hunger, refugee camps, flash floods and severe flooding, elicit not the banishment of the tales' bearer, but telepathic exchange through which the reels of memory are respun. Sheltered by the guitarist's refrain, a flowing river of tones, a gentle listening to haunting memories, and levity, birth a retuning of the heart.

From the balcony of the hotel, I followed the gaze of the camera across the river, then retraced my steps and descended into the pandemonic sound of trucks, cars, dogs, birds, and motor scooters along the river road. A man is digging for something next to the walk. A backhoe excavates the muddy riverbank. A person strolling beside the Mekong reaches down to touch the water and, for a moment, wades in. As one dream diary merges with another, a slight figure on a bicycle pedals by slowly, then more swiftly.

Beneath the evening skies, jet skis circle and jump freestyle, cutting figures on the river's surface. A motorboat, its wake unfurling, cruises beyond the bridge. A longboat with fishers glides past. Following its own course, roots stretched in the air, a floating log.

Late in the day, to rest, and to dream, a jet ski skims across a pale shape floating in the water. My feet lightly on the pedals, Turbo began to frolic with the luminous jellyfish, the tremulous shimmer of a bright and full moon. A whir of spinning wheels, I reached to take a picture, but Turbo, ever eager to partake of nightly movies with the sleeping nagas of Muang Badan, leapt above the camera's eye and plunged through the translucent orb. Like a hot air lantern that danced the night away before tumbling into the current, I, too, dreamed, engulfed by the river's song.

---

[59] Rayns, 2015.

[60] Weerasethakul, *Mekong Hotel*, http://www.kickthemachine.com/page80/page1/page20/index.html.

Bibliography

Bjerkem, Brynjar, ed. *Apichatpong Weerasethakul: Photophobia*. Oslo. Transnational Arts Production. 2013.

von Boehm, Felix. "Apichatpong Weerasethakul, On Memories". *CINE-FILS, Online Interview Magazine*. September 2010. https://www.youtube.com/watch?v=SeDS612TQ8M.

Brzeski, Patrick. "Cannes: 'Cemetery of Splendor' Director on his Obsession with the Surreal (Q&A)". 14 May 2015. https://www.hollywoodreporter.com/movies/movie-news/cannes-2015-cemetery-splendor-director-795576/.

Butler, Maeve and Eimear O' Raw, eds. *Apichatpong Weerasethakul: For Tomorrow For Tonight*. Dublin. Irish Museum of Modern Art. 2011.

Camia, Giovanni Marchini. "Interview with Apichatpong Weerasethakul". *Fireflies, A Film Zine* 1 (July 2014): 8–9.

Carrington, Damian. "Flying Squirrel and Eyeless Spider Discovered in Greater Mekong". *The Guardian*. 4 June 2014. https://www.theguardian.com/environment/2014/jun/04/flying-squirrel-and-eyeless-spider-discovered-in-greater-mekong.

Carrion-Murayari, Guy. "Interview with Apichatpong Weerasethakul". In *Apichatpong Weerasethakul: Primitive*. Ed. Guy Carrion-Murayari and Massimiliano Gioni. New York. New Museum. 2011. 10–14.

Carrion-Murayari, Guy and Massimiliano Gioni, eds. *Apichatpong Weerasethakul: Primitive*. New York. New Museum. 2011.

Casman, Daniel. "A Shared Memory: Talking to Apichatpong Weerasethakul". 26 May 2015. https://mubi.com/notebook/posts/a-shared-memory-talking-to-apichatpong-weerasethakul-about-cemetery-of-splendour.

Cook, Adam. "Five Questions with Apichatpong Weerasethakul". 9 August 2012. https://filmmakermagazine.com/49959-five-questions-with-apichatpong-weerasethakul/#.YHCJT4Xj6gp.

Draper, John. "Draft Constitution Neglects Minority Rights of Millions". *The Isaan Record*. 23 April 2015. https://theisaanrecord.co/2015/04/23/draft-constitution-neglects-minority-rights-of-millions/.

van Duijnhoven, Sergr. "Interview with the Winner of the Palme d'Or 2010, Apichatpong Weerasethakul". 8 June 2010. http://sergevanduijnhoven.blogspot.com/2010/06/interview-with-winner-of-palme-dor-2010.html.

Glavin, Terry. *Waiting for the Macaws*. Toronto. Viking Canada. 2006.

Hunt, Matthew. "Exclusive Interview with Apichatpong Weerasethakul". *Encounter Thailand* 2, no. 13 (2013): 36–39. https://www.google.com/url?esrc=s&q=&rct=j&sa=U&url=http://www.matthewhunt.com/portfolio/exclusiveinterviewwithapichatpongweerasethakul.pdf&ved=2ahUKEwiet9y8OfHvAhXITd8KHQTHBGsQFjAAegQIA-BAB&usg=AOvVaw3l_7bocJBp18F6pptuMUPp.

EFFULGENCES PARTICLES IN MOTION   175

Ingawanij, May Adadol. "Playing for Real". *Singapore: Future Perfect.*
2011. https://www.academia.edu/3365764/Playing_for_Real.

Ingawanij, May Adadol and Benjamin McKay, eds. *Glimpses of Freedom:
Independent Cinema in Southeast Asia.* Ithaca. Southeast Asia Program
Publications. 2011.

Kim, Jihoon. "Learning About Time: An Interview with Apichatpong
Weerasethakul". *Film Quarterly* 64, no. 4 (2011): 48–62.

Koresky, Michael. "Transformers, More than Meets the Eye: A
Conversation with Apichatpong Weerasethakul". 13 April 2005. http://
reverseshot.org/interviews/entry/492/apichatpong-weerasethakul.

Lin, Aimee Lin. "Apichatpong Weerasethakul: Darkness Visible".
23 March 2012. http://www.leapleapleap.com/2012/03/
apichatpong-weerasethakul-darkness-visible/.

Lissoni, Andrea. "Apichatpong Weerasethakul, *Vampire,
M Hotel*". *VDrome.* N.d. http://www.vdrome.org/
apichatpong-weerasethakul-vampiresud-vikal-m-hotel/.

Mansfield, Matt. "Apichatpong Weerasethakul's Double
Vision, an Interview". April 2014. Removed from http://
www.dazeddigital.com/artsandculture/article/19508/1/
apichatpong-weerasethakul-double-visions-interview.

Menzel, Randolf. "Spectral Sensitivity and Color Vision in Invertebrates".
In *Comparative Physiology and Evolution of Vision in Invertebrates.* Ed.
H. Atrum. Berlin. Springer Verlag. 1979. 503–580.

Miller, Terry E. *Traditional Music of Lao: Kaen Playing and Mawlum
Singing in Northeast Thailand.* Westport and London. Greenwood
Press. 1985.

Mullin, Kyle. "Brimming Waters: A Thai Director Presents his Latest
Work in Beijing". November 2011. http://www.bjreview.com.cn/Cover_
Stories_Series_2013/2011-11/22/content_515200.htm.

Nagara, Masashi. "Photophobia, Art Gallery@KCUA". June 2014.
https://m.www.youtube.com/watch?v=gEogkNnUN8c.

Ngaosrivathana, Mayoury and Pheuiphanh. *The Enduring Sacred
Landscape of the Naga.* Chiang Mai. Mekong Press. 2009.

Peranson, Mark and Kong Rithdee. "Spotlight, Ghost in the Machine:
Apichatpong Weerasethakul's Letter to Cinema". N.d. https://
cinema-scope.com/spotlight/spotlight-ghost-in-the-machine-apichat-
pong-weerasethakuls-letter-to-cinema/.

Quandt, James, ed. *Apichatpong Weerasethakul.* Vienna. Synema. 2009.

Quandt, James. "Exquisite Corps: An Interview with Apichatpong
Weerasethakul". In *Apichatpong Weerasethakul.* Ed. James Quandt.
Vienna. Synema. 2009. 125–131.

Quandt, James. "Push and Pull: An Exchange with Apichatpong
Weerasethakul". In *Apichatpong Weerasethakul.* Ed. James Quandt.
Vienna. Synema. 2009. 182–191.

Rayns, Tony. "Interview with Apichatpong Weerasethakul, Memories, Mysteries". July 2006. http://www.kickthemachine.com/page80/page24/page12/index.html.

Rayns, Tony. "Mekong Hotel: Apichatpong Q&A". 2015. https://whatson.bfi.org.uk/lff/Online/default.asp?doWork::WScontent::loadArticle=Load&BOparam::WScontent::loadArticle::article_id=361BA69A-05E0-449F-BE84-4AB9553D218A.

Ryan T.J., D.S. Roy, M. Pignatelli, A. Arons and S. Tonegawa. "Engram Cells Retain Memory Under Retrograde Amnesia". *Science* 348, no. 6238 (2015): 1007–1013. doi: 10.1126/science.aaa5542.

SCAI. "Apichatpong Weerasethakul, *Fireworks (Archives)*". September 2014. https://www.scaithebathhouse.com/en/exhibitions/2014/09/fireworks_archives/.

Tatarska, Anna. "Under Water: Apichatpong Weerasethakul". 1 August 2012. https://keyframe.fandor.com/under-the-water-apichatpong-weerasethakul/.

Tossa, Wajuppa. Trans. and ed. *Phadaeng Nang Ai: A Translation of a Thai-Isan Folk Epic in Verse*. Lewisburg. Bucknell University Press. 1990.

UCCA. "Apichatpong Weerasethakul, *For Tomorrow for Tonight*". November 2011. https://ucca.org.cn/en/exhibition/apichatpong-weerasethakul-tomorrow-tonight/.

Walengen, Sveinung. "En samtale mid film regissor og kunstner Apichatpong Weerasethakul". 16 October 2013. https://montages.no/2013/10/en-samtale-med-filmregissor-og-kunstner-apichatpong-weerasethakul/.

Weerasethakul, Apichatpong. "17 August, 2008". In *PRIMITIVE*. CUJO 2:1. Milan. Edizioni Zero. 2009. n.p.

Weerasethakul, Apichatpong. *A Letter to Uncle Boonmee*. http://www.animateprojects.org/films/by_date/2009/a_letter_to.

Weerasethakul, Apichatpong. "Apichatpong on *Blissfully Yours*". https://www.secondrundvd.com/release_more_by.html.

Weerasethakul, Apichatpong. "Apichatpong Weerasethakul Artist Talk in Photophobia Exhibition, Oslo". 9 October 2013. https://vimeo.com/76932283.

Weerasethakul, Apichatpong. *Cactus River*. http://www.kickthemachine.com/page80/page1/page17/index.html.

Weerasethakul, Apichatpong. "February 7, 2554" and "March 11, 2553". In *Apichatpong Weerasethakul: For Tomorrow For Tonight*. Ed. Maeve Butler and Eimear O' Ra. Dublin. Irish Museum of Modern Art. 2011. n.p.

Weerasethakul, Apichatpong. *Fireworks (Archives)*. http://www.kickthemachine.com/page80/page22/page33/index.html.

Weerasethakul, Apichatpong *For Tomorrow for Tonight*. http://www.kickthemachine.com/page80/page22/page11/index.html.

Weerasethakul, Apichatpong. *Mekong Hotel.* http://www. kickthemachine.com/page80/page1/page20/index.html.

Weerasethakul, Apichatpong. *Monsoon.* http://www.kickthemachine. com/page80/page1/page37/index.html.

Weerasethakul, Apichatpong and Brynjar Bjerkem. "On Photophobia". In *Apichatpong Weerasethakul: Photophobia.* Ed. Brynjar Bjerkem. Oslo. Transnational Arts Production. 2013. 2–21.

Weerasethakul, Apichatpong and Chai Siri. "On Photophobia". In *Apichatpong Weerasethakul: Photophobia.* Ed. Brynjar Bjerkem. Oslo. Transnational Arts Production. 2013. 22–23.

Weerasethakul, Apichatpong and TrAP. "Nasjonalgalleriet NRK-ApichatpongWeerasethakul i Oslo". https://www.youtube.com/ watch?v=w28QnZK3_n4.

Yoon, Lina. "'Uncle Boonmee' Maker Explores Art". 30 November 2011. http://blogs.wsj.com/scene/2011/11/30/ uncle-boonmee-maker-explores-visual-art-in-beijing/.

Forms and Representations

8

Transmedia Plot in Apichatpong Weerasethakul's *Primitive*

Jade de Cock de Rameyen

When Apichatpong Weerasethakul's team and the young men of Nabua, a village in northeastern Thailand, had finished building a womb-like spaceship, the artist did not ship it to Haus der Kunst (Munich) with his traveling multimedia exhibition *Primitive* (2009). It did not become a sculptural centerpiece and formidable narrative anchor in the white cube. Instead, he left it there, at the far end of Isan. First used as a haven for the youngsters' alcoholized encounters, it soon became the village's wheat storage. Until its restoration by the Thai Film Archive years later,[1] the site was run down, taken over by vines. As a narrator prophetically recounts in one of *Primitive*'s videos: "Somewhere in time, someone will discover my time machine. It will be covered in plants, roots and moss. They will think that it is a prop from a movie shot a century ago."

Just like the versatility of the derelict spaceship, Weerasethakul's multiplatform project *Primitive* seems infinite in its narrative potentialities, though none is explicit. Set against the backdrop of the 1960s–1970s abuse of local communities by the Thai military, *Primitive* gathers seven videos of an installation designed for the museum, two shorts commissioned by the online platform Animate Projects, a 400-page artist book filled with story bits, pictures and drawings, two photographs, and the prize-winning feature film *Uncle Boonmee Who Can Recall His Past Lives* (2010). Far-off from the central government, the northeast of Thailand has a history of persecution and resistance. Apichatpong wanted to reflect "an active force of inertia"[2] he felt in Isan's political atmosphere. Yet curators emphasize that *Primitive* is not meant

---

[1] Thai Film Archive, "The Spaceship of Nabua", *Google Arts & Culture*, 2021, https://artsandculture.google.com/story/the-spaceship-of-nabua/oAVxEi3VrCGhSw.

[2] Apichatpong Weerasethakul, *Apichatpong Weerasethakul Sourcebook:*

to be experienced as "the political history of Nabua".[3] We struggle to find details about the past of the village in the videos. The exhibition text barely mentions the violent repression of communist-sympathizing farmers by the military.

Only if we were to read Apichatpong's artist book would we learn about the rural community of Nabua's specific role in this conflict.[4] A Nabua resident recalls that "when there were shooting it would light up the sky".[5] It was there that fighting broke out for the first time, on the 7 August 1965. Afterwards and until the early 1980s, the military made camp in the village. Men went into hiding into the jungle for they were beaten or killed. Left alone, women were raped. Since then, legend has it that it is a widow's village: to avoid mysterious death, men of Apichatpong's film crew were advised to paint their nails with colorful nail polish. This traumatic history is only one of the numerous stories included in the book: other texts tell us of reincarnation, ghosts, domestic abuse and hypnotism. Excerpts of Apichatpong's diary and *Uncle Boonmee*'s original script are equally included.

Such are Weerasethakul's filmic worlds. The most spectacular motives of his films are only referenced in passing or deleted in the final edit. "I've always liked to cut out big scenes", he confesses. "Often, the more I invest in the scene, the more I cut out."[6] Despite its title, never does uncle Boonmee remember his past lives. Diverse storylines succeed one another but the classical devices of flash-back are carefully avoided. The same strategy is used in the exhibition. When visitors entered the *Primitive* show at the New Museum (New York), their first vision was a modest Giclée print of a distant fire in a nightly landscape, titled *The Field*. Visibility is minimal and the shot is far from noteworthy. Yet it raises a host of questions: questions that will receive responses so partial that they only encourage digging deeper.

The Serenity of Madness (New York: Independent Curators International, 2016), 61.

[3] Massimiliano Gioni and Gary Carrion-Murayari, "Apichatpong Weerasethakul: Primitive", *New Museum*, 2011, http://www.newmuseum. org/exhibitions/view/apichatpong-weerasethakul-primitive.

[4] For a more thorough account of the book and how it references the political landscape of Thailand see Pandit Chanrochanakit, "Deforming Thai Politics: As Read through Thai Contemporary Art", *Third Text* 25, no. 4 (2011): 419–429.

[5] Andrea Amichetti and Andrea Lissoni, "Apichatpong Weerasethakul: Primitive" (2009) *Cujo*.

[6] Weerasethakul, 2016, 53.

More and more artists engage with the cinema industry while sustaining a gallery film practice in parallel. Apichatpong Weerasethakul's practice is nevertheless remarkable as *Uncle Boonmee* and his artistic work are explicitly embedded within a single project. The project's disparate ingredients should make for an explosive aggregate, but the whole stubbornly resists dispersion. *Primitive* inaugurates therefore a broader though still niche phenomenon, where feature and installation are part of filmic universes extending across platforms and media (e.g. the works of Salome Lamas, Dora Garcia and Ben Rivers). *Uncle Boonmee* has received extensive critical attention, but little has been said on the consequences of its articulation with the more overtly political videos of *Primitive*.

Resisting the avant-garde denominator, Apichatpong describes his approach both in the art world and the cinema as an "experimental narrative".[7] Critics generally agree on Weerasethakul's features' narrativity, but they struggle to describe its logics other than as "spatialized", "broken" or "interstitial".[8] Drawing from and created in contiguity with his artistic practice, his cinema challenges linear emplotment. Speaking of narrativity in moving-images installations is all the more problematic, images being scattered across the exhibition space. Nevertheless, *Primitive* reviewers often describe their experience in narrative terms.[9] What makes such a spatially and temporally dispersed filmic universe narrative?

Addressing this problem requires us first to take a detour by recent research in narratology, which remains largely ignored in film studies. Raphael Baroni's rhetorical narratology and its functionalist approach to plot[10] focus on the workings of discordance *against* its embeddedness into causal configuration. Defining narrative as representation of action

---

[7] Weerasethakul, "Around the World of Apichatpong Weerasethakul. Interview by Eungie Joo", 2011, http://ca.newmuseum.org/index.php/Detail/Object/Show/object_id/8463.

[8] See Jihoon Kim's chapter on the spatialization of broken narrative; no doubt the most serious attempt at defining Weerasethakul's intermedia narratives so far. Jihoon Kim, "Between Auditorium and Gallery: Perception in Apichatpong Weerasethakul's Films and Installations", in *Global Art Cinema: New Theories and Histories*, ed. Rosalind Galt and Karl Schoonover (New York: Oxford University Press, 2010), 125–141.

[9] Ken Johnson, "Youth, With Hopes and Bliss Intact", *The New York Times*, 27 May 2011, sec. Arts; "Gustav Metzger and Apichatpong Weerasethakul", e-flux, 2011; Aily Nash, "WE ARE PRIMITIVE: Apichatpong's Ineffable Experience of Nabua", *The Brooklyn Rail*, 2011.

[10] Raphaël Baroni, *L'œuvre du temps: poétique de la discordance narrative* (Paris: Seuil, 2009).

misses the ambiguity of the event, precisely that which makes it *narrative*. It is a narrative tension irreducible to univocal causation that enables immersion within the heterogeneous storyworld of *Primitive*. How does exhibition scenography, and Apichatpong's textural soundscapes in particular, affect the workings of plot in the installation? Paying close attention to acoustic phenomena provides a fresh methodology to consider plot in multiscreen installations, where sonic territories directly affect narrative articulation. Secondly, I will examine how the loop and mobile spectatorship affect our horizon of expectation. Moving-image installations such as *Primitive* bring narrative communication to its limits. Even retrospectively, linear rearticulation of on-screen events fails. This will lead me to address a final issue: to what extent can we speak of transmedial narrative in artists' cinema? How do filmic worlds shot in distinct locations, reflecting a strong generic, stylistic and medial diversity intersect or overlap? While the first inquiries concern the *Primitive* exhibition, the latter involves its articulation with the feature.

My analysis is based on the installation at the New Museum (New York) which was abundantly documented, as well as the screeners that Apichatpong generously provided for my research.[11] Running from May to July 2011, after having been shown in Munich, Liverpool and Paris, the *Primitive* exhibition at the New Museum was the most complete to date: in addition to the seven videos of the *Primitive* installation, it included the short *Phantoms of Nabua* and two photographs. The only works missing were the feature, which had had its theatrical release shortly beforehand, and *Letter to Uncle Boonmee*, a short commissioned by and available online on the Animate Projects platform. American visitors had therefore access to all the works embedded in the multiplatform project. Providing practically optimal conditions for an ideal(ized) reception, the American show will ground our interrogation of transmedial narrativity in *Primitive*.

---

[11] Because I could not experience the installation in person, I rely on visitors' reviews, museum archives, exhibition designs and additional documentation made available by Apichatpong. My viewing experience allows a detailed and in-depth analysis, which is somewhat difficult to achieve in the museum given the overall length of *Primitive,* but lacks the very contingencies inherent to a visit in situ. The material conditions of my analysis also bespeak a broader phenomenon: the digital web of solidarity established between researchers, curators and artists of experimental cinema, atoning for its limited access.

Aural Temporality

Speaking of narrativity in film installations is disputable, for exhibition scenography often composes with a disparity of media, aesthetics, filmmaking styles. Pulled between two opposing forces—fragmentation and continuity—installation art becomes by definition, as Catherine Elwes argues, an art of montage. Moving-image installations "activate the space between frames, both actual and imaged, as much as they coalesce concentrations of meaning within their provisional borders".[12] But when does the spatialized and thematic connectivity typical of installation art become narrative? To answer this, an analysis of the material, spatial and temporal circumstances of experience is required. So let us visit the third floor of a futuristic New York tower and take a virtual walk through the fields of Nabua.

An architecture graduate, Apichatpong pays special attention to exhibition design and scenography. The *Primitive* show at the New Museum is separated into five different, though porous spaces. The interstice between walls and ceilings, as well as the absence of doors and curtains, allows obstacle-free roaming of people and sounds. Lighting is dimmed and light spills are relatively contained. Apart from the projectors, only directional lightings are used, pointed at two photographs facing the entrance. Walking past the panel, one could sit on a square bench, opposite any of four videos (Fig. 1): *Nabua* (9'), *Making of the Spaceship* (28'), *A Dedicated Machine* (1') and *An Evening Shoot* (4'). Though routes vary, all reviewers began their visits with *Nabua*.

The first video to be visible from the entrance, *Nabua* is the most spectacular piece and the only non-silent one in the main room. A series of tracking shots feature the village of Nabua as it is repeatedly struck by lightning. Immediately immersive, *Nabua* layers a thick jungle soundscape, windy noise and sudden lightning bolts. As the looping video reaches its end—or its new beginning—the pitch of the jungle lowers to an agreeable tone, insects coming together in quasi-musical harmony for an instant. Soon, we hear the rumble of thunder far away—but the storm never breaks out. Suspense keeps building as bass thickness is boosted or cleared up, reverb is added and taken out, cicadas' and fireflies' singing comes to foreground and recedes to the background. Images do not evacuate tension. Shot entirely at night, strong light sources (neon, lightning, fireworks, spotlight) blind us. Human contours dissolve into darkness. A shadow takes a few steps

---

[12] Catherine Elwes, *Installation and the Moving Image* (New York: Columbia University Press, 2015), 34.

Fig. 1: Apichatpong Weerasethakul, *Primitive*, 2011. Exhibition view. New Museum. Photo by Benoit Pailley.

back. Camera moves slowly, but constantly: panning, tracking, zooming out—searching the land from a distance. We are at pains to understand what villagers are doing, but they do not seem to notice and go about their evening business.

Turning to adjacent videos offers no relief. The ominous soundscape penetrates silent images, making villagers' peaceful daytime routine in *Making of the Spaceship* feel like the deceptive quiet before the storm. This phenomenon is known as spatial magnetization: sound is captured by our vision, despite inconsistencies.[13] Thus, although *Making* embraces the realist documentary genre, the people of Nabua seem to be preparing for what is coming: a spaceship is designed and put together, piece by piece. Slowly, its dark shadow is seen fluttering in the air, upwards and downwards in *A Dedicated Machine*. Silent gunshots of *An Evening shoot* are made explosive as the lightning strikes the villages on the opposite wall. Soldiers inside a house shoot target through open windows. In the field, a man walks and is shot down. Caught in a loop, the man keeps on dying, at the mercy of a cyclical time.

The main space leads to three separate rooms. The *Primitive* diptych, the longest (30') and most traditionally narrative work, was exhibited

---

[13] Michel Chion, *L'audio-vision*, 4th edition (Paris: Armand Colin, 2017), 78.

Fig. 2: Apichatpong Weerasethakul, *Primitive*, 2011. Exhibition view. New Museum. Photo by Benoit Pailley.

in a smaller L-shaped, significantly darker room. It features a lengthy voice-over. Throughout the film, a teen's soft voice recounts his encounters with spirits of past reincarnations in the jungle, his dream of the future and his time machine travel. The visual channels first focus on teens hanging out on a dam. As darkness falls, they play with torches and fireworks. A draped figure sets on fire in the sunset. Mainly shot at night, *Primitive* experiments with all kinds of light sources: moonlight, flames, dancing flashlights, neon, fireworks. The red hue inside the spaceship bathes the viewers (Fig. 2). The room thus repeats the cozy surroundings on-screen and reminds us of *Uncle Boonmee*'s memorable cave;[14] viewers are shaded from the outside world and sprinkled with mysterious lights.

A smaller screen with headphones was installed in the corner (*Nabua Song*), showing a much less enthralling scene: an apathic soldier chews on some food with a blank look. The subtitles encourage using the

---

[14] The feature follows Boonmee's last days. As he is about to die, Boonmee and his family go to a cave, where he recounts his dream of the future under the moon's eye.

headset. Off-screen, a guitarist sings the heroic fate of Nabua and calls for rebellion:

> Nabua is a small patch of land. Here we grow rice and farm peacefully. [...] Until we have become legend. 7 August. It's time to hear about our heroes and their bravery. So that our kids in the future can learn from them. Fight for your freedom. Take out your guns and knives to fight. [...] We will fight for justice.

The soundtrack produces non-natural meaning:[15] the relation of non-equivalence between music and images suggests the author's intention of producing bipolar meaning and our need to recognize such intentionality. Here, musical promises of future revolutions transform the soldier's lethargy and prompt the spectator to infer another idea: Nabua's inertia may be less peaceful than it seems.

In the adjacent room, a video's flickering light leaks above the wall where *Primitive* is projected, infiltrating the protective environment of darkness. Moving to that space, we find one work, also on headphones: *I'm Still Breathing*. Handheld shot, the dynamic rock music video was described as "the most immediately engaging"[16] piece. Running boys pass a camera to each other and kick a fireball, then hop in the back of a truck, jumping and dancing extatically, bare chested. Finally, at the opposite end of the gallery, *Phantoms of Nabua* (10', also available online) is projected in a small dark room. It is the most meta-cinematic work and picks up various elements from the other videos. A projector screens *Nabua* in a field at night. Youngsters kick a fireball until setting the screen on fire. Only the sound of the lightning bolts remains, blending with the burning frame.

This short exhibition tour reveals how Apichatpong and the curators (Massimiliano Gioni, Gary Carrion-Murayari, Eungie Joo) carefully configured light and darkness—motives that are constantly thematized on-screen. But more significantly, the construction of experiential territories is acoustic. Sound plays a crucial role in *Primitive*. As mentioned, the tension between autonomous worlds—each demanding concentrated contemplation—and the totalitarian universe of the exhibition—intruding into our singular experience of an artwork—is characteristic of installation art. Yet artists' moving-image benefits from an additional factor of synthesis: sound. "Where sound pulls together

---

[15] Dominique Nasta, *Meaning in Film: Relevant Structures in Soundtrack and Narrative* (Berne: Lang, 1991).
[16] Johnson, 2011.

TRANSMEDIA PLOT IN WEERASETHAKUL'S *PRIMITIVE*

physically distinct elements in an installation", Elwes writes, "the audio track of a film is used as a smoothing device for linking one scene to the next and rationalizing potentially illogical juxtapositions of locations and characters".[17]

In this regard, it is striking that headphones are limited to musical pieces (*I'm Still Breathing* and *Nabua Song*). Aural contamination is controlled so that neither soundtrack would set the tone of the exhibition. Because all speakers establish a similar aural experience, ambient sounds are grounded on multiple frames at once in *Primitive*. Sound maintains a unified experience despite videos disconnected in space, style and subject. This is what Michel Chion calls territory-sounds: a multiplicity of punctual sources inhabiting a space without raising the question of their visual location.[18] Here, territory-sounds make visitors' choreography more fluid, instantaneously building a concrete sense of the whole through which to seamlessly navigate. Reverberation and composite texture provide volume to the place, granting it an expansive presence, beyond our visual field.

Additionally, a vibrant aural temporality heightens the irreversible flow of our experience. Michel Chion has noted that irregular, uneven sounds—such as fire, wind and cicadas—have a strong temporalizing effect on images.[19] Visitors enter a living space, characterized by diverse, deeply enmeshed temporal processes. Apichatpong has argued that feature films length allows for a "gradual accumulation of feelings" while the installation should immediately offer "the whole sensual experience of space and time".[20] In the exhibition the accumulation is horizontal—an affective layering of sounds that seeps through space and inscribe our visit over a specific duration, that of Nabua and its off-screen jungle.

But *Primitive*'s aural environment exceeds its unifying and temporalizing functions. More importantly, sound plays here a dramatizing role. A dense auditory field envelops the viewers, one that is sometimes soothing, but more often ominous. At times, the nightly soundscape meshes with *Primitive* narrator's calm voice. At other times, silence is counterpointed by barking dogs, creaking branches, a flying fireball, and the excited voices of the youngsters kicking it around. A series of lightning bolts, first muffled, later explode in full

---

[17] Elwes, 2015, 98.
[18] Chion, 2017, 84.
[19] Chion, 2017, 84.
[20] Jihoon Kim, "Learning About Time: An Interview with Apichatpong Weerasethakul", *Film Quarterly* 64, no. 4 (2011): 48.

crispiness. It is "an alarming sound like gunfire fill[ing] the gallery".[21] *Primitive* sound designer Akritcharlerm Kalayanamitr heightens and amplifies on-location field recordings (by Chalermrat Kaweewattana), thus "denaturaliz[ing]" them.[22] Modulations in bass reverberation add to this disquieting effect. Relatively dry and directional sounds are heavily charged with resonance. Soon, bass dominates, cicadas lose intensity, human voices recede into the distance until disappearing entirely. Sound from afar envelops us as if coming from within. Nabua's open fields now feel like a large, enclosed space. Because reverberation challenges our ability to localize a sound, it triggers "either anxiety or a heightened state of arousal, which is a biological state of enhanced alertness".[23] Through these aural crescendos, sound vectorizes and dramatizes what should otherwise look like quiet nightly scenes.

Aural Plot

Primitive has been described as "disorienting fantastical",[24] "unsettling" and "scary",[25] "welcoming and dangerous".[26] Ambient sounds favour immersive and progressive listening, though not without an element of foreboding, while aural shocks punctuate time and have a startling effect on the viewer. These sudden bursts of energy actualize the tension accumulated by a thick aural environment. Along with curiosity, suspense and surprise are understood by functionalist and rhetorical narratology as defining effects of narrativity. According to Meir Sternberg's seminal work, these are the *why* of narrativity that shape—separately or in combination—the interplay between the telling/told sequences.[27] Each

[21] Johnson, 2011.

[22] Philippa Lovatt, "'Every Drop of My Blood Sings Our Song. There Can You Hear It?': Haptic Sound and Embodied Memory in the Films of Apichatpong Weerasethakul", *The New Soundtrack* 3, no. 1 (2013): 70.

[23] Barry Blesser and Linda-Ruth Salter, *Spaces Speak, Are You Listening? Experiencing Aural Architecture* (Cambridge, MA: MIT Press, 2009), 62.

[24] Aparna Sharma, "Apichatpong Weerasethakul: Primitive (Review)", *Leonardo* 45, no. 2 (2012): 168.

[25] Wise Kwai, "Apichatpong-a-Rama: Primitive, Hangover, Jury in Venice, Morning in Finland", *Wise Kwai's Thai Film Journal* (blog), 24 June 2011, http://thaifilmjournal.blogspot.com/2011/06/apichatpong-rama-primitive-hangover.html.

[26] Dennis Lim, "Apichatpong Weerasethakul", *Artforum International* 50, no. 1 (2011): 341.

[27] Meir Sternberg, "How Narrativity Makes a Difference", *Narrative* 9, no. 2 (2001): 115–22.

interest reflects a gap about the storyworld, which the viewer needs to supply with multiple gap-filling hypotheses. In *Primitive*, it is first and foremost sound that conveys both suspenseful ambiguity and surprising instability.

In film studies embodied engagement with sound is often understood as disrupting or exceeding narrative; diverting our attention away from what is identified as the rational and verbal.[28] Philippa Lovatt studies Weerasethakul's idiosyncratic sonic environments, and shows how, by enabling "haptic hearing", they blur the border between the personal and social. For Lovatt, such haptic sound may only have a dysnarrative function. The perceived incompatibility of haptic soundscape with narrative identification in affect film theory lies on its formalist understanding of narrativity, as the delivery of plot information, from which the viewer can elaborate a cause-effect chain of events. However, as cognitive narratologists[29] have shown, the causal determinism of formalist models does not reflect narrative fascination and interest. Univocal causality rationalizes time, explains temporality away by making each effect the product of its cause. Cognitive desire stems instead from the underdetermined and probabilistic dynamics of events. Uncertainty is at the heart of narrativity.

Recently rhetorical narratology has shifted focus away from the content of representation to acts of production and reception. In line with Sternberg's functional model, Raphaël Baroni in particular has reframed the debate on the affective dynamics of plot; studying how narrative sparks our interest. In his analysis, Baroni spotlights narrative tension as the living core of narrative engagement. What matters lies in the middle of the sequence: an intentional dissonance, embodied in the interpreter's feeling of surprise, curiosity or suspense.[30] Internal instability provides time with its affective depth, it eroticizes it and dramatizes our experience of being in time. For such aesthetic effect

---

[28] Lisa Coulthard, "Haptic Aurality: Resonance, Listening and Michael Haneke", *Film-Philosophy* 16, no. 1 (2012): 16–29; Laura U. Marks, *The Skin of the Film: Intercultural Cinema, Embodiment, and the Senses* (Durham: Duke University Press, 2000); Lovatt, 2013.

[29] David Herman, *Story Logic: Problems and Possibilities of Narrative* (Lincoln: University of Nebraska Press, 2002); Hilary P. Dannenberg, "Ontological Plotting: Narrative as a Multiplicity of Temporal Dimensions", in *The Dynamics of Narrative Form*, ed. John Pier (Berlin: De Gruyter, 2004), 159–190.

[30] Raphaël Baroni, "Tensions et résolutions: musicalité de l'intrigue ou intrigue musicale?", *Cahiers de Narratologie. Analyse et théorie narratives* 21 (2011): 5.

to arise, the telling needs to be irreversible and reticent. There is a progressive becoming of the story in time, which is moved by something that escapes representation. Narrative tension is the uncertain anticipation of a possible resolution in the form either of a *prognosis* or a *diagnosis,* both of which are based on contextual information and intertextual and/or actional scenarios stored in the memory of the reader.[31] Stories hinge less on the final resolution of such gaps than on the number of virtualities we fill it with.

Baroni's model emphasizes how textual *reluctance* and a specific environment of reception configure a horizon of expectations. Plots are experiential phenomena instead of textual ones, exhibiting their temporal contours as they unfold in time. They have more to do with the dramatized rhythmics of the musical phrase than with the architectural form of structuralism. Plot and musical sequence, Baroni argues, could be ultimately defined as a play of tensions and resolutions; the staging of a relation, harmonious or dissonant, between the repetition of an awaited structure and the relatively unpredictable becoming of a dynamic form.[32] This echoes research on vocalized interactions between toddler and mother as the common origin of music and narratives.[33] Early vocalized interactions are identified in Daniel Stern's developmental psychology as protonarrative envelopes, "hold[ing] both a discrete feeling shape and bound[ing] the unfolding of a motive".[34] Protonarrative is the prelinguistic ability to shape an interactive world in terms of narrative events and motives. A desire temporally distributes and coordinates elements and events of an experience on a line of dramatic tension, from which a temporal feeling shape is created. The progression toward the end state is a dramatized and irreversible trajectory. But more profoundly, Stern argues, affective shifts in suspense and pleasure are what carries narrative. An emphatic constellation of affects forms a specific temporal sweep that transforms our sense of passing time into a discrete narrative unit. It provides coherence and boundaries to a moment. This goal-oriented interpersonal structure of tension and

---

[31] Raphaël Baroni, "Virtualities of Plot and the Dynamics of Rereading", in *Narrative Sequence in Contemporary Narratology*, ed. Françoise Revaz and Raphaël Baroni (Columbus: Ohio State University Press, 2016), 89.

[32] Baroni, 2011, 10.

[33] Jean-Jacques Nattiez, "La Narrativisation de la musique. La musique: récit ou proto-récit?", *Cahiers de Narratologie: Analyse et théorie narratives* 21 (2011), http://journals.openedition.org/narratologie/6467.

[34] Daniel N. Stern, *The Motherhood Constellation: A Unified View of Parent-Infant Psychotherapy* (New York: Routledge, 1995), 85.

release is the first form of temporal organization and the foundation of both plot and music.[35]

Music is a dramatized sequence of events, with crisis point, beginning and end. It also features an ambiguous sort of causation that reflects better the natural uncertainty haunting our attributions of causation in life. Devoid of necessary consequences, music foregrounds the event as a contingent, highly circumstantial occurrence. Arguing against an "overprivileging of language itself in some models of narrativity that exclude music",[36] Michael Toolan suggests a reconsideration of *contingent consequences* in narrative theory. "In its seeming explicitness", he writes, "language can make causal relations overdetermined, simplified, and reduced; we can be misled by it into thinking we have learned true causes".[37] Shifting emphasis away from semantic content, Baroni's model enables such a non-linguistic approach to narrativity. Focusing on the concrete dynamics of plot requires foregrounding the progressive and embodied experience of discordance and contingency. Modulations of affective contour are the very dynamic of plot; what makes a series of event tellable. Between variations and repetitions, preparation and surprise, progression, acceleration and fading, narratives resemble more cresting waves than linear sequences of events.

Strongly grounded on the temporal irreversibility of our aural experience, *Primitive* shapes a vectorized tension based on a series of affective shifts. Moments of suspense, surprise and quiet follow one another. But, like music, Apichatpong's soundscapes lacks determined semantic content. Kalayanamitr's compositions for Apichatpong's cinema (compiled in 2017 for an album release *Metaphors*) profoundly remix on-location recordings from various places and times, shuffling different realms in rhythmic modulations. Sonic narrativity is more

---

[35] Jean Molino and Raphaël Lafhail-Molino, *Homo fabulator: théorie et analyse du récit* (Montreal: Leméac, 2003).

[36] Michael Toolan, "Musical Narrativity", in *Narrative Sequence in Contemporary Narratology*, ed. Françoise Revaz and Raphaël Baroni (Columbus: Ohio State University Press, 2016), 138. Jean-Jacques Nattiez, for instance, does not grant full narrativity to music. The strongest argument against musical narrativity is its lack of determined semantic content. In response to this, Bryon Almén suggests that narrative regards less referentiality than the relations between elements. A functional approach to narrative would enable narrative analysis of music. For an account of the debate regarding musical narrativity see Byron Almén, "Narrative Archetypes: A Critique, Theory, and Method of Narrative Analysis", *Journal of Music Theory* 47, no. 1 (2003): 1–39.

[37] Toolan, 2016, 138.

cinetic than mimetic. We are immersed into "the unpredictable flux of history", as a critic puts it.[38] The hypnotic aural environment of *Primitive* is an object-less drama, full of living and multivocal noises, seamlessly oscillating between quiet and thunder. As they move to the fore or recede in the background, all sonic entities have the potential to be agentive, effectively blurring the character/setting distinction.

Violence seeps through the landscape, forgotten memories of past state repression and rebellions to come. In *Primitive*, earth is dense with memories. Deleuze speaks of "stratigraphic" landscape shots in Straub-Huillet's cinema: where "the earth stands for what is buried in it".[39] Only, whereas Straubian bare landscapes could be read, Apichatpong's can only be heard. Strata are porous, land is messy. Sound oozes out in every direction. Thai words are deeply enmeshed in earthly noises. Kalayanamitr's noises are often indistinguishable: is it a roaring blaze or the buffeting wind wrapping the microphone? Are those lightning strikes, gunshots or crackling speakers? More radical effects are also used, such as sound transformations, where timbral migrations enact changes of sonic identity. In *Nabua*, a tiger's roar gradually becomes a roaring thunder. By meddling with our fixed categories of description, Kalayanamitr prevents aural causalism, i.e. the restriction of a sound to a determined spatial cause.[40] Narrative agency is redistributed into constellations of meteorological, animal and human forces. In fact, *Primitive* transports us into the following stage: "how memory is transformed and reborn" as he puts it in an interview.[41] The land cannot contain anymore all that it had covered up. Filled to the brim with silent memories of past executions and tortures, it erupts. And this eruption is first and foremost non-human: lightning, flames, fireworks, barking dogs. With Apichatpong's electrical landscapes, the environment regains the agency it was denied as narrative background.

"Of course, if things get too weird", as a critic puts it, "you can always adjourn to another room and clamp on the headphones to jam to Modern dog while watching the video *I'm Still Breathing*".[42] Headphones provide what Francesco Casetti names "existential bubbles":[43] ad-hoc

---

[38] Johnson, 2011.

[39] Gilles Deleuze, *Cinema 2: The Time-Image*, trans. Hugh Tomlinson and Robert Galeta (Minneapolis: University of Minnesota Press, 1989), 244.

[40] Michel Chion, *Le son: Ouïr, écouter, observer*, 3rd edition (Paris: Armand Colin, 2018), 114.

[41] Kim, 2011, 50.

[42] Kwai, 2011.

[43] Francesco Casetti, *The Lumière Galaxy: Seven Key Words for the Cinema to Come* (New York: Columbia University Press, 2015), 71.

refuges where spectators might regain a sense of intimacy. Thus, as we seek refuge into the musical bubbles Apichatpong has set for us, this extraordinary ambient electricity ignites human bodies through dance (*I'm Still Breathing*) and songs (*Nabua Song*). Pop rock music is often used by Apichatpong to counterpoint his dense ambient soundscapes. *Uncle Boonmee* ends with a Thai pop score bridging two incompossible narrative directions: the characters are in two places at once. It sets an optimist and mundane tone to on-screen aberrations. In the installation too, music allows the non-human strangeness to be more relatable to us. In *I'm Still Breathing*, the teens' exhilaration is contagious, while in *Nabua* Song, the boy's call for revolution finally offers a concrete political echo to the environmental eeriness.

Endless Plot

Primitive's looping wave crests move us, body and mind, along distinct storyworlds, but the wave never settles. Suspense finds some punctual moments of musical release but no definitive resolution. The lack of teleology of moving-image installations poses a significant difficulty for narratology. Peter Brooks[44] argues that it is our desire for an ending that energizes storytelling. Narrative closure has also been understood as what provides completeness to a text, what "gives ultimately unity and coherence to the reader's experience".[45] Closure is thus an effect that a text may produce—or not. Following Sternberg's model, Eyal Segal[46] sees it as the resolution of narrative interest, when all informational gaps are filled. For Baroni, cognitive resolution is not necessary for a plot to exist, but the chronology and the teleology of the telling is. Narrative negotiates over time our expectations of final disclosure—whether it will happen or not. All approaches to narrative closure (or openness) rely on a material fact: the text's termination point, its ending. But how can viewers project their expectations of possible endings without an actual ending?

Primitive takes rhetorical narratology further, for teleology and chronology do not reflect visitors' experience of looping films, nor

[44] Peter Brooks, *Reading for the Plot: Design and Intention in Narrative* (Cambridge, MA: Harvard University Press, 1992).
[45] Barbara Herrnstein Smith, *Poetic Closure: A Story of How Poems End* (Chicago: University of Chicago Press, 1968), 36.
[46] Eyal Segal, "Ending Twice Over (or More)", in *Narrative Sequence in Contemporary Narratology*, ed. Françoise Revaz and Raphaël Baroni (Columbus: Ohio State University Press, 2016), 71–86.

the spatial dynamics of interplay and contamination across screens and sound channels. Typical of artists' moving-images, the loop finds its roots in the early years of cinema. Charles Musser[47] has shown that Vitascope films and the Lumiere Cinematographe were characterized by temporal repetition, just like the optical devices that preceded cinema. Before the teleological unfolding of film through the projector became the norm, films were either spliced end to end in a continuous band or repeated on the audience's request. Today gallery films exacerbate the circumstances of early loops. What amounted to repeated spectatorship has become a contaminated and provisory one. Multiscreen projection has often been said to eliminate linearity altogether.[48] Visitors rarely stay put in front of one video throughout its duration. Most often, they roam in between screens, eyes and ears shifting back and forth, from one film to the other. Installations like *Primitive* do not only challenge teleology, they also problematize the chronology of *each* viewing through simultaneous and adjacent projections.

Nevertheless, even if tentative, scattered and contaminated, the progression of our experience remains irreversible. *Primitive* lacks a material ending, but not an experiential one. *De juris,* all videos are looping, allowing repeated viewing and problematizing the very ideas of beginning and end. The installation could also be experienced anew in each one of our paths, discovering novel articulations between sounds and screens. *De facto,* neither the loop nor mobile spectatorship mitigate irreversibility.[49] *Primitive* makes this especially clear. Kalayanamitr's soundscape temporalizes, vectorializes and dramatizes the duration of our visit. It makes the arrow of time tangible. Yet, as Raymond Bellour points out, one of the critical differences between gallery films and cinema is that there is nothing that keeps us inside

---

[47] Charles Musser, "Rethinking Early Cinema: Cinema of Attractions and Narrativity", in *The Cinema of Attractions Reloaded*, ed. Wanda Strauven (Amsterdam: Amsterdam University Press, 2006), 389–416.

[48] Françoise Parfait, *Vidéo: un art contemporain* (Paris: Éd. du Regard, 2001), 314; Erika Balsom, *Exhibiting Cinema in Contemporary Art* (Amsterdam: Amsterdam University Press, 2014), 163–167; Catherine Fowler, "Room for Experiment: Gallery Films and Vertical Time from Maya Deren to Eija Liisa Ahtila", *Screen* 45, no. 4 (2004): 324–343.

[49] Herein we disagree with Mary Ann Doane, according to which the loop allows a reversible spectatorship. Mary Ann Doane, *The Emergence of Cinematic Time: Modernity, Contingency, the Archive* (Cambridge, MA: Harvard University Press, 2002), 132.

TRANSMEDIA PLOT IN WEERASETHAKUL'S *PRIMITIVE*

a black box.[50] Apichatpong's gripping sonic plots incline us to stay, but for how long? Visitors decide when their experience ends, either having seen each video several times or, as it is most often the case, without having seen all videos in full-length. This decision hinges on our expectations of disclosure. When does the installation answers, or fails to answer, our expectations? More specifically, what kind of (dis)closure is expected here?

Mobile spectatorship in *Primitive* challenges the chronological ordering of our experience. Instead of a sequence of videos,[51] the exhibition scenography provides clusters of contamination, by way of spatial proximity—namely sound and light spills—or through the repetition of motives, which weaves unexpected associations. Multiple lines of exploration that are yet to explore invade our field of experience. Each walking route through the exhibition will actualize different connections between the storyworlds on screen. As Dennis Lim[52] puts it, *Primitive* is not a puzzle to solve but a space to explore. Dramatic denouement has little to do with how Weerasethakul's installation intrigues us. For we cannot expect narrative closure from an *end*-less journey. The maze coalesces afresh at each crossing.

But could chronological order be retrospectively realized? Could our experience recover causal linearity upon its termination? After all, the embedded narrative of reincarnation is available to us both in *Uncle Boonmee* and the exhibition. This interpretation would make all videos fit within an integrative frame-narrative as nested stories of someone's past lives. "They call me a guy who can recall his past lives", a narrator tells us in *Primitive*. Light dots would visit him in the rice fields, and he would chase them into the jungle. The images he would see were "like a television", only a walking one: "When I followed the light and its story, I also walked a long distance. My walking and the animal's were like a dance". Visitors' and narrator's walk through the jungle are alike. We too chase light beams around the exhibition space. Human

---

[50] Raymond Bellour, *La Querelle Des Dispositifs: Cinéma - Installations, Expositions* (Paris: P.O.L., 2012), 60.

[51] Fowler has noted how gallery films are often installed into a "joined up soundscape" (Catherine Fowler, "On Sound and Artistic Moving Images: Anri Sala's Acoustic Territories", *Senses of Cinema* 86 (2018)): where sounds from another video simultaneously breaks our attention and provides guidance through the space. Some exhibitions strictly plan the choreography of its visitors, so that a degree of linearity, albeit patched-up, is maintained in the viewer's experience of the works.

[52] Lim, 2011.

and animal stories visit us, each one is its own piece of quilt, accounting for itself in its own way.

Apichatpong's cinema is replete with the magical and the strange. Discussing its lack of hierarchization of human characters over other beings, Nathalie Boehler highlights a "naturalism of the supernatural",[53] whereby spirits and animals are casually and non-hierarchically integrated in the narrative. Monkey ghosts and dead wives join their family for dinner, princesses mate with fishes, sci-fi spaceships struggle to take off, men are countlessly resuscitated, a peaceful village is caught in a lightning spree. Nevertheless, these magical things happen less to a character, than to an interconnected world. Memories do not come from within but from without. I have argued elsewhere[54] that *Uncle Boonmee* is not the story of a man remembering his past lives. Scenes involving a traditional voice-over flashback, supporting the anthropocentric focus on Boonmee's past lives, were carefully deleted in the final cut. Nothing indicates that the stories following one another—the princess' transformation, the buffalo's fly the Jen and Thong's duplication—are indeed Boonmee's memories. Apichatpong exploits the possibilities of filmic narration to complicate the hypothesis put forth in the feature's title. Here, too, we must engage with the ambiguities of the installation.

The question of reincarnation mirrors a tension between local superstitions and Buddhism in Thailand, a tension that Apichatpong leaves unsettled. In northeastern Thailand, the animist belief in the transmigration of souls across time and species is deeply rooted in the Cambodian Khmer. Buddhism, however, and Thai monk Ajahn Buddhadasa Bhikkhu (1906–93) in particular, for whose teachings Apichatpong has expressed enthusiasm, is at odds with folk beliefs in reincarnation. "Because there is no one born, there is no one who dies and is reborn", he writes. "Therefore, the whole question of rebirth is quite foolish and has nothing to do with Buddhism at all."[55] According to the principle of *suññatā* (voidness of self), no stable sense of self can ground the migration of souls. Voidness allows one to be free of ego to fully know the interdependent co-arising of all things, a reality without ends or bounds, pure stream of transformation. Thus, grasping things—such as past lives—as mine merely reflects one's ignorance.

[53] Natalie Boehler, "The Jungle as Border Zone: The Aesthetics of Nature in the Work of Apichatpong Weerasethakul", *Austrian Journal of South-East Asian Studies* 4, no. 2 (2011): 302.

[54] Jade de Cock de Rameyen, "Narrative Difference: A Non-Human and Speculative Paradigm for Uncle Boonmee", *Film-Philosophy*, forthcoming.

[55] Bikkhu Buddhadasa, *Heartwood of the Bodhi Tree: The Buddha's Teaching on Voidness* (Boston: Simon and Schuster, 2014).

The *suññatā* doctrine of radical immanence provides a suitable lens to approach contingent causation in *Primitive*. Characters have little grasp in Apichatpong's worlds. In fact, teenagers are far from narrative agents: they wander around, play, sleep, eat, daydream or set fireworks. These are aimless movements rather than deliberate, intentional actions. In the three videos on speakers (*Nabua, Primitive* and *Phantoms of Nabua*), the human is made anecdotal—as mere shadows or muffled chatter. Strong backlights in the darkness make facial features indistinguishable. As a reviewer puts it, "many images are shot in twilight or the dark hours of night—thereby straining viewers' identification with the profilmic".[56] Nabua's teenagers represent an anonymous collectivity, lacking agency but bursting with unchanneled energy. This energy is echoed in the aural field, in which an essential part is played by the jungle surrounding the village. Forest sounds install a sensorial consciousness of some ongoing transformation, a nonhuman potential for change. Adam Szymanski[57] argues that *Uncle Boonmee* calls for an ecosophicalaesethetic, i.e. a broadening of feeling and perception to the nonhuman and imperceptible forces of our world. Kalayanamitr's soundworks make this particularly clear: they dilate our perception of space and time and open it to metaphysical speculation.

In *Primitive*, even retrospectively, causal necessity fails. Suspense does not relate to the chronological development of characters' actions. The pieces are not expected to fit but to enfold. There is an enigmatic superposition of filmic worlds that should not have anything to do with one another. For Dominique Païni, the semantic shortfall of looping moving-image and their lack of closure entails spectators' disappointment.[58] Narratology provides an alternative perspective: instead of disappointing our expectation; the loop shifts its focus. While ignorance about what happens next does not resist a repeated viewing, suspense may outlive cognitive resolution. This paradox—coined anomalous suspense—has drawn narratologists' attention. Baroni[59]

---

[56] Sharma, 2012, 168.

[57] Adam Szymanski, "Oncle Boonmee, celui qui se souvient de ses vies antérieures et l'esthétique écosophique de la paix", in *Fabulations nocturnes: Écologie, vitalité et opacité dans le cinéma d'Apichatpong Weerasethakul*, ed. Érik Bordeleau et al. (London: Open Humanites Press, 2017), 52–83.

[58] Dominique Païni, *Le temps exposé: le cinéma de la salle au musée* (Paris: Cahiers du cinéma, 2002), 71.

[59] Raphaël Baroni, "Virtualities of Plot and the Dynamics of Rereading", in *Narrative Sequence in Contemporary Narratology*, ed. Françoise Revaz and Raphaël Baroni (Columbus: Ohio State University Press, 2016), 87–103.

has argued that narrative tension may change over time in *nature*: from being based on cognitive uncertainty, it can turn into emotional involvement. Marie-Laure Ryan suggests shifting the phenomenon from the epistemic to the "emotional, almost existential plane"[60]—empathy. Our concern for the beings entangled in the uncertainties of fate resists cognitive disclosure and allows for looping suspense to persist.

Where worlds are plenty and resolution is infinitely delayed, *Primitive* remains filled with unactualized plot virtualities. Something has happened in some other time and some other place that keeps on having effects in the present. Aural dramatization immerses us into temporal process not as cognitive disclosure (anticipating what is next) but as eviential creativity, suspenseful generation of virtual worlds. Narratology suggests that such affective immersion may be autonomous from the causal sequence of events to which we can prospectively or retrospectively reduce a text. Through the vertical expression of an event, one never fully actualized, a different kind of story is built, one where disparate storyworlds contaminate each other without ever blending, and contaminate us in the meantime. It is an atmospheric empathy: "As viewers we are constructed to both witness actions we see and to follow those indirect, shared sentiments—anticipation, anxiety, loss, absence, idleness, energy—that quietly yet heavily linger in the air."[61] We quickly understand that *Primitive*'s mysteries will remain unsolved, eschewing horizontal articulation of cause–effect, but we feel for what is happening around us.

Transmedia Plot

So far, we have approached narrativity across channels in the installation. For all its non-chronological and non-teleological narrativity, the *Primitive* exhibition remains a spatio-temporal unit, shaping a bounded, irreversible experience, with a beginning, middle and end. Narrative articulation of the installation and the feature is yet another problem, for there is no such given unit. It involves the broader issue of transmedia storytelling. According to Henry Jenkins' initial conceptualization, transmedia storytelling refers to "a unified and coordinated

---

[60] Marie-Laure Ryan, *Narrative as Virtual Reality: Immersion and Interactivity in Literature and Electronic Media* (Baltimore: Johns Hopkins University Press, 2001), 148.

[61] Sharma, 2012, 168.

entertainment experience"[62] where elements of a fiction are dispersed across multiple channels, each contributing to the unfolding of a story. Jenkins emphasizes the unity of narrative experience across channels, time and space. For Marie-Laure Ryan this is not necessarily the case. She distinguishes between top-down and bottom-up distribution of content across media. The first is a deliberate distribution of a story or a storyworld across various channels. The latter is the posteriori exploitation of an already successful narrative by the same or different authors, where each story adds another layer to a core narrative—the phenomenon best characterizing Hollywood franchises like *Star Wars*. Ryan argues that bottom-up transmedia are often "random, uncontrolled",[63] whereas top-down ones keep the unicity of experience intact. Because top-down storytelling creates "experiences that cannot be achieved within a single medium", Ryan suggests that "transmedia could very well be regarded as a novel means of expression, and, thereby, as a medium in its own right".[64]

Grouping installations, feature film, book, photographs and whatnot, artistic projects like Weerasethakul's may be considered as top-down transmedia. Apichatpong constantly opens storylines that he picks up elsewhere. On the one hand, the diptych mentions a dark skin princess and a dream of the future, but both stories are really elaborated in the feature film. On the other hand, like the spaceship, the cave is a shelter and time-travel machine, allowing Boonmee to meet Nabua's youth. As Boonmee recounts his dream of the future in the cave, Apichatpong inserts a diaporama of the teenagers of Nabua dressed up as soldiers and posing with the monkey ghost. This makes little sense for those who have not seen the exhibition. It opens the film to political interpretations, more explicit in the installation.

Primitive is a unified and coordinated experience—or rather, a coherent conglomerate of experiences. In the exhibition storyworlds, coordination is achieved through contamination—both aural and visual. Lightning bolts sound like gunshots. Smoke, flames, shining lights accompany us all along. Whether it is a visiting memory or some threat to come, light is constantly brought to the fore as having its own agency. Thus, visual micro-rhythms provide coherence to the whole. Fire blazes in the fields, takes hold of a screen, is kicked around

---

[62] Henry Jenkins, "Transmedia Storytelling 101", *Henry Jenkins* (blog), 2007, http://henryjenkins.org/blog/2007/03/transmedia_storytelling_101.html.

[63] Marie-Laure Ryan, "Transmedia Narratology and Transmedia Storytelling", *Artnodes* 18 (2016): 4.

[64] Ryan, 2016, 8.

by teenagers. And lyrical repetition is not limited to the installation. Inside the spaceship, a red hue recalls Monkey ghosts' eyes, spotlights blind us like the moon in Boonmee's death scene or the projector's beam in *Phantoms of Nabua*. Dressed in military uniforms, the teenagers re-enact the oppression of their dead fathers, while monkey ghosts may be communists coming out of hiding in the jungle. The universe of *Primitive* is more than the sum of its part: each storyworld contains the germ of another story.

Jenkins predicts a shift from storytelling to worldmaking: "More and more, storytelling has become the art of world building, as artists create compelling environments that cannot be fully explored or exhausted within a single work or even a single medium."[65] Baroni proposes instead an alliance of plot and world narratology,[66] so far isolated subfields. If, according to Baroni's paradigm, plots involve storyworld virtualities rather than the logical planification of story and its discursive organization, then the concept is adequate for the analysis of worldly construction in transmedia storytelling.[67] Furthermore, Alain Boillat postulates that the multiworldliness of a transmedia universe might be already at stake in a work, when its universe carries the seeds for multiple declinations of a world.[68] We can therefore speculate that the plot of the installation might shed light to the one underlying the feature, and *Primitive* at large.

We have discussed the integrative force of aural narrativity in the exhibition; how the unifying, temporalizing and plotting effects of territorial sound allow affective immersion in a stream of transformation that is both full and void. *Primitive* provides an interior perspective to the contingency of time; an event pervading Nabua, its jungle and its inhabitants, animals and humans, a metamorphosis that has happened, is happening and will keep on happening. In *Uncle Boonmee* too bass reverberation marks the repetition of a single event of transformation across storyworlds. On three key occasions, the landscape becomes a sonic envelope. Just before the arrival of Boonmee's son Boonsong, now a monkey ghost, the camera frames the nightly jungle. We hear the crunch of leaves underfoot in the roaring landscape, Tong asks "what is that sound?". Later, as the princess enters the water and removes

---

[65] Henry Jenkins, *Convergence Culture: Where Old and New Media Collide* (New York: NYU Press, 2008), 114.

[66] Alain Boillat, *Cinéma, machine à mondes: essai sur les films à univers multiples* (Chêne-Bourg: Georg, 2014).

[67] Baroni, 2017, 187.

[68] Boillat, 2014, 101.

TRANSMEDIA PLOT IN WEERASETHAKUL'S *PRIMITIVE*   203

her jewelry to mate with the fish, the sound of the waterfall loses its crispness. It is gradually overwhelmed by a heavy drone. Finally, Boonmee's death sequence gives free rein to reverberation. Cicadas gradually recede into the background, bass come to the fore and so does Boonmee's heavy breathing. Inside the cave, acoustics abolish the distance between body and environment. The density of auditory field reaches its highest degree. We understand this to be the living core of the storyworld. Bonmee too, as he reflects: "This cave it's like a womb, isn't it? I feel like I was born here in a life I can't recall."

Although inscribed in the linearity of theatrical experience, sonic narrativity is also key to *Uncle Boonmee*. Resisting linear emplotment and cognitive disclosure, *Primitive* articulates storyworlds around a narrative tension, a suspenseful transformation expressed through sonic shifts. Transmedia storytelling thus maintains a tension between two poles: dissemination and constellation. While the aural event allows centrifugal generation of compossible storyworlds, territorial sounds, rhymes and repetitions play a centripetal part, so that "disparate stories connect that wouldn't in reality".[69] Like the feature's title, the voice-over in the diptych offers a story that guides our interpretation of the heterogenous composite and non-linear sequences of images, but its narration does not elucidate what hides underneath the soil. It only adds an extra layer of sedimentation. Suspenseful dynamics of gap-filling hypotheses waiting to be solved are hardly at play here. Chronological lacks cease to be what drives our interest. In the looping world of *Primitive,* suspense changes in nature. Apichatpong dramatizes the dependent co-arising of things, in which communists, soldiers, film crew, monkey ghosts and us meet, now or then, here or there.

Baroni's model allows a methodological turn: from the structural semantics of story to the pragmatic dynamics of plot. What moves us is temporal discordance, not its configuration. Weerasethakul's narratives are less represented than performed; aural plot makes autonomous events conspire and intrigue us. A periodic disturbance travels through media, in different milieus, at different speeds. Upon the wave-crest of plot, our experience lies in these transitions more than in the journey's end. *Primitive* is an environmental narrative, within which leakages open worlds that exist in parallel, yet intimately connected ones. Rather than lying in some cognitive denouement, the object of our narrative desire is ontologically removed, perhaps a distant life we cannot recall, but one that already queers our present.

[69] Nash, 2011.

Bibliography

Almén, Byron. "Narrative Archetypes: A Critique, Theory, and Method of Narrative Analysis". *Journal of Music Theory* 47, no. 1 (2003): 1–39.

Amichetti, Andrea, and Andrea Lissoni. "Apichatpong Weerasethakul: Primitive". *Cujo.* 2009.

Balsom, Erika. *Exhibiting Cinema in Contemporary Art.* Amsterdam. Amsterdam University Press. 2014.

Baroni, Raphaël. *L'œuvre du temps: poétique de la discordance narrative.* Paris. Seuil. 2009.

Baroni, Raphaël. "Tensions et résolutions: musicalité de l'intrigue ou intrigue musicale?". *Cahiers de Narratologie: Analyse et théorie narratives* 21 (2011): 1–15.

Baroni, Raphaël. "Virtualities of Plot and the Dynamics of Rereading". In *Narrative Sequence in Contemporary Narratology.* Ed. Françoise Revaz and Raphaël Baroni. Columbus. Ohio State University Press. 2016. 87–103.

Bellour, Raymond. *La Querelle Des Dispositifs: Cinéma—Installations, Expositions.* Paris. P.O.L. 2012.

Blesser, Barry and Linda-Ruth Salter. *Spaces Speak, Are You Listening? Experiencing Aural Architecture.* Cambridge MA. MIT Press. 2009.

Boehler, Natalie. "The Jungle as Border Zone: The Aesthetics of Nature in the Work of Apichatpong Weerasethakul". *Austrian Journal of South-East Asian Studies* 4, no. 2 (2011): 290–304.

Boillat, Alain. *Cinéma, machine à mondes: essai sur les films à univers multiples.* Chêne-Bourg. Georg. 2014.

Brooks, Peter. *Reading for the Plot: Design and Intention in Narrative.* Cambridge MA. Harvard University Press. 1992.

Buddhadasa, Bikkhu. *Heartwood of the Bodhi Tree: The Buddha's Teaching on Voidness.* Boston. Simon and Schuster. 2014.

Casetti, Francesco. *The Lumière Galaxy: Seven Key Words for the Cinema to Come.* New York. Columbia University Press. 2015.

Chanrochanakit, Pandit. "Deforming Thai Politics: As Read through Thai Contemporary Art". *Third Text* 25, no. 4 (2011): 419–429.

Chion, Michel. *L'audio-vision.* 4th edition. Paris. Armand Colin. 2017.

Chion, Michel. *Le son: Ouïr, écouter, observer.* 3rd edition. Paris. Armand Colin. 2018.

Cock de Rameyen, Jade de. "Narrative Difference: A Non-Human and Speculative Paradigm for Uncle Boonmee". *Film-Philosophy.* Forthcoming.

Coulthard, Lisa. "Haptic Aurality: Resonance, Listening and Michael Haneke". *Film-Philosophy* 16, no. 1 (2012): 16–29.

Dannenberg, Hilary P. "Ontological Plotting: Narrative as a Multiplicity of Temporal Dimensions". In *The Dynamics of Narrative Form.* Ed. John Pier. Berlin. De Gruyter. 2004. 159–190.

Deleuze, Gilles. *Cinema 2: The Time-Image*. Trans. Hugh Tomlinson and
 Robert Galeta. Minneapolis. University of Minnesota Press. 1989.
Doane, Mary Ann. *The Emergence of Cinematic Time: Modernity,*
 Contingency, the Archive. Cambridge MA. Harvard University Press.
 2002.
e-flux. "Gustav Metzger and Apichatpong Weerasethakul". 2011.
Elwes, Catherine. *Installation and the Moving Image*. New York. Columbia
 University Press. 2015.
Fowler, Catherine. "Room for Experiment: Gallery Films and Vertical
 Time from Maya Deren to Eija Liisa Ahtila". *Screen* 45, no. 4 (2004):
 324–343.
Fowler, Catherine. "On Sound and Artistic Moving Images: Anri Sala's
 Acoustic Territories". *Senses of Cinema* 86 (2018).
Gioni, Massimiliano and Gary Carrion-Murayari.
 "Apichatpong Weerasethakul: Primitive". *New Museum*.
 2011. http://www.newmuseum.org/exhibitions/view/
 apichatpong-weerasethakul-primitive.
Herman, David. *Story Logic: Problems and Possibilities of Narrative*.
 Lincoln. University of Nebraska Press. 2002.
Herrnstein Smith, Barbara. *Poetic Closure: A Story of How Poems End*.
 Chicago. University of Chicago Press. 1968.
Jenkins, Henry. "Transmedia Storytelling 101". *Henry Jenkins* (blog). 2007.
 http://henryjenkins.org/blog/2007/03/transmedia_storytelling_101.
 html.
Jenkins, Henry. *Convergence Culture: Where Old and New Media Collide*.
 New York. NYU Press. 2008.
Johnson, Ken. "Youth, With Hopes and Bliss Intact". *The New York Times*.
 27 May 2011. sec. Arts.
Kim, Jihoon. "Between Auditorium and Gallery: Perception in
 Apichatpong Weerasethakul's Films and Installations". In *Global*
 Art Cinema: New Theories and Histories. Ed. Rosalind Galt and Karl
 Schoonover. New York. Oxford University Press. 2010. 125–141.
Kim, Jihoon. "Learning About Time: An Interview with Apichatpong
 Weerasethakul". *Film Quarterly* 64, no. 4 (2011): 48–52.
Kwai, Wise. "Apichatpong-a-Rama: Primitive, Hangover, Jury in Venice,
 Morning in Finland". *Wise Kwai's Thai Film Journal* (blog). 24 June
 2011. http://thaifilmjournal.blogspot.com/2011/06/apichatpong-ra-
 ma-primitive-hangover.html.
Lim, Dennis. "Apichatpong Weerasethakul". *Artforum International* 50,
 no. 1 (2011): 341.
Lovatt, Philippa. "'Every Drop of My Blood Sings Our Song. There Can
 You Hear It?': Haptic Sound and Embodied Memory in the Films of
 Apichatpong Weerasethakul". *The New Soundtrack* 3, no. 1 (2013): 61–79.
Marks, Laura U. *The Skin of the Film: Intercultural Cinema, Embodiment,*
 and the Senses. Durham. Duke University Press. 2000.

Molino, Jean, and Raphaël Lafhail-Molino. *Homo fabulator: théorie et analyse du récit*. Montreal. Leméac. 2003.

Musser, Charles. "Rethinking Early Cinema: Cinema of Attractions and Narrativity". In *The Cinema of Attractions Reloaded*. Ed. Wanda Strauven. Amsterdam. Amsterdam University Press. 2006. 389–416.

Nash, Aily. "WE ARE PRIMITIVE: Apichatpong's Ineffable Experience of Nabua". *The Brooklyn Rail*. 2011.

Nasta, Dominique. *Meaning in Film: Relevant Structures in Soundtrack and Narrative*. Berne. Lang. 1991.

Nattiez, Jean-Jacques. "La Narrativisation de la musique. La musique: récit ou proto-récit?" *Cahiers de Narratologie: Analyse et théorie narratives* 21 (2011). http://journals.openedition.org/narratologie/6467.

Païni, Dominique. *Le temps exposé: le cinéma de la salle au musée*. Paris. Cahiers du cinéma. 2002.

Parfait, Françoise. *Vidéo: un art contemporain*. Paris. Éd. du Regard. 2001.

Ryan, Marie-Laure. *Narrative as Virtual Reality: Immersion and Interactivity in Literature and Electronic Media*. Baltimore. Johns Hopkins University Press. 2001.

Ryan, Marie-Laure. "Transmedia Narratology and Transmedia Storytelling". *Artnodes* 18 (2016): 1–10.

Segal, Eyal. "Ending Twice Over (or More)". In *Narrative Sequence in Contemporary Narratology*. Ed. Françoise Revaz and Raphaël Baroni. Columbus. Ohio State University Press. 2016. 71–86.

Sharma, Aparna. "Apichatpong Weerasethakul: Primitive (Review)". *Leonardo* 45, no. 2 (2012): 167–169.

Stern, Daniel N. *The Motherhood Constellation: A Unified View of Parent-Infant Psychotherapy*. New York. Routledge. 1995.

Sternberg, Meir. "How Narrativity Makes a Difference". *Narrative* 9, no. 2 (2001): 115–22.

Szymanski, Adam. "Oncle Boonmee, celui qui se souvient de ses vies antérieures et l'esthétique écosophique de la paix". In *Fabulations nocturnes: Écologie, vitalité et opacité dans le cinéma d'Apichatpong Weerasethakul*. Ed. Érik Bordeleau, Toni Pape, Ronald Rose-Antoinette, and Adam Szymanski. London. Open Humanites Press. 2017. 52–83.

Thai Film Archive. "The Spaceship of Nabua". *Google Arts & Culture*. 2021. https://artsandculture.google.com/story/the-spaceship-of-nabua/oAVxEi3VrCGhSw.

Toolan, Michael. "Musical Narrativity". In *Narrative Sequence in Contemporary Narratology*. Ed. Françoise Revaz and Raphaël Baroni. Columbus. Ohio State University Press. 2016. 130–150.

Weerasethakul, Apichatpong. "Around the World of Apichatpong Weerasethakul. Interview by Eungie Joo". 2011. http://ca.newmuseum.org/index.php/Detail/Object/Show/object_id/8463.

Weerasethakul, Apichatpong. *Apichatpong Weerasethakul Sourcebook: The Serenity of Madness*. New York. Independent Curators International. 2016.

9

Home Away From Home
Apichatpong Weerasethakul's Filmed Images of Home and Homeland Envisioned

Palita Chunsaengchan

> With a feeling of uneasiness I kept revisiting Nabua.
> —Apichatpong Weerasethakul[1]

Around the end of 2019, in a world sans COVID-19 where the prospect of practicing what was "normal"—our productivity, mobility and routine—seemed inexhaustible, the community of global cinephile might have been quite enlivened by the news about Apichatpong Weerasethakul's new project—the shooting of *Memoria*.[2] The enthusiasm evolved partly around the fact that this was Weerasethakul's first feature film of full scale in many years (the most recent one before *Memoria* was *Cemetery of Splendour* in 2015). More importantly, one could say that the thrill around *Memoria* definitely comes from the fact that this is the director's first internationally co-produced film. Of course, on the level of funding, it is true that Weerasethakul's former projects have always been successful at attracting transnational financial support. But *Memoria*, shot mainly in Colombia rather than in the director's homeland, Thailand, and equipped with full international casting and production crew, undeniably amplifies, let alone reaffirms, the director's status as a director of world cinema and, consequentially, his access to resources abroad.

The film is about a sleep-deprived woman constantly bothered by an omnipresent noise that could perhaps be identified as construction noise or is simply an auditory hallucination.[3] Though the thematic focus on insomnia might echo that of *Cemetery of Splendor* (2015), the fact that

[1] Apichatpong Weerasethakul, "The Memory of Nabua: A Note on the *Primitive* Project", in *Apichatpong Weerasethakul* (Vienna: Synema, 2009).
[2] See Giovanni Marchini Camia, "Set Diary: Memoria", https://www.filmcomment.com/blog/category/journals/set-diary-memoria/.
[3] This chapter was written during the last quarter of 2020 and submitted

Memoria was inspired by the history of politics and places—the very locality of Colombia—rather than the northeast of Thailand (or Isan in Thai) must not be overlooked. In late October 2020, Weerasethakul published a note reflecting on the crisis of the global pandemic and how he had had to come back to Thailand and, unfortunately, pause the filmmaking of *Memoria* in Colombia. Instead of being away from home shooting a film inspired by an unfamiliar place, Weerasethakul was *back* to his home in Thailand and instead offered us *October Rumbles* (2020)—a short lamenting reflection of rain, regeneration and Buddhism in the time of crisis.[4] One thing that this instance makes clear is the way in which filmmaking outside the studio system—or one could even argue for the filmmaking in and of the Global South—relies so much on and is facilitated by real places and uncompromising access to them. It underlines not only the significance of travel, mobility, encounters with places that are unfamiliar, and unpredictably homely or unhomely[5] but also of aesthetic possibilities emerging from attempts to make sense of such encounters and ever-changing conditions.

to the editors in February 2021. The film, *Memoria,* was not officially released until 26 December 2021.

[4] *October Rumbles* is also a commissioned project supported and sponsored in conjunction with "The Third Realm Exhibition". The film was screened virtually only for a limited period of time. The access to the film was restricted to YouTube channel and the file itself was uploaded by this gallery, The Polygon. More information can be found in an article written by the gallery: "Apichatpong Weerasethakul – October Rumbles". *The Polygon.* https://thepolygon.ca/news/apichatpong-weerasethakul-october-rumbles/.

[5] Using the term "unhomely" of course requires us to pay attention to the Freudian psychoanalytic tradition of the *Unheimlich*, in Sigmund Freud's essay in 1919 "Das Unheimliche". Unhomely in the Freudian sense is meant for something that arouses gruesome fear, eerie, weird and was developed from the encounters with the "undead" or the "uncanny", often associated with the "repressed" and "trauma". In the poststructuralist reading, *Unheimlich* "is actually a condition of the Heimlich, insofar as heimlich, which denotes comfort, familiarity, and safe enclosure, always already contains within it connotations of withdrawal, concealment, secrecy, even danger". See Claudette Lauzon, *The Unmaking of Home in Contemporary Art* (Toronto: University of Toronto Press, 2017), 20. However, this chapter only loosely refers to this German psychoanalytic tradition of *unheimlich* because it seeks to resist a psychoanalytical viewpoint that focuses only on the intersubjectivity of an individual. This chapter is more interested in the way in which the director deploys his resources, networks and political surroundings to create a sense of unhomeliness that is more collective via his cinema.

This chapter weaves together places in the real material world; home; homeland, mobility, memory and filmmaking in Weerasethakul's works, in order to trace how his filmed images were conditioned by these elements and, especially, by the stage of being in an unfamiliar place and yet desiring to film it. The chapter focuses, on the one hand, on how the filmed images depict places that *are not* the director's original home (as in the sense of where he grew up or a place to which he associated his origin, childhood, past memories and personal attachment) and yet *feel* like home. On the other hand, it investigates filmed images of places that are not the director's home and might also feel unhomely—or might appear as a discomfort or disruption. I contend that the way in which Weerasethakul turns those places into the filmed images render possible not only a way to understand his philosophy and aesthetic practices of filmmaking but also to approach the real places conscious of their historical remnants and political futures. I trace my assumption of the first category of "being not at home but feeling homely" in his commissioned non-feature short, *Cactus River* (*Khong Lang Nam*, 2012) and the first quarter of the film *Ashes* (2012). The second and third quarters of *Ashes*, however, open up possibilities to discuss the second category in which the filming and visualization of places offer a political critique of the national politics of contemporary Thailand. For this particular reason, I find Weerasethakul's *Ashes* and his famous art installation *Primitive* (2009), in which he collaborated with local teens in Nabua in Thailand, very informative and helpful to the conversation about the politics of places. As we shall see, places that were filmed dominate his film aesthetic. And yet, in return, the filmed images of those places reveal alternative ways in which each place could be understood along the political history of the nation. The significance of Nabua as a place that is neither his home nor feels homely, for example, lies in the fact that, on the one hand, it drives the creative project of *Uncle Boonmee Who Can Recall His Past Lives* (2010)—his *tour de force* that saw him awarded the *Palme d'Or* at the Cannes Film Festival. On the other hand, Nabua brings back to the surface state violence in the form of an anti-communist operation in the 1970s. Nabua and the filmed images of the village becomes a potential site in which political critiques could be achieved and materialized.[6]

There is no doubt, as the themes and topics of this volume might have already suggested, that Weerasethakul has arguably ascended to the

---

[6] See Palita Chunsaengchan, "The Critique of Anti-Communist Violence in *Uncle Boonmee Who Can Recall His Past Lives*", *Asian Cinema* 32, no. 1 (2021): 95–111.

position of an "auteur" director. Most scholarly essays and journalistic attention on Weerasethakul definitely reflect this claim. The archive that has been built around the director consists of different thematic points, his cinematic styles across different films, years and production teams, his background and training first in architecture in Khon Khaen, Thailand and in cinema studies in Chicago—all of which underscore the auteuristic focuses. It is, of course, not rare to see this generation of successful Thai film directors graduate or have a degree or training in film studies from abroad, especially in the West. But the fact that Weerasethakul was one of the very few Thai film directors who was considered to have "made it" at the Cannes Film Festival several times from the early 2010s has been one of the milestones and inspirations for the Thai film community.

Given his status and contribution to the Thai film industry, the Thai Film Archive recently announced that they were humbled to receive an important gift from Weerasethakul. It is an installation of a spaceship from his project *Primitive*. The spaceship was co-created by teens in Nabua and is now installed in the hallway of the Archive's new building.[7] His status as an important auteur has also been proved by the fact that he has often been invited to exhibitions, talks and events, which have often attracted attention from scholars and cinephiles alike. A couple years ago, for example, the news that Weerasethakul visited the Archive with Tilda Swinton, the lead actress of *Memoria*, thrilled his followers in his home country.[8] Although this news did not, unfortunately, reach the Thai general public, due to the lack of interest in independent film culture and to poor governmental and cultural support for the infrastructure of film and art industry, it is still not at all difficult to see how Weerasethakul has reached the prestigious status of one of Thailand's most important directors.

In highlighting this trajectory of attention toward Weerasethakul as an auteur, or for his auteurship, it is of course important to acknowledge the tradition of studies that have long accompanied the use of the terms. The tradition of the "auteur theory", first developed by the critics

---

[7] In this newsletter, Thai Film Archive chronicles Weerasethakul's exhibition of his *Primitive* project including the installation of the spaceship of Nabua. See Natthapol Sawasdee, "Nitadsakarn awakard hang baan nabua" ("Exhibition on Extraterritoriality of Nabua"). *Film Archive (Public Organization)*. https://www.fapot.or.th/main/information/article/view/319 (in Thai).

[8] This news appeared on the official Thai Film Archive's Facebook account: Thai Film Archive, "Today Apichatpong brought Tilda Swinton ... to visit Thai Film Archive". *Facebook*. 30 October 2018. https://www.facebook.com/ThaiFilmArchivePage/posts/2103048203078702.

of *Cahiers du Cinéma* in the 1950s, may have proven useful to some drafts of the history of filmmaking,[9] to myriad explorations of the styles and consistency of various directors, and to the argument that seeks to develop a theory of cinema as a form of art. However, some critics have famously disapproved of this trajectory, pointing to the fact that filmmaking actually consists of many aspects other than just the auteur or director.[10] Although this claim has rightly underlined an important ethical nuance for film historiography and the roundedness of inclusivity in film industry, it is no less important to justify why an auteurist study of Weerasethakul is still relevant and very much needed.

Firstly, as I mentioned above, the infrastructure of the national cinema of Thailand has been, more or less, centralized to the studio system and very much dependent and contingent on support from private investment and on governmental policy on rating and censorship. However, collaborations from cultural and academic institutions in the past two decades have started to move more toward smaller-scale or independent productions, as well as to broaden the scope of what cinema means both in the national and global paradigms. Thus, to have a director like Weerasethakul, whose works have been motivated mostly by his own "homeland", undoubtedly underscores potential growth for the Thai film industry on the global stage and greatly motivates a new generation of directors, critics and scholars.[11] Therefore, it is fair to claim that the rationale behind such an auteurist attention as seen in this volume also sheds light on the conversations both around film historiography and the genealogy of film aesthetics and ideologies that are often involved in the making of a film in a particular national context. It opens up, for example, questions as to why non-Western national film histories often have to begin and end with figures of directors and their films, and as to whether or not there are other ways in which film histories could be captured in such contexts.[12]

---

[9] Seung-hoon Jeong and Jeremi Szaniawski, "Introduction", in *The Global Auteur: The Politics of Authorship in 21st Century Cinema* (London: Bloomsbury Academic, 2016), 1–20.

[10] See James Naremore, "Authorship, Auteurism, and Cultural Politics", in *An Invention Without a Future: Essays on Cinema* (Oakland: University of California Press, 2014), 15–32.

[11] My claim here works only to captivate the concrete tangible reality of film production in Thailand as well as the disparity between domestic and international markets. Yet my claim, by no means, attempts to diminish the significance of works in the fields of transnational cinema, ethnography and so on.

[12] In the context of the hegemonic narrative of the Thai film history, we

PALITA CHUNSAENGCHAN

Secondly, although there are several interviews on Weerasethakul's cinematic aesthetic and various aspects of his filmmaking, works that focus on the relationship between his practices, his professional network—support from and attachment to his people—and what they might mean for his filmed images and film structure are still quite scarce. If the debate around the auteur theory suggests that an auteur is someone who possesses and performs a distinct style and sensibility regardless of genres and the lack of a studio system, I want to push this argument further; on the one hand, by incorporating an aspect of his network, attachment and intimacy both with people and places into the understanding of this auteurship; on the other hand, by considering Weerasethakul's conceptualization of "home" in its abstraction in relation to the thematic visualization, cinematic practices and the constructedness of the filmed images in some of his exemplary works, I elaborate not so much on the claim of uniqueness of his aesthetic vision, but more on the realm of network and proximity of a political subject that he embodies to the contemporary political history of Thailand. This, I argue, is intricately intertwined with the history of places, which includes the lived experiences and memories of places of the locals vis-à-vis the political events that occurred in those places. I also contend that the director's filmed images of places and his cinematic style reveal the injuries of the people, which, on one hand, were caused by the losses of home and preemptive fears of further potential destruction, and, on the other hand, by the inescapable unfortunate history of national political turmoil and violence.

Not Any River but "Cactus River"

After *Syndromes and a Century* (2006)—the film that Weerasethakul identified as closest to his memories of his hometown, Khon Khaen, in the northeast of Thailand or Isan—few of his films dealt directly with the concept of home. Although it is true that *Uncle Boonmee Who Can Recall His Past Lives,* the film that adorned him the *Palme d'Or* in 2010, was also shot in the northeast, the film was more of a collaborative

---

often start with how cinema came to Siam and how certain pioneers invested in the technology and built the industry. It is also common to see the narrative of the "first person". For example, it deals with the stories of who was the first film director or the first person who promoted public film screenings. See, for instance, Mary J. Ainslie and Katarzyna Ancuta, eds, "Key Directors", in *A Complete Guide to Thai Cinema* (London: I.B. Tauris, 2018).

politically charged project that came out of his art installation, *Primitive,* rather than being a diary, or memories of his home, during the time of his parents' residency in Isan. From the director's background, given the fact that he moved a lot both for educational and professional purposes—for instance, from his undergraduate degree in architecture in Khon Khaen to his Master's degree in film histories in Chicago, then back to Bangkok and Chiang Mai, a province in northern Thailand—it is not overstating it to say that travels and changes of places definitely affect his way of thinking about home, including the sense of longing and belonging one might want to capture.

Aligning the information we knew about Weerasethakul's mobility and how it might have informed his artistic practices to the period post-*Palme-d'Or* (after the Cannes Film Festival in 2010) in which the director gained much support and recognition from international audiences and various types of cultural institutions, I was interested in some of the projects he produced after he arguably gained this auteurship. Among a couple of commissioned short films available on YouTube, *Cactus River (Khong Lang Nam),*[13] a project commissioned by the Walker Art Center located in Minneapolis, Minnesota, in 2012, strikes me as an important constituent work of Weerasethakul for a couple reasons. Firstly, this short, commissioned non-featured film remains quite overlooked or, rather, unknown, to a wider global audience, despite the general attention toward Weerasethakul and the fact that this film actually shares significant similarities, especially the location of shooting and the cast that compliment his Cannes special-screened feature film, *Mekong Hotel* (2012). The Walker Art Center even premiered *Mekong Hotel* in their auditorium just a week after the release of the online short film. Yet it is *Mekong Hotel* that remains more visible to the general public.

Secondly, I believe that it is important for those who are interested in Weerasethakul's cinematic and artistic tradition also to explore practices and rationales behind the director's commissioned works, especially those that involve art or cultural institutions apart from the film industry. This is precisely because such works could potentially reveal certain networks and contributions that could have been underdiscussed among film scholars, and yet are constituent of the director's overall aesthetic and identity. In general, Weerasethakul had received financial and cultural support from, and was more or less

---

[13] Walker Art Center. "Cactus River (Khong Lang Nam)". 12 October 2012. https://www.youtube.com/watch?v=H5vToT_ionU.

closer to, European or Asian cinematic and art institutions.[14] *Cactus River*, on the other hand, was tasked by an American art institution so that, upon its completion, the film would inaugurate the Walker Channel in which streaming content of various types of art is available in real time. The museum, known for its focus on contemporary art and the modern architectural design of its building, also strives to become more engaged with new media and expansive ways in which the concept of art can be understood and institutionalized. The museum explained the decision to select Weerasethakul as the first figure to be commissioned and to have the honor for the inauguration as follows: "He was asked to inaugurate artist presence on the Walker Channel because he is truly a modern renegade, someone who *moves freely* across artistic practices."[15]

It is widely agreed that Weerasethakul's ability to "move freely across artistic practices" has always informed not only his aesthetic toward cinema but also our reception of his works regardless of whether it is a full-length feature films or an art installation. One of the early discussions on Weerasethakul's characteristics by James Quandt, for instance, concurs with the Walker Art Center's statement. Quandt asserts that the director is someone whom "the art world calls a 'glocal,' someone whose works draws on the international language of modernism while remaining rooted in his native culture".[16] On the institutional level, for instance, *Cactus River* crosses the threshold of cinema and art precisely because it is a film that would be screened in an art museum and would later be available online for a global audience on a media platform, YouTube. Specifically, given the issue of boundary-crossing, the film shot from the border of Thailand on the shores of the Mekong river and yet sent across the Pacific Ocean to the Midwest of the United States not only brings back the time in which the director spent in the Midwest but also conjures up the memories of his past that dated back prior to his arrival in the United States: the period in which his "home" was in northeastern Thailand and in which the strong

---

[14] For example, the director won the 2013 Fukuoka Prize, the 2014 Yanghyun Art Prize, one of the most prestigious awards in South Korea, and the 2016 Prince Claus Award in the Netherlands. He also exhibited his artworks and video installations in Munich, Liverpool, Dublin, etc. See Dana Linssen, "If Light Was Un/Folding, The Measure of Time", in *Apichatpong Weerasethakul* (Amsterdam: Eye Filmmuseum, 2017).

[15] Sheryl Mousley, "Cactus River: Apichatpong Weerasethakul Film Debuts on Walker Channel". *Walker Crosscuts*. https://walkerart.org/magazine/cactus-river-apichatpong-weerasethakul-film-debuts-on-walker-channel.

[16] James Quandt, "Resistant to Bliss: Describing Apichatpong", in *Apichatpong Weerasethakul*, ed. James Quandt (Vienna: Synema, 2009), 16.

connection to the Mekong, the river of life for the people, defined the perspective of life and space. The boundaries that seem to be solid and that separate different homes fade away if we consider this dimension.

From the beginning of *Cactus River,* the presence of filmed images of a river is prominent. But for those who do not know the context of the short film or the director's background, or who just randomly encounter this video on YouTube, the image of the river or the term *Cactus River* itself offers no specific geographical information. Additionally, given the director's choice to film in black and white, it is even harder to make any reference between the filmed space we see in the diegetic world and the image of places we see in the real world—or non-diegetically. In other words, the images of the river in the film are not confined to any sense of realism—they do not claim to "represent" or to "look like" the Mekong river. Even though this might be the case on the level of ontological discussions of the filmed images, there is, in fact, guidance, or rather instruction, provided by the director himself. Below is the director's statement intended to accompany the film release at the Walker Art Center:

> Since she appeared in my film in 2009, Jenjira Pongpas has changed her name. Like many Thais, she is convinced that the new name will bring her good luck. So Jenjira has become Nach, which means water. Not long after, she was drifting online and encountered a retired soldier, Frank, from Cuba, New Mexico, USA. A few months later they got married and she has officially become Mrs. Nach Widner. The newlyweds found a house near the Mekong River where Nach had grown up. She spends most of her day crocheting baby socks for sale, while he enjoys gardening and watching television (sometimes without the sound because most of the programs are in Thai). *Cactus River* is a diary of the time I visited the couple—of the various temperaments of the water and the wind. The flow of the two rivers—Nach and the Mekong, activates my memories of the place where I shot several films. Over many years, this woman whose name was once Jenjira has introduced me to this river, her life, its history, and to her belief about its imminent future. She is certain that soon there will be no water in the river due to the upstream constructions of dams in China and Laos. I noticed too, that Jenjira was no more.[17]

---

[17] The director's statement can be found along with the film on https://www.youtube.com/watch?v=H5vToT_ionU.

It is clear from the director's note which river has inspired *Cactus River*. The film was shot on his trip to visit Jenjira or, rather, Nach's new home in Nhong Khai—a province in Isan that shares the natural border of the Mekong river with the Lao People's Democratic Republic. Those who are familiar with Weerasethakul's filmography over the years might have been able to identify the name, Jenjira, right away. It was Jenjira Pongpas—the one who appeared, for instance, as Orn, a desperately passionate mid-life woman, in *Blissfully Yours,* as Aunt Jen in *Syndromes and a Century* and *Uncle Boonmee Who Can Recall His Past Lives* and again as Jenjira in *Cemetery of Splendor*. The relationship that the director shares with the actress—he mentioned that she introduced him to "this river, her life, its history, and to her belief in its imminent future"—also evokes a sense of familiarity, intimacy and, perhaps, comfort. It is in this professional network that his peer's home becomes intricately linked to his own home in Khon Khaen.

Another important point in the director's writing lies in how he equates, on the one hand, the new name of Jenjira—Nach, which means river—to the indispensable Mekong river and, on the other hand, how he aligns where Jenjira grew up (Nhong Khai) to his previous film projects shot intentionally in various provinces and places in Isan. What is interesting is how a conception of home can be understood as

Fig. 1: JenjiraPongpas, who appeared in many of Weerasethakul's films. This still is from *Cactus River*. Courtesy of the Walker Art Center, Minneapolis.

HOME AWAY FROM HOME

a place that relies not only on the professional relationship but also on the commonality that all the provinces in the region of the northeast of Thailand share, as well as what they could constitute together. The point of association that the director made between Jenjira's home and his home is very significant to my argument. Because I argue that it is in this process of associative identification that the director realigns unfamiliarity to familiarity, his absence from home to homeliness envisioned. It is in the association that Nhong Khai (a province where Jenjira resides) is also part of Isan as much as Khon Khaen (the province where he grew up and later inspired one of his films, *Syndromes and a Century*), as well as how his life has been intertwined with Jenjira's life, that makes the concept of home viable. It is as much about the kinship of his professional network as the process of regional identification that makes home a broader and flexible area—a possibility within which the director could process his memories of his real home.

According to the director, *Cactus River* is also "a diary of the time [he] visited the couple—of the various temperaments of the water and the wind"; therefore, it is no doubt a personal take on spatial formation and deterioration. What I mean by spatial formation, on the one hand, is the fact that the director constructs a filmed space of home as an extension of *his* home as well as in the process of associative identification that allows him to unite his professional network and a region of Isan to his homemaking and his memories of home. On the other hand, the deterioration can be acknowledged by the negation at the ending of his note that "Jenjira was no more" and in the Thai subtitle *Khong Lang Nam*, which can be literally translated as "the draught of the Mekong river", stating quite explicitly the concern about inevitable changes and transformations on the level of environmental crisis and transnational projects of dam constructions. If he aligns his home to Jenjira's home and Nach to the Mekong river, what is quite interesting is how he also aligns his realization that "Jenjira was no more" to his realistic take on the natural decay and impermanence of things—in this case of both the sense of home constituted in his network, attachment and intimacy with the subjectivity of Jenjira and the potential decay of home that is associated with the Mekong river—the river of life and the symbolic image of his home in northeastern Thailand.

What I have discussed thus far could be affirmed by the textuality of *Cactus River*. Without any dialogue, but noises that sound like the operation of a vintage camera, the film starts with black-and-white footage of a woman sitting next to the river. She would be accompanied by a man only briefly after the first scene. Then, in fewer than five seconds, the cut shifts to a scene of a man lying down looking into the river. Given the unnatural speed of the film, which implies post-production digital editing, by the eighteenth second of the film we can already see one of the many potentials of cinema, one that lies in editing and its capacity to manipulate time. In this case, Weerasethakul deploys the formal aspect of filmmaking to shed light on the thematic concern that he had, for example, on how fast people were forced to move or transform, how certain things stay static while others flow quite arbitrarily and, most importantly, how unnatural a place could look in and as a filmed space. All of these textual possibilities were enabled by the medium that is cinema, and yet it was also because of cinema that the themes of impermanence as informed by Buddhism, and as always informing Weerasethakul's philosophy and filmmaking, was connected to the idea of home, potential destruction and disappearance.

This means that, in a way, the filmed images of the river—the one that flows at an unnatural speed—were not only annotated and made clear to us as depicting the reality of the Mekong river by the director's paratextual note. But also, the filmed images of the river were constructed during the profilmic event—what was in front of the camera was being linked to the director's memories of his past and his home in Isan. In a way, it was the Mekong in front of Weerasethakul's camera—a decisive moment that turned the profilmic space to a filmed image—that made possible the visualization of home. But, apart from that, it is also in the post-production or the editing process that the making of what was previously homely or what was associated to home in the moment of film production was connected to the concept of impermanence combined with anxiety and fear for changes and destructions. This complex operation thus creates a home that belongs both to the past or the realm of memories as well as to the future of the realm of home envisioned.

This intricate relationship between profilmic space (in front of the camera) and the filmed images of places that also undergo post-production editing in Weerasethakul's *Cactus River* underlines the different stages of relationships between cinema, temporalities, spaces and the director's formation of home. That cinema ties together the director's past (memories of how this place has been understood, pictured, archived in relation to his memories of his childhood home, etc.), present (possible choices and decisions taken for what is happening in the filming process), and future (possibilities of editing, presenting and circulating) is undeniably paramount in Weerasethakul's outstanding style and contribution to world cinema and even to the art sphere at large.

"My Homeland that Is Unhomely": The Cases of *Ashes* (2012) *and Primitive* (2009)

At the first public screening of *Ashes* at the Cannes Film Festival in 2012, Weerasethakul asserts that this project is "like a home movie". He explained that, because of the Lomography LomoKino camera offered to him by Mubi—one of the online streaming sites that monthly rotates global art films to its users—he was able to experience the "imperfections" that analogue could bring. This practice, he emphasized, was drastically different to his usual spoiled habits, and the comfort of having the digital format available. Weerasethakul further commented in his speech that he wished everyone would shoot whatever they love as well as "whatever mistakes".[18]

The LomoKino is a vintage-inspired camera by Lomography. The film camera is advertised for its analogue 35 millimeter movie-making format. In fact, Weerasethakul highlighted this particular point, stating that, with this camera, the filming required him to roll the film like in the old days and that, for him, he could shoot only up to 30 seconds of *silent* footage per roll. The director ended up using about 100 rolls for this project and he only deployed parts of the collection for this short film. *Ashes* starts simply with a shot of someone walking a dog in a village. The environment in the setting looks familiar to that of *Blissfully Yours, Syndromes and a Century, Tropical Malady,* his art installation, *Primitive,* and many other of the director's films that were set in the provincial areas of Thailand. Because of the technicality of the camera—the specificity of the medium itself—that requires film rolling and does not support sound in film, *Ashes* gives us an appearance of stop motion, grainy colorful images and the sound of dialogue camera, rumbling motorcycle engine, dog barking, chicken crowing, that we knew were all adjusted into the film in the post-production process. The combination of filmed images that come from an analogue camera and the post-production editing of sound into the film together offer us a comprehensive image, and even a sentiment, of a daily life in a village. One thing that we could notice for sure in the first half of *Ashes* is the director's contemplative, and yet nonchalant, observation of lives that are far from a city—arguably removed, to some degree, from the complexities of political lives—and the unpretentious simplicity of what he referred to in his interview as "whatever you love, whatever mistakes".

---

[18] Revista Lumière, "Ashes Q&A Apichatpong Weerasethakul Cannes 2012". 2012. https://vimeo.com/42505347.

Fig. 2: A scene of dogwalking from *Ashes* (2012), dir. Apichatpong Weerasethakul. Courtesy of Mubi and director Apichatpong Weerasethakul.

Moreover, it is important to note that the film is not simply a commissioned film without rules and restrictions, but a film with a prescription for a specific camera—a condition that could have guided Weerasethakul's style and filmmaking practice in certain directions. In other words, for whichever topic he has at hand, the director had to also be mindful of the particularities, conditions and what the analogue LomoKino entails. In the very first part, for example, *Ashes* started off with a very mundane observation of a walk in a neighborhood, a small local pig farm and tropical plants that are familiar to his audience, especially to those who have indulged his filmography before. And yet, though all these images that I mentioned possess the qualities of verisimilitude—of being the replica or even of indexing the real world in front of Weerasethakul's camera—they always remind us that they are mediated, that they are part of the process of filmmaking and of particular technical conditions.

Given the specificity of the camera used for this film and the fact that *Ashes* is less concerned with narrative structure, the film apparently signifies the conversations about the nature of images, the ontology of cinema and the technicality of filmmaking itself. This also means that it is quite challenging and counterintuitive to try to describe details of scenes or sequences with words, especially when this type of film is quite experimental with the making of the images and less interested in

Fig. 3: The protest sign that says "No 112". From *Ashes* (2012), dir. Apichatpong Weerasethakul. Courtesy of Mubi and director Apichatpong Weerasethakul.

classical narrative cinema. However, for the purpose of argumentation, I would like to point us to a roll of celluloid that marks the change of places and locations in *Ashes*. This change of locations is very apparent not only to the natives but arguably to all audiences. It is the change from the images of the rural to the images of the city. And, in this case, with specific signs such as congested traffic, colorful caps, motorcycle services and the cardboard signs written in Thai, Weerasethakul makes it clear that he wanted to take us to Bangkok. And yet the implication of this itinerary also involves what was happening in Bangkok—a series of political crises during 2009–2012, which coincided with the years prior to the making of this film project.[19]

Despite the brevity of this city sequence, some cardboard signs with big legible fonts and political messages stand out. One of them looks more like a sign with only a number and a cross on it—signifying "No 112". This refers to section 112 of the *Lèse Majesté* law—a law that defines the crime against the monarch (or to do "wrong to the majesty" in French), and that it is "illegal to defame, insult or threaten the king, queen, heir-apparent, heir-presumptive or regent according to section 112 of the Thai Criminal Code".[20] Those who are on the progressive

---

[19] At the end of the film, the film credits give us some information about the period of time in which the film was completed—August 2012.

[20] Section 112 can be found in the Criminal Law of Thailand. Apart from the definition of the law, it specifies that those who commit this crime "shall be punished with imprisonment of three to fifteen years". "Offences

pro-democratic side argue that, because of the obvious ambiguity in the way in which the phrase "defaming, insulting and threatening" could be interpreted, this law has been instrumentalized—or, more precisely, weaponized—by the royalist party in order to silence the opposition. It is, to them, a deep fracture in the development of the human rights, freedom and equality of the Thai citizen, since it has led to many incidents of authoritarian abuses and juridical maltreatment.

For instance, during the years 2011–12, during which *Ashes* was produced, one of the most frightening and controversial convictions under the *Lèse Majesté* law was the case of "Uncle SMS", or *Ah-Kong* in Thai. Ampon Tangnoppakul was charged for anonymously sending four defaming SMS messages to the phone number of Somkiat Khrongwattansuk, personal secretary to the then prime minister of Thailand, Abhisit Vejjajiva. It only took the Criminal Court 11 months from the first day the files were submitted to them (18 January 2011) to convict Ah Kong for the crime stated in section 112. The court sentenced him to 20 years in prison (five years per SMS sent).[21] Ah Kong died in prison while serving his sentence. His trial and the sentence he received drew much serious criticism, as well as disillusionment in the institutions (such as the juridiciary) that had held together Thai politics, and led to demands for the abandonment of the *Lèse Majesté* law in Thailand and court reform. However, despite these demands, so far none of the requests of the pro-democracy supporters has been realized or adopted by the major political institutions of Thailand. And the *Lèse Majesté* law remains today as one of the sites where political violence resurfaces.[22]

In 2010, Bangkok became, once again, a central location for protesters—the Red Shirt protest—who demanded a general election after the prime minister, Abhisit Vejjajiva, was appointed after the intervention of the Constitutional Court of Thailand in 2008. The political demand of the Red Shirts was a reaction to military intervention—a 2006 coup d'état to overthrow Thaksin Shinawatra, the former

---

against the King, the Queen, the Heir-Apparent and the Regent". *Criminal Code B.E. 2499: Book I.* http://www.thailandlawonline.com/Laws/criminal-law-thailand-penal-code.html.

[21] Unfortunately, most reports of the case and of legal proceedings are in Thai. iLaw, "Judgement of Uncle SMS case". *iLaw.* https://ilaw.or.th/node/1229.

[22] Association for Thai Democracy. "ATD Official Report on the Deterioration of Freedom of Expression in Thailand". https://thaidemocracy-us.org/our-works/atd-official-report-on-the-deterioration-of-freedom-of-expression-in-thailand.

prime minister, whose populist support was generally mobilized from the "grassroots" social class outside the bourgeois sphere of Bangkok. The Red Shirt protest in 2010 was therefore an event that resulted from an accumulation of the people's angst and anger toward deeply rooted injustices at the institutional level. The fact that the Red Shirt protesters were pro-democracy, pro-election and found unfairness in the military coup d'état—a recurring part of the problems in Thai politics since the Revolution of Siam in 1932—connotes a sense of anti-institution and, therefore, inevitably incites tendencies of suppression from the part of the state and government. Former prime minister Vejjajiva—generally considered to be on the side of the "Yellow Shirt" or the anti-Thaksin movement—ordered a military crackdown on the Red Shirt protesters, starting from 9 May and ending in outrageous violence on 19 May. Official reports state that 53 people, including paramedic volunteers, died during the series of crackdown operations. Yet, only a few days later, on 23 May, the then-governor of Bangkok, Sukhumbhand Paribatra, promoted a campaign called "Bangkok Big Cleaning Day",[23] which destroyed all remaining forensic proof of the widespread violent military crackdowns. It remains one of the most injurious incidents in Thai politics—one that was often cited by pro-democratic protesters during the most recent protests in 2020–21.

Ashes may have brought up these traumatic incidents and political crises only briefly, through the director's nonchalant observation of the cardboard signs and the photographic image of the late king, Bhumibhol Aduljadej, in front of the Court of Justice. However, I argue that, despite the brevity of this city sequence, the cinematic structural shift in *Ashes*—from the mundane daily lives and the sense of homeliness in the village to a radically chaotic political unhomeliness in Bangkok—emphasizes not only the history of state violence inscribed in the bourgeois space of Bangkok but also the harsh reality of how national politics works always as a governing force that could wreck homes both in the physical sense and in the abstract sense of affect, sentiment, subjectivity and well-being. As for the national discourse, locals are often taught to appreciate Thailand for its richness in natural resources, its culture and progress derived from the sacred institutions of the monarchy and Buddhism, as well as to simultaneously aspire to achieve Bangkok's middle-class way of life. And yet, the ruptures from a long history of unresolved political turmoil not only often disrupt the way in which one makes sense of the surrounding but also disintegrate

---

[23] "Bangkok Cleaning Day—May 10". 25 May 2010. https://www.youtube.com/watch?v=DHi8RnmJSQw.

the beliefs in the sovereign of the state, politics of the nation and the claimed virtues of any institutions. Additionally, the capital city that used to be a space of hopes and dreams for better lives became a killing field of rural grassroots citizens. It became a place that shunned demands for fairness, equality and democracy.

Weerasethakul is one of the prime examples of Thai directors whose worldviews lie in these political entanglements. He comes from the generation whose early years saw the rise of totalitarian government, military intervention and right-wing conservative over-protection of the sacred institutions of Thailand, like the monarchy and Buddhism, in the wake of communism in the region. He is also a political subject who witnessed unfair treatment and violence in rural areas in contrast to the undeniably increased opportunities in the metropolitan area. Seeing the result of such political realities and confrontations between oppositions, it is often an ongoing struggle to find ways to critique and yet also to acknowledge that many injustices still remain and are often untouchable.

After the Bangkok sequence, Weerasethakul takes us to a new part of the film where he cuts back-and-forth between a black-out screen and photographic images of random people, where Weerasethakul's monologue not only transitions us to the second part of the film but also designates the theme of home and the making of home out of past memories. The director states in his monologue:

> I realized it was a dream. It's a dream within a dream. I reached out to a 2B pencil. I drew a picture on the paper, my back to the dream. I kept turning back to look at them. The large images trying to copy them... to mimic the colors. The picture I drew turned out to be my hometown [in KhonKhaen]. Buildings in my memory. From my memory, they were houses. A town that hadn't changed.

In a way, *Ashes* is driven not only by the memory of home but also by the impulse of homemaking. As we have seen throughout this chapter, I have insisted that homemaking is always a political project that involves dealing with past histories and simultaneously enforcing a vision of a radical future or a hope for change. After the monologue ends, Weerasethakul leads us to the final part of the film. It is a rather grim observation of the darkness of the night and vivid blasting light coming from explosive fireworks, and of the crowd gathering to see this spectacle of contrast. This contemplation on the dialectical play between the light of the fireworks and the darkness of the night in the background also resembles the collaborative production of *Primitive*, in

Fig. 4: The sign in Thai can be translated as following: "Stop killing the people with unjust law." Apparently, there is a "no 112" sign at the bottom. From *Ashes* (2012), dir. Apichatpong Weerasethakul. Courtesy of Mubi and director Apichatpong Weerasethakul.

which video installations of interviews with local teens from Nabua, for example, require the setting up between the brightly lit screen and the ultimately dark surrounding or backdrop.

One can also find in Weerasethakul's production of *Ashes* and his art project *Primitive* the fact that both of the projects worked closely, on the one hand, with the idea of "homeland"—the nation-state of Thailand— and, on the other hand, disrupts this continual sense of comfort of home by bring up national pasts of various incidents of state violence. Weerasethakul's essay "Memories of Nabua" recollects that "Nabua earned its nationwide reputation, when the first gun battle between the farmer communists and the totalitarian government broke out in the rice fields. As a result, Nabua was heavily occupied and controlled by the military. The torture intensified. Fear proliferated."[24] Undeniably, the political context of Thailand during 2009–12, underlined by the short city sequence in *Ashes*, also emerged from the military interventions and the totalitarian government—one that was not elected by the democratic process of the nation but was one of the various results of the 2006 coup d'état.

Lastly, let me point to one of the cardboard signs in *Ashes* which states "Stop killing Thai people with unjust law." In less than a second, the camera moves on to other signs and random lyrical images of Bangkok, including random streets and traffic congestion. Yet it is in this very brief moment when the filmed images of the sign appear on screen that unhomeliness resurfaces in the space of the director's homeland. It

---

[24] Apichatpong Weerasethakul, "The Memory of Nabua", 197.

is in these filmed images—done particularly in the analogue fashion—that the mundane life was contrasted so radically with the political turmoil concomitantly occurring in Bangkok. It is in these filmed images that, in the first half, home was remembered and, in the second part, homeland was envisioned in relation to the politics of the nation. *Ashes* brings to fore not only any streets of Bangkok—but the streets filled with protests, with historical weights and burdens, with hopes and dreams of a country without *Lèse Majesté*, military intervention and state violence. They thus become another record of the memories, wounds and injuries of the people. Most importantly, perhaps, it insists to reproduce the images of the people's attempt to envision a space that would be homely, comforting and less precarious to them.

Bibliography

"Apichatpong Weerasethakul – October Rumbles". *The Polygon*. 29 October 2020. https://thepolygon.ca/news/apichatpong-weerasethakul-october-rumbles/.

Ainslie, Mary J. and Ancuta Katarzyna. *A Complete Guide to Thai Cinema*. London. I.B. Tauris. 2018.

Association for Thai Democracy. "ATD Official Report on the Deterioration of Freedom of Expression in Thailand". Accessed 12 August 2021. https://thaidemocracy-us.org/our-works/atd-official-report-on-the-deterioration-of-freedom-of-expression-in-thailand.

"Bangkok Cleaning Day—May 10". 25 May 2010. https://www.youtube.com/watch?v=DHi8RnmJSQw.

Camia, Giovanni Marchini. "Set Diary: Apichatpong Weerasethakul's Memoria, pt. 1". *Film Comment*. 18 February 2020. https://www.filmcomment.com/blog/category/journals/set-diary-memoria/.

Chunsaengchan, Palita. "The Critique of Anti-Communist State Violence in *Uncle Boonmee Who Can Recall His Past Lives*". *Asian Cinema* 32, no. 1 (2021): 95–111. https://doi.org/10.1386/ac_00035_1.

iLaw. "Judgement of Uncle SMS case". *iLaw*. 17 October 2011. https://ilaw.or.th/node/1229.

Jeong, Seung-hoon and Jeremi Szaniawski. "Introduction". *The Global Auteur: The Politics of Authorship in 21st Century Cinema*. Ed. Seung-hoon Jeong and Jeremi Szaniawski. London. Bloomsbury Academic. 2016.

Lauzon, Claudette. *The Unmaking of Home in Contemporary Art*. Toronto. University of Toronto Press. 2017.

Linssen, Dana. "If Light Was Un/Folding, The Measure of Time". *Apichatpong Weerasethakul*. Amsterdam: Eye Filmmuseum. 2017.

Lumière, Revista. "Ashes Q&A Apichatpong Weerasethakul Cannes 2012". 2012. https://vimeo.com/42505347.

Mousley, Sheryl. "Cactus River: Apichatpong Weerasethakul Film Debuts on Walker Channel". *Walker Crosscuts*. 12 October 2012. https://walkerart.org/magazine/cactus-river-apichatpong-weerasethakul-film-debuts-on-walker-channel.

Naremore, James. *An Invention Without a Future: Essays on Cinema*. Oakland. University of California Press. 2014.

"Offences Against the King, the Queen, the Heir-Apparent and the Regent". *Criminal Code B.E. 2499: Book I*. 2021. https://www.thailandlawonline.com/laws-in-thailand/thailand-criminal-law-text-translation#penal-1.

Quandt, James, ed. *Apichatpong Weerasethakul*. Vienna. Synema. 2009.

Walker Art Center. "Cactus River (Khong Lang Nam)". 12 October 2012. https://www.youtube.com/watch?v=H5vT0T_ionU.

Sawasdee, Natthapol. "Nitadsakarn awakard hang baan nabua" ("Exhibition on Extraterritoriality of Nabua"). *Film Archive (Public Organization)*. 3 September 2019. https://www.fapot.or.th/main/information/article/view/319.

Thai Film Archive. "Today Apichatpong brought Tilda Swinton (...) to visit Thai Film Archive". *Facebook*. 30 October 2018. https://www.facebook.com/ThaiFilmArchivePage/posts/2103048203078702.

Weerasethakul, Apichatpong. "The Memory of Nabua: A Note on the *Primitive* Project" in *Apichatpong Weerasethakul*, ed. James Quandt. Vienna. Synema. 2009.

10

Between an Erased Past and an Uncertain Future
Hybrid Forms in the Films of Apichatpong Weerasethakul

Sivaranjini

> I would say that there is really no reality in cinema. To quote Manoel de Oliveira's Visita ou Memórias e Confissões, "Fiction is cinema's reality".
>
> —Apichatpong Weerasethakul[1]

The representations of reality have been an ongoing discussion in film theory and practice. The equivocation of cinema as a record or evidence of reality and as an art or representation of thoughts culminated in the evolution of two distinct filmmaking practices, labeled popularly as documentary and fiction, respectively. Since the beginning of cinema, there have been both realistic and illusionistic tendencies and explorations in the medium.

Hybrid cinema combines non-fiction elements with fiction, creating a new representation that reflects upon itself and raises doubts about the very nature of reality in film. Every film is a fiction film,[2] as the structures of representation in cinema presented and perceived are essentially "false" or unreal. Once sieved through the cinematic apparatus, everything attains the value of a spectacle. On the contrary, every film is a documentary,[3] as it records and reproduces the evidence of the culture and the people who perform within it. The hybrid film form becomes

---

[1] Susana N. Duarte, and José Bértolo, "Another kind of Primitive Dream. Interview with Apichatpong Weerasethakul", *Cinema: Journal of Philosophy and the Moving Image* 8 (2016): 135.

[2] Christian Metz, *The Imaginary Signifier: Psychoanalysis and Cinema*, trans. Celia Britton, Annwyl Williams, Ben Brewster and Alfred Guzzetti (Bloomington: Indiana University Press, 1982), 44.

[3] Bill Nichols, *Introduction to Documentary* (Bloomington: Indiana University Press, 2001), 1.

an evolutionary and experimental step to maintain a fluid, uncertain interaction between truth and falsity, escapism and hypermediacy.

The term "hybrid" becomes a homonym as it is often used in film studies to specify diasporic cultural cinema, cross-genre cinema and documentaries that incorporate fictional filmmaking practices. When looking at Apichatpong Weerasethakul's oeuvre, I use the term "hybrid" to defy the categorization of the fragmented, composite nature of his films (in both content and form) mostly dwelling into the tension between fiction and non-fiction in cinema. By enquiring into the same, I try to make parallels with the socio-geopolitical history of Thailand, particularly the northeastern part, Isan, which essentially appears as a recurring subject in his films. Weerasethakul's own transitory style between video art and cinema is influenced by regional texts, old Thai horror cinema, television, Iranian and Taiwanese films, and structural/avante-garde American films.

It is fascinating to note the etymological underpinnings[4] of the word "hybrid" in the context of Weerasethakul's films. The Latin word *hybrida* indicates an offspring from a cross-breed of various animal or plant species. *Sat Pralat*, the Thai title of his film *Tropical Malady* (2004), means a monster born to two different species, with the lead character Keng transforming to a beast in the second part. This attribute goes one step ahead in *Uncle Boonmee Who Can Recall His Past Lives* (2010) (hereafter *Uncle Boonmee*), where Boonmee's son transforms into a monkey ghost and the princess, who is one of Boonmee's past incarnations, loses her virginity to a catfish in a stream. The Greek word *hubris* (excess) indicates a form that stretches an existing system's boundaries. In cultural studies, the term "hybrid" denotes the blending of cultures in forming heterogeneous forms called third places.[5] Bangkok-based curator Gridthiya Gaweewong comments that Thai cultural identity is all about hybridization; Thai people blend other cultures and adapt them as their own.[6]

To delve deeper into the layered composition of Apichatpong films it is important to have a quick peep into the socio-political history of

---

[4] Jihoon Kim, *Between Film, Video, and the Digital Hybrid Moving Images in the Post-Media Age* (London: Bloomsbury Academic, 2016), 3.

[5] Yvonne Spielmann and Jay David Bolter, "Hybridity: Arts, Sciences, and Cultural Effects", *Leonardo* 39, no. 2 (2006): 106. Also mentioned by Kim, 2016.

[6] Gridthiya Gaweewong, "On Thai Artists and an Issue of Cultural Identity", *Apex Art*, July 2001. Mentioned in James Quandt, "Resistant to Bliss: Describing Apichatpong", in *Apichatpong Weerasethakul*, ed. James Quandt (Vienna: Synema, 2009), 16.

Thailand. Situated in the southeast Asian peninsula, Thailand, formerly Siam, shares its borders with Myanmar, Laos, Cambodia and Malaysia. With a majority Buddhist population, Thailand was never a colony of a European power, unlike many other southeast Asian countries, but was influenced by interactions with colonial powers like the British and the French and having close relations with the United States, especially during and after World War II. Many dynasties ruled over Thailand. The Siamese revolution of 1932 resulted in the constitutionalization of the monarchy. The name Siam was changed to Thailand then. In 1957 the monarchy was replaced after a military coup. Since then, military rule and democracy have alternated in Thailand.

In the 1960s and 1970s, there was a brief period of revolutionary uprisings with the support of neighboring countries (Vietnam and Laos) coupled with student movements, which were successfully suppressed by paramilitaries and state forces. In 2014 a military *junta* took over Thailand and, since then, the country has been under military rule, led by army chief turned prime minister Prayuth Chan-ocha, with a constitutional monarchy at the head.

Royalty is worshipped and the king is treated as god in Thailand. The *Lèse Majesté* laws that prohibit any insult or defamation of royalty, paired with *junta* rule, created frequent political turmoil in Thailand. The first election after the 2014 takeover happened in 2019, which was meant to transfer the power from the *junta* to an elected government, was suppressed even before the results came, and Prime Minister Prayuth retained power. Since then, there have been multiple resistance movements, especially from students across the country rising up against the autocratic powers of the monarchy and the *junta*.

Isan, the northeastern part of Thailand where Apichatpong grew up with his parents, who were medical doctors, is a constant character in most of his films. Sharing a border with Laos, the Isan region is the poorest in Thailand, geographically, socially and historically isolated from the rest of the country, and therefore discriminated against. The border between Laos and Isan was only demarcated during early twentieth-century French Indo-China colonization. Most locals still speak a dialect of Lao.[7] There was a rise in communism and anti-state movements from the mid-nineteenth century in the region, which were consistently suppressed by the military. Through his films and video works, Apichatpong traces the memory of a region whose history is consciously and conspicuously forgotten and has become a folk tale

---

[7] Chistopher J. Baker and Pasuk Phongpaichit, *A History of Thailand* (New York: Cambridge University Press, 2009), 172.

of past lives lived, haunted and passed. The ghost becomes an allegory for the transient lives of innumerable people who have been treated as invisible and non-existent by the state. The present situation and the future are not any different in Isan or Thailand; any voice of resistance and freedom is suppressed before it is heard outside.

The content of all Thai cinema was regulated from 1930 by the Film Act (B.E.2473), a system of prior censorship, which was replaced by a new film rating system by the Film and Video Act 2008. The Thai Board of Censors had demanded to cut four scenes from Apichatpong's film *Syndromes and Century* (2006), which led to him starting the "Free Thai Cinema" movement to reflect on censorship practises in Thailand. Apichatpong refused the domestic release of the film, rejecting the cuts, instead replacing the scenes with black frames to protest and inform his audience about the censorship.

The essence of a hybrid form in Apichatpong's films can be identified in the liminal zone of the narrative settings: between life and death, geopolitical border of nations, past and future, interior and exterior, primitive and modern, protagonists living on the fringes of society, like immigrants, sexual minorities, ghosts and the disabled. These interims of the narrative settings are inseparably interconnected to the form of the film, which marries the fictional to the non-fictional.

The following analysis of his films tries to elucidate the idea of hybrid cinema through three different lenses: film realism, film form and film medium. In the first section, I try to map his films against the background of realist film theories, movements and practices. In the second section, I look at the films formally and try to find patterns in their intersections to identify the correlations between his films' formal structures and their content. In the third section, I look at his experiments in reflexivity and incorporating of transmedial practises in cinema, which stretches and questions the possibilities of the medium in the light of contemporary media theories.

The Reality Effect

Apichatpong shares in multiple interviews his skepticism over the dichotomy of fact and fiction in cinema as what led him to make films that blend both. We are conscious of even the slightest shifts in our attention while watching his films; the long durational shots that make one aware of the presence and passage of cinematic time, actors staring back at us when we look at them on screen, spatial-temporal-sonic crossovers within and across multiple films.

One can observe a strong documentary quality in his films, a conscious effort to bring more life as opposed to the exuberantly fantastical Thai popular cinema. Two of his films, *Mysterious Objects at Noon* (2000) (hereafter *Mysterious Objects*) and *Mekong Hotel* (2011), in fact developed their fictional elements while conceived as documentaries. Apichatpong's first feature film, *Mysterious Object at Noon,* shot on a black-and-white 16 millimeter reversal film, has the Thai name *Dogfahr nai meu marn,* which translates as "Dogfahr in the Devil's Hand". Travelling across Thailand, the film team plays the surrealist game "exquisite corpse" ("cadavre exquis", originally invented by André Breton), where each film segment inspires and drives the next. *Mysterious Objects* opens with a cinéma vérité thirst for reality. Long shots from a fish vendor's truck prowling around the city run through the opening credits, accompanied by the microphone voices of the day's deals. Then, while the female vendor shares her disturbingly poignant story of her parents selling her to her uncle for 1700 baht, we hear the filmmaker's voice breaking the flow, suspending our indulgence of her pain, demanding from her another story, either real or fiction. What follows is the fictional recreation of a story started by the vendor about a boy in a wheelchair and his home-school teacher, Dogfahr.

Apichatpong and his crew travel across Thailand, from the north to the south (Bangkok, Chiang Rai, Chiang Mai, Phitsanulok, Khon Kaen, Panyi Island), with her story traversing the urban and rural landscapes and asking people to contribute to the narrative, transforming the rest of the film into a documentary about the making of a fiction film. As the narrative flows in the hands of different people, Dogfahr becomes an evasive entity, metamorphosing from a mysterious round object that appears one afternoon to an alien boy. In the fictional re-enactments, different women in different narrative situations play the role of Dogfahr, like two actresses playing Conchita in Luis Buñuel's *That Obscure Object of Desire* (1977). Intertitles are used between segments to separate and connect the fragmented narrative. The text is fairly straightforward, like the captions of silent era films, but very unlike them in function. They are initiated as a tool for holding the narrative together but, as we progress with the film, its very nature becomes questionable. Many found footage elements from a separate time zone, like the Asia-Pacific war, also contribute to the narrative storyline. The film seamlessly segues from the documentary segments to the fictional, so that the separation between the actors and the characters they play becomes non-existent.

A traditional Lao folk song group, Mor Lam, performs their own version of the story in one segment; in another two deaf children contribute to the story with hand gestures. *Mysterious Objects* thus presents a new contemporary genre of myth-making; ghosts, witches and similar Thai folklore elements make their way in the film through the participants, leading to the evolution of a new art form called village surrealism.[8] Surrealism, born out of its practice as an art movement, extended to the cinema in the late 1920s in Paris. James Clifford's identification of surrealist aesthetic, which values fragments, curious collections, and unexpected juxtapositions,[9] perfectly fits *Mysterious Objects*. Apichatpong thus creates a poem-object, with a heterogeneous mix of counter-realities in the same cinematic plane. David Teh calls *Mysterious Objects* "a history without dates, a map without place-names and a documentary without facts".[10] While remapping Thailand through fiction intervening people's lives, Apichatpong unmaps the geo-body of the nation, a constructed, fabricated homogeneous idea of nationhood and national identity, *khwampenthai* (Thainess),[11] to a new cartography inclusive of its marginalized communities, who are forcefully fitted into the nationalistic imagination. We also trace a soundscape of the nation—different accents (teenagers speaking the Karen language), dictions lost in translation, not just for foreign audiences but even for Thai natives. Thus, *Mysterious Objects* becomes a journey across a foreign land, seeing the unseen and listening to the voiceless.

When tracing the meeting place of ethnography and surrealism, one can draw parallels between Luis Buñuel's landmark 1933 hybrid film *Land Without Bread* and *Mysterious Objects*. *Land Without Bread* goes against the grain of ethnographic fieldwork, misleading us with an unreliable narrator's voice mimicking an objective matter-of-fact commentary on the miseries in the Las Hurdes region in Spain. The ethnographic search, expedition, a certain indifference to the subjects and the absurdity of the narrative connects *Mysterious Objects* to *Land Without Bread*. While the voice-over in *Land Without Bread* connects the dissociated fragmented images, but at the same time misleads us, it is the intertitles that does the job in *Mysterious Objects*.

---

[8] Term mentioned in Elvis Mitchell, "Film Review: From Thailand, Adventures in Collective Storytelling", *NY Times*, 2001, https://www.nytimes.com/2001/11/01/movies/film-review-from-thailand-adventures-in-collective-storytelling.html.

[9] James Clifford, "On Ethnographic Surrealism", *Comparative Studies in Society and History* 23, no. 4 (1981): 540.

[10] David Teh, "Itinerant Cinema: The Social Surrealism of Apichatpong Weerasethakul", *Third Text* 25, no. 5 (2011): 609.

[11] Thongchai Winichakul, *Siam Mapped: A History of the Geo-Body of a Nation* (Honolulu: University of Hawaii Press, 1994), 172.

BETWEEN AN ERASED PAST AND AN UNCERTAIN FUTURE   235

Apichatpong takes on the path of Jean Rouch, exchanging the objective gaze of ethnography to "shared anthropology", where the "Other" speaks of and for themselves. Rouch saw cinema as an art of the double transitioning from the real world to the imaginary world.[12] Rouch had anticipated two directions cinéma vérité would take: one being an observer of the reality when it happens and capturing an incident with the most possible closeness and the best equipment. The other is leaning towards using fiction to tell stories, but still leaving space for improvisation and chance.[13] He identifies these as two truths: the former being the documentary reporting and the latter the dramatic truth. He prefers the latter, where we do not capture life as it is but capture life as provoked by the filmmaker. *Mysterious Objects* takes the latter path where the camera intrudes on the reality to provoke a reaction to produce a form of cinematic reality rather than the filmmaker observing it as "a fly on the wall", capturing the before and after of the shifting frontiers of the real and the fictional. Ethnographic filmmaking is an iterative process for Rouch, with constant interaction and feedback from his participants. Apichatpong, as part of one of his art projects, paid homage to Rouch's *Chronicles of Summer* (1961)—a bunch of balloons were released into the sky with prepaid postcards tied to them bearing the text "Are you Happy?" A few who received the cards replied. He describes the process as a search for "collaborators with the help of nature".[14]

Apichatpong blends the actors into the environment as if the camera is invisible or captures crowds and passersby "performing" as if they are acting for the camera. One can observe the latter tendencies, particularly in the "pillow shots"[15] he employs. Consider these cutaway shots from *Cemetery of Splendour* (2015)—a line of school children crossing the road with their teachers, a hen with her chicks playing around her, a night street food vendor's conversation over the cell phone to her boyfriend about her gay work buddy, mass aerobics classes

---

[12] Jean Rouch, *Ciné-Ethnography*, trans. Steven Feld (Minneapolis: University of Minnesota Press, 2003), 185.

[13] James Blue, "Jean Rouch in Conversation with James Blue", *Film Comment* 4, no. 2 (1967): 86.

[14] Conversation with Apichatpong Weerasethakul by art curator Hans Ulrich Obrist, Locarno Film Festival, accessed from YouTube, 5 August 2020, 31:46.

[15] Term coined by film critic Noël Burch referring to Yasujiro Ozu's films. Noël Burch, *To the Distant Observer: Form and Meaning in the Japanese Cinema*, ed. Annette Michelson (Berkeley: University of California Press, 1979).

in the park, shopping malls, homeless people sleeping under a street lamp—such chance encounter with reality are shown in vivid detail and playful curiosity in cinema.

We also see detailed documentation of various vocations—an elaborate ice-cutting process in *Tropical Malady*, boxing matches during a local fair and a quotidian fragment from the life of elephant trainers in *Mysterious Objects*, the extended medical diagnostic discussions in *Syndromes and a Century* (2006), factory scenes in *Blissfully Yours* (2002), film sets in *Worldly Desires* (2005)—to name just a few. What we witness here is a reminiscence of neorealist ideas; extras whose otherwise insignificant lives become more than mere background of the film's constructed inner landscape. Such brief yet memorable invasions to mundane lives balance out the overarching presence of the lead actors. That way, every actor shares a democratic presence on the screen, being an "extra" in the cinematography of the film's being, an antithesis to heroes and their journeys.

In his experiments with cinematic realism, Weerasethakul acknowledges the influences of Iranian new cinema, particularly films of Abbas Kiarostami and Mohsen Makhmalbaf. The many subjectivities of reality and a lack of absolute truth form a philosophical realm in which these filmmakers place their films. Makhmalbafs' "truth" as espoused by Rumi's broken mirror[16] runs parallel to Apichatpong's subjective construction of real worlds in Buddhist beliefs.

There are noticeable cross-references between different films and video works of Apichatpong, almost as if his characters and narratives live a parallel life in an alternate cinematic universe—a bunch of school children sharing the story about a tiger witch in the coda sequence of *Mysterious Objects* finds its way into *Tropical Malady*, a hospital scene with Dogfahr and her father in *Mysterious Objects* repeats in *Blissfully Yours* with the same doctor. Hospitals and strange ailments, jungles, men in military uniforms, monks, obsession with skin lotions and creams, picnics to the pastoral are some of the recurring themes in his films that evoke déjà vu. Characters carrying their names and physical form also recur from film to film; Jenjira Pongpas appears as Jen in many films, in *Blissfully Yours* the girl talks of a soldier named Keng who

---

[16] "Rumi, who is one of the greatest Persian poets, said that the truth was a mirror in the hands of God. It fell and broke into pieces. Everybody took a piece of it, and they looked at it and thought they had the truth": Mohsen Makhmalbaf in *Makhmalbaf's Broken Mirror: the Socio-Political Significance of Modern Iranian Cinema*, ed. Lloyd Ridgeon (Durham: University of Durham, Centre for Middle Eastern and Islamic Studies, 2000), 14.

would appear in a later film *Tropical Malady*, Tong (Sakda Kaewbuadee) from *Tropical Malady* reappears in *Uncle Boonmee*.

Apichatpong is conscious of his power and privilege as a filmmaker who struggles to grapple with his own gaze on his film subjects as an outsider.[17] He overcomes it by blending with his crew—they spend time together, share meals and get to know each other as people. That is when his openness to contributions from his crew and authorial humility benefits him. In addition to the feature-length works, there are other short films like *Malee and the Boy* (1999), where he follows a ten-year-old boy who roams around Bangkok capturing sounds in a recorder. This aspect of authorial openness can be seen in the way he credits himself in the films *Mysterious Objects*, *Blissfully Yours* and *Tropical Malady*, not as a director but as someone who conceived the idea.

Filmmaking can thus be looked at as a collective lucid dreaming activity in the context of Apichatpong's films. Cinema being a fluid medium (light, movement, acting), filmmaking becomes a delicate act, like conducting an orchestra.[18] Working mostly with non-actors in his films, these practices have made them relax and bring their own life elements to the cinema, where life and cinema share instances from each other. Apichatpong is in constant search for his actors in public places like bars and restaurants, observing the mannerisms and gestures of people who have the traits of his characters. Sometimes, it is the other way: adapting the script to accommodate the actor's characteristics (Orn in *Blissfully Yours*, and Tong in *Tropical Malady*)[19].

Quite often the life stories of his actors find their way into the narrative: Jenjira Pongpas, Apichatpong's longtime collaborator, appears as a namesake character Jen in many films—sharing her own life stories over time. Even after her legs were crippled following a major accident, she continued her presence in his films with crutches. In *Cemetery of Splendour*, her American husband, the story of them meeting over the internet and their recent marriage slips in between conversations and scenes. Similarly, in the film *Mekong Hotel* we see her narrating to her daughter her childhood memories with her father, who was from Lao, about the political conflicts of the Isan region in the 1960s and 1970s.

---

[17] Lawrence Chua, "Apichatpong Weerasethakul", *Bomb* 114 (2010): 47.
[18] "I really try to control, or better, to conduct the elements of a given setting, as if it were an orchestra": Duarte and Bértolo, 2016, 133.
[19] Quandt, 2009, 17.

The element of chance, what Rouch calls "grace",[20] plays a huge role in Apichatpong's films, where sudden serendipitous moments, which could never be scripted, rehearsed and performed, permeate the filmic setting. Noel Burch connects this to Heisenberg's uncertainty principle, where the filmmaker, despite whatever control he has on the profilmic, should embrace the tension between the camera and the irretrievably alien life that it is trying to capture.[21] Hence, cinema becomes an unforeseeable aleatory, one in which we experience a virgin state of events, a phenomena, life that is untouched by human intervention, an art that gets richer with human absence rather than presence.[22]

Fragmentation and Alienation of Pleasure

Narrative intransitivity is by far the most commonly used reflexive technique in modernist films. Peter Wollen identifies this as a significant feature of counter cinema, along with alienation, unpleasure, multiple diegesis and foregrounding.[23] By interrupting the narrative flow the spectators are forced to reconcentrate and refocus their attention, disrupting the emotional spell cast on them. Apichatpong often follows a fragmented narrative structure in his films—quite often dyadic; *Blissfully Yours, Tropical Malady, Syndromes and a Century.* Even the title credits appear at conventionally odd places in these films to demarcate the boundaries of the segments. In *Blissfully Yours*, the credits appear at 41 minutes into the film, over a car journey and the landscape changing from urban to pastoral. *Tropical Malady* has two credit sequences, one at nine minutes from the beginning of the film and the second at 58 minutes, almost at the halfway point of the film, with the opening of the new segment. In *Syndromes and a Century*, although there are no evident demarcations between the sections, towards 51 minutes we witness an abrupt shift. The setting, lighting and appearances of actors

---

[20] "We must have luck; we must have what I call 'grace.' And grace is not something learned; it arrives all of a sudden, it works": Jean Rouch and Enrico Fulchignoni, "Cine-anthropology", in Rouch, 2003, 147.

[21] Noël Burch, *Theory of Film Practice* (New Jersey: Princeton University Press, 1981), 121.

[22] "All the arts are based on the presence of man, only photography derives an advantage from his absence": Andre Bazin, "The Ontology of the Photographic Image", in *What is Cinema?* Vol. 1 (London: University of California Press, 1967), 13.

[23] Peter Wollen, "Godard and Counter Cinema", in *European Film Studies Reader* (London, New York: Routledge, 2002), 75–82.

BETWEEN AN ERASED PAST AND AN UNCERTAIN FUTURE 239

are different in both segments, signifying a change in time from past to present. Similarly, scenes and actions of the first part are repeated with the same actors, but with changes in the way they are seated or the camera is positioned—like axis jumps and pace of editing. It is natural for us to make parallels between the past and present in the two segments—mirroring, repetition and contrast.

Uncle Boonme Who Can Recall His Past Lives follows more of an episodic structure—the film is divided into six different fragments, each made from a different film reel, following a different style, setting, lighting and acting. The film traces a history of Thai visual culture by taking different stylistic inspirations from early Thai cinema, Thai television dramas and horror movies. This heterogeneity and varying influences contribute to the fragmented structure of the film.

Jihoon Kim calls these narrative divides interstices,[24] which breaks the spatial temporal continuity of the films, and compares it to two parallel screen video projections in a gallery. The perception of passage of time in cinema projected in a movie hall and a video watched in a gallery space become very different experiences. Time is accumulated linearly in cinema, but it forms a circular loop in video art. Apichatpong often explores his video installations as primary sketches for his feature films, sometimes parts of it finding presence in the other.

Apart from these visible separations and fragmentations, there are certain subtle narrative disjunctures that play a huge role in Apichatpong's films; certain individual sequences carry more emotional weight and strength than a conventional coherent linear narrative. Identification with the characters does not happen in a linear series of building the belief through events in his films, rather a single slice of life—a shot, a scene or a gesture. We are left often wanting to know a little more of his characters—one experiences a familiar strangeness with them. They are often unpredictable, drifting from what we attribute them, to behaving exactly like the narrative.

In *Tropical Malady*, set in a small town in Thailand, a slow, relaxed romance develops in the first part of the film between Keng (Banlop Lomnoi), a patrol officer on duty, and a native boy Tong (Sakda Kaewbuadee). But Apichatpong never leaves us to savor the beauty of the two of them being in love. The second part starts with a new credit sequence and unveils a shamanistic ghost tale of a soldier's expeditions in the woods searching for a tiger's spirit, played by the same two actors. The gaze is never one-sided in *Tropical Malady*, between the characters or between us, the spectators, and the characters. While

[24] Kim, 2010, 161.

we take pleasure in looking at the men falling in love, they look right back at us through the camera, making us aware that we are also being looked at, thus killing the onlooking voyeur in us. We do not see them exchanging gazes in a classical action–reaction shot; rather we see them looking at us instead. These self-reflexive strategies are another way of stifling identification with the narrative and characters. Identification with the characters would mean a complete or partial removal of one's self and identity as a viewer. As an effort to break this, Wollen brings in the alienation effect (*verfremdungseffekt*), popularized by Bertolt Brecht in theatre, inspired from the Russian formalist concept of *ostranenie* (estrangement). Brecht defines the alienation effect as "attempts to act in such a manner that the spectator is prevented from finding his way into the characters. Acceptance or rejection of the characters' words is thus placed in the conscious realm, not, as hitherto, in the spectator's subconscious".[25]

Early French impressionist filmmakers used the term *photogenie* to imply the power of cinema to transform the mundane to the magical by defamiliarizing the familiar. *Photogenie* makes us look at ordinary things in an extraordinary manner. The French alluded to defamiliarization as a medium-specific essence of cinema, distinguishing it from photography's realness and authenticity. Defamiliarization was employed in early French films through certain techniques–mostly a playful visual effect created within or outside the camera or in an unfamiliar way of looking at a familiar object or instance. With the often-used static camera long take style in his films, Apichatpong draws us to invest in the film while also distancing us from it by making us aware of the passage of time and the realization that we are watching a film. One is drawn into a blissful languor, a hypnotic state of passive awareness. Apichatpong so appreciates the audience falling asleep watching his films that he created an installation called *SLEEPCINEMAHOTEL*—guests were invited to sleep and rest with images projected on screen.[26]

Apichatpong's cinema has one foot in Bazinian realism, acknowledging and embracing cinema's indexical virtues being a photographic record, and the other in the phantasmagorical absurdities of illusion and dream. In the most casual way, he presents the most absurd objects—the dead wife of Boonmee gradually appears as an apparition during a dinner table conversation, pretty much at the beginning of

---

[25] Bertolt Brecht, "On Chinese Acting", *Tulane Drama Review* 6, no. 1 (1961): 130.

[26] International Film Festival of Rotterdam (IFFR), "SLEEPCINEMAHOTEL", 2018, www.iffr.com. https://iffr.com/en/2018/films/sleepcinemahotel.

the film *Uncle Boonmee*, followed by their disappeared son returning home to the same scene as a monkey ghost. Similar unceremonious entrances occur in *Cemetery of Splendour*, when two goddesses appear casually as young women in front of Jen dressed in fashionable modern outfits. While presenting such exotic eastern fantastical objects—gods and ghosts—Apichatpong consciously disenchants the viewer from the stereotypical oriental pleasures. Thailand being a tourist haven, a place imagined for visual and erotic pleasures, his films consciously break the Western gaze to present an alternative. But he is not subscribing either to the alternate exotic trope of the "uncivilized" and "beastly" rural in oriental cinema—rather he portrays filmic truth as a lived experience of a few insignificant people, their beliefs and dreams. May Ingawanij calls these instances "performative realism" as opposed to the fantasy genre, where the characters respond readily to the marvel of the lifeworlds they inhabit without expecting a rational explanation for it.[27]

Ingawanij also associates with the films of Apichatpong the Thai word *jing*, which means to express the inexpressible or difficult truths playfully.[28] In *Cemetery of Splendour,* which is the most direct narrative film of Apichatpong, a playful switch happens almost halfway into the film. Itt, the soldier with a weird sleeping sickness, and his caretaker Jen, spend an afternoon near the lakeside park, when Itt falls asleep during their conversation. What follows is an uncanny sequence of a group of young men and women sitting on multiple benches near that lakeside park, shifts seating positions like a musical chair but in a more synchronized, choreographed manner—like the winding of an instrument that makes music with movements. This performance leads to the subsequent opening of a beguiling portal; one where Jen and the medium Keng, to whom the soldier Itt's soul is now transmigrated, interacts. Itt-as-Keng takes Jen on a journey from the real world of the park to a fantastical royal palace, which is never seen on screen by us or Jen, but is described through words and made felt through gestures. Keng-as-Itt paints the picture of the palace in eerie detail; her voice takes us for a walk into the historical pasts of the land through Itt's unconscious mind. While the visual stays with Jen, who is observing the sculptures installed in the park, orchids, proverb boards and flood

---

[27] May A. Ingawanij, "Animism and the Performative Realist Cinema of Apichatpong Weerasethakul", in *Screening Nature: Cinema Beyond the Human*, ed. Anat Pick and Guinevere Narraway (New York: Berghahn Books, 2013), 97.

[28] May A. Ingawanij, "'Playing for Real' On Apichatpong Weerasethakul's video Haunted Houses", in *Fiction Exhibition Catalogue* (Future Perfect, 2013).

marks on trees. Jen shares her memories of the political past of the region—one of the sculptures reminds her of the where shelter she stayed during the bombing of Laos. As both characters break their connections occasionally from their own worlds to step into others, we are thrown to question the very nature of real and imaginary. By the end of this sequence, Jen, like us, doubts if it was all a dream, while Keng metamorphoses to Itt completely—we believe she is him, her gestures, smile all start looking like him. Jen opens her eyes wide and the portal closes with a similar shift in the movements of people on park benches.

Film becomes solely a mnemonic medium in Apichatpong; even the sound design goes against the norms we are accustomed to in cinemas. The dominance of natural/environmental sounds, the soundscape of the jungle—crickets, cicadas, electronic hums over voices of characters in *Uncle Boonmee*—encourages a sensorial and embodied engagement with the film.[29] The sound–image dissociation also helps in spatial delineation within and between the scenes; the music track that overflows the line of action in *Mekong Hotel*, the conversations placed over tracking in shots of landscapes in *Syndromes and Century*, the non-diegetic radio commentary in *Mysterious Objects*.

Cinema goes beyond mere storytelling and emancipation of a manipulative narrative flow. Found stories find their way with the organic flow of life. They appear in no order and not following the cause and effect of events. By the fragmented nature in his films, we dissociate each time from the wholeness of the plot, hence democratizing the narrative from falling into an authoritarian structure.

Material, Medium and Meta Cinema

> Documentary? Fiction? Halfway through this film, there's a bridge [...]. Without wishing to sound like Confucius, I would say that from either one of the riverbanks, the bridge unites, the other is perfectly visible. And the river is always the same.
>
> —Miguel Gomes[30]

---

[29] Philippa Lovatt, "'Every Drop of My Blood Sings Our Song. There Can You Hear It?': Haptic Sound and Embodied Memory in the Films of Apichatpong Weerasethakul", in *The New Soundtrack 3.1* (Edinburgh: Edinburgh University Press, 2013), 61–79.

[30] Miguel Gomes' description in his director's note for *Our Beloved Month of August* (2008).

The Mekong river, the transboundary river, the bridge between Lao and Thailand, symbolizes the fluidity and the material presence of Apichatpong's cinematic genre that blends fact and fiction, presenting an exciting discourse on self-reflexivity and boundaries between cinema and consciousness. *Luminous People* (2007), a short film set on a boat running against wind on the Mekong river, has a group of people in it performing a ritual for the dead, casting the ashes off the stream, and throwing flowers as they pass the Thai–Lao friendship bridge. The villagers of Nong Khai who have participated in the film recreated the fake ceremony and their voiceovers, responses, songs have been added to the film's soundscape. The swinging boat carries the fleeting memories of the living and the dead passing across the border zone.

Apichatpong returns to the river with another film *Mekong Hotel* (2012), set during the 2011 floods in Thailand at a hotel on the shores of the river, with his ensemble actors Jenjira Pongpas, her daughter and Sakda Kaewbuadee. It unfolds as a rehearsal for an imaginary film, an unfulfilled project of Apichatpong called *Ecstasy Garden. Mekong Hotel* is a self-conscious horror film; it portrays the interactions between a mother, a daughter, and a man around a cannibal Pob ghost, who transmigrates to all of their bodies at least once in the film. *Mekong Hotel* is also an experiment with extra diegetic sounds where an unedited recording of a rehearsal session with classical guitarist Chai Bhatana plays over the entire film without any distinction or connection to the image, over the dialogues, voices, ambient sound.

A boat across the river and a hotel both form transitory zones, temporarily occupied between journeys from place to place. These deliberate choices to foreground the process of filmmaking become another recurring device in his films. Actors read from the scripts, break from character and look directly into the camera in *Mekong Hotel*. Even in the fictional sequences in *Mysterious Objects*, Apichatpong and the technical crew are seen appearing in front of the camera interacting with actors. We see glimpses from quick break sessions in between the filming process. The boom mic hangs visibly in frame in the last sequence of interaction with school children; thus, the process also becomes a part of the film. Some physically damaged, technically imperfect footage, which would otherwise be removed during the edit, is also included in the final version of the film.

Worldly Desires (2005) is another experimental film about the making of another film. A film crew in a jungle is seen shooting a love story with a recurring song shot at night; the technical equipment—lights, light stands, camera, the crew—are all visible to us. The display grid lines as seen through the viewfinder of a camera, takes and retakes of the same scenes elucidate the profilmic procedural details of the film production.

The influences of structural/materialist films can be observed in these tendencies, where the form and content of the medium becomes inseparably blended as one. Every film becomes a record of its own making.[31] Apart from the rejection of narrative manipulation and meaning, it is also a play on the material aspects of cinema: the physical material—the shifting choices with film and digital in video works and films, the fleeting, disintegrating images from the hand-cranked film *Ashes*; but also the dialectical materialism—film as a constant interaction between two opposing terms, between the materiality and the reality represented in the film. In some sense, his films embrace the medium-specific limitations of the cinema, light and the flatness of the screened surface, grain and texture of film, repetition and duration of time. But transmedial practices which stretch and question the possibilities of the cinematic medium are also incorporated by him— text and illustrations coming on screen over the scenes in *Blissfully Yours*, paintings in *Tropical Malady*. James Quandt identifies his work as a Buddhist version of *Gesamtkunstwerk*, total work of art.[32] The use of visual effects in many of his films can be seen as a remediation maintaining the multiplicities of text, image, sound, and movement in the cinematic medium.[33] Ingawanij refers to these as a "catalogue of references, citations and allusions ... a diverse array of preexisting media, texts, myths, stories, rituals and other communicative practices".[34]

The freeze frames in *Uncle Boonmee* remediate the photographic immediacy of automatic reproduction in film. It refers back to its parent project, *Primitive* (2009), an installation consisting of seven short, intersecting art pieces. *Primitive* is set in the Nabua region of northeastern Thailand, which was occupied by the Thai army between the 1960s and the 1980s to repress the communists, which led to many episodes of violent abuses and subsequent deaths. Many villagers, mostly men, took refuge in the forest. Apichatpong worked with the teenage boys, from the communist farmer families, to develop the video works, where they wore military clothes and played soldiers, and constructed a spaceship to the future. In *Uncle Boonmee*, Apichatpong

[31] Peter Gidal, "Theory and Definition of Structural/Materialist Film", in *Structural Film Anthology* (London: British Film School (BFI), 1976), 1.

[32] Quandt, 2009, 19.

[33] Jay D. Bolter and Richard Grusin, *Remediation: Understanding New Media* (New York: MIT Press, 2000).

[34] Ingawanij, "Animism and the Performative Realist Cinema of Apichatpong Weerasethakul", 2013, 93.

picks ten stills from the videos of *Primitive* to form a sequence. Boonmee awaits his death inside a cave, his vision slowly fades and the photoplay begins alone with his voiceover about a time machine taking the past people to the future. The staged photographs thus evoke the past and future at the same time; the authenticity of the photographic image to replace the erased memories of collective trauma of the people of Nabua and as a transitory medium to share the anxieties and speculations of an uncertain future of both cinema and Thailand. "I feel hope for cinema, but at the same time, I feel hopeless for the country." Apichatpong talks of *Cemetery of Splendour* as the last of his feature films to be shot in Thailand.[35]

Cinema returns to its roots in Apichatpong Weerasethakul's films, not just to the immediate history of Thai cinema or to the Lumières', but to its most primitive, an embryonic cave. The womb of visual arts, photography and cinema—from cave paintings to Plato's allegory of the cave, shadows cast on the cave wall questioning our perception of reality.[36]

A flaming football burns the projected screen on the ground in Nabua,[37] but cinema never succumbs or surrenders to Death; Life flows outside the screen, light emanates from our bodies. Histories—both personal and collective repeat, recur and reloop over time. The film material reincarnates to its new form; to the numeric code of digital. Even after the characters leave a scene, their doubles occupy the screen space.[38]

---

[35] C.J. Prince, "Apichatpong Weerasethakul Talks 'Cemetery of Splendour'", *Way Too Indie*, 9 March 2016, http://waytooindie.com/interview/apichatpong-weerasethakul-on-cemetery-of-splendor/.

[36] Susan Sontag, *On Photography* (London: Penguin Modern Classics, 1977), 3.

[37] Shot from "Phantoms of Nabua", part of *Primitive* (2010) installation.

[38] Reference to the coda sequence of the film *Uncle Boonmee Who Can Recall His Past Lives*.

Bibliography

Baker, Chistopher J. and Pasuk Phongpaichit. *A History of Thailand*. New York. Cambridge University Press. 2009.

Bazin, Andre. *What is Cinema?* Vol. 1. London. University of California Press. 1967.

Blue, James. "Jean Rouch in Conversation with James Blue". *Film Comment* 4, no. 2 (1967): 86.

Bolter, Jay D. and Richard Grusin. *Remediation: Understanding New Media*. New York. MIT Press. 2000.

Brecht, Bertolt. "On Chinese Acting". *Tulane Drama Review* 6, no. 1 (1961): 130–136.

Burch, Noël. *To the Distant Observer: Form and Meaning in the Japanese Cinema*. Ed. Annette Michelson. Berkeley. University of California Press. 1979.

Burch, Noël. *Theory of Film Practice*. New Jersey. Princeton University Press. 1981.

Chua, Lawrence. "Apichatpong Weerasethakul". *Bomb* 114 (Winter 2010): 40–48.

Chuang, Una. "Crossing over Horror: Reincarnation and Transformation in Apichatpong Weerasethakul's 'Primitive'". *Women's Studies Quarterly* 40, no. 1–2 (2012): 211–222.

Clifford, James. "On Ethnographic Surrealism". *Comparative Studies in Society and History* 23, no. 4 (1981): 539–564.

Duarte, Susana N. and José Bértolo. "Another Kind of Primitive Dream. Interview With Apichatpong Weerasethakul". *Cinema: Journal of Philosophy and the Moving Image* 8 (2016): 132–137.

Gidal, Peter. "Theory and Definition of Strcutural/Materialist Film". In *Structural Film Anthology*. London. British Film School (BFI). 1976.

Ingawanij, May A. "Animism and the Performative Realist Cinema of Apichatpong Weerasethakul". In *Screening Nature: Cinema Beyond the Human*. Ed. Anat Pick and Guinevere Narrawa. New York. Berghahn Books. 2013. 91–109.

Ingawanij, May A. "'Playing for Real' On Apichatpong Weerasethakul's Video Haunted Houses". In *Fiction Exhibition Catalogue*. Future Perfect. 2013.

International Film Festival of Rotterdam (IFFR). "SLEEPCINEMAHOTEL". 2018. www.iffr.com. https://iffr.com/en/2018/films/sleepcinemahotel.

Kim, Jihoon. "Between Auditorium and Gallery: Perception in Apichatpong Weerasethakul's Films and Installations". In *Global Art Cinema: New Theories and Histories*. Ed. Rosalind Galt and Karl Schoonover. Oxford. Oxford University Press. 2010. 125–141.

Kim, Jihoon. "Learning About Time: An Interview with Apichatpong Weerasethakul". *Film Quarterly* 64, no. 4 (2011): 48–52.

Lovatt, Philippa. "'Every Drop of My Blood Sings Our Song. There Can You Hear It?': Haptic Sound and Embodied Memory in the Films of Apichatpong Weerasethakul". In *The New Soundtrack 3.1*. Edinburgh. Edinburgh University Press. 2013. 61–79.

Metz, Christian. *The Imaginary Signifier*. N.p. Screen. 1975.

Metz, Christian. *The Imaginary Signifier: Psychoanalysis and Cinema*. London. MacMillan. 1982.

Mitchell, Elvis. "Film Review: From Thailand, Adventures In Collective Storytelling". *NY Times*. 2001. https://www.nytimes.com/2001/11/01/movies/film-review-from-thailand-adventures-in-collective-story-telling.html.

Nichols, Bill. *Introduction to Documentary*. Bloomington. Indiana University Press. 2001.

Prince, C.J. "Apichatpong Weerasethakul Talks 'Cemetery of Splendour'". *Way Too Indie*. 9 March 2016. http://waytooindie.com/interview/apichatpong-weerasethakul-on-cemetery-of-splendor/.

Quandt, James. "Resistant to Bliss: Describing Apichatpong". In *Apichatpong Weerasethakul*. Ed. James Quandt. Vienna. Synema. 2009. 13–30.

Ridgeon, Lloyd. *Makhmalbaf's Broken Mirror: The Socio-Political Significance of Modern Iranian Cinema*. Durham. University of Durham, Centre for Middle Eastern and Islamic Studies. 2000.

Rouch, Jean. *Cine-ethnography*. Minneapolis. University of Minnesota Press. 2003.

Sontag, Susan. *On Photography*. London. Penguin Modern Classics. 1977.

Spielmann, Yvonne and Jay David Bolter. "Hybridity: Arts, Sciences, and Cultural Effects". *Leonardo* 39, no. 2 (2006): 106.

Teh, David. "Itinerant Cinema: The Social Surrealism of Apichatpong Weerasethakul". *Third Text* 25, no. 5 (2011): 595–609.

Winichakul, Thongchai. *Siam Mapped: A History of the Geo-Body of a Nation*. Honolulu. University of Hawaii Press. 1994.

Wollen, Peter. "Godard and Counter Cinema". In *European Film Studies Reader*. London; New York. Routledge. 2002.

11

Post-Interstitial Authorship in Apichatpong Weerasethakul's Cinema

Anchalee Chaiworaporn

Typically, they are educated or work abroad temporarily, acquiring practical savvy and developing international contacts. Their films are, in most cases, financed internationally. They regularly spend extended periods abroad, but then return to work at home. They are globetrotting to fundraise and for festivals, yet they see advantages in shooting within their domestic environment and opt to stay in the region for the most intense periods of their work.

—Dina Iordanova[1]

Dina Iordanova's assertion about Asian filmmakers and their contemporary temporary "artistic migration"[2] becomes one of the characteristics that have been seen in the works of many global art cinema-makers all over the world, including Apichatpong Weerasethakul. Arguably, this changing paradigm of migration and movement which appear in temporaries, rather than in permanence, also affect the authorship of many border-crossing directors' works. Under a trait of interstitial mode of production—as addressed by Hamid Naficy—they might not continue to enunciate the traditional politics of diaspora or identity crisis seen in the work of earlier filmmakers. Apichatpong is also one of these changing auteurs whose transnational film practices enable him to acquire various supports so that he can maintain his avant-garde styles in his works. Nevertheless, it also does not mean that all of them will ignore tackling the social issues surrounding their filmmaking

---

[1] Dina Iordanova, "East Asia and Film Festivals: Transnational Clusters for Creativity and Commerce", in *Film Festival Yearbook 3: Film Festivals and East Asia,* ed. Dina Iordanova and Ruby Cheung (St Andrews: St Andrews Film Studies, 2011), 22.

[2] Iordanova, 2011, 21.

careers. Some of them have their own social integration in ways that might be different from one another. This chapter tries to explore the contemporary portrayal of global film finance and its effect on the construction of cinematic authorship in Apichatpong's works, in which I prefer to define it as "(post)-interstitial" authorship. In this study, I propose two dimensions of Apichatpong's "(post)-interstitial" mode of production. The first part will explore the characteristics of local and global film financing surrounding Apichatpong's filmmaking trajectories in order to see how the interstitial mode of production is characterized nowadays, especially in relation to global arts cinema. In the final part, the hybrid identity and aesthetics that have been accentuated in Apichatpong's cinema will be analyzed by using both textual and contextual methods. The interviews of Apichatpong and his teacher, existing reviews of the director's works, as well as my own analysis/reflection—will be integrated. Contexts and texts permeate each other, in order to challenge the debates over the changing paradigm of interstitial cinema that can be either intentionally constructed by the arguments of structuralists or deconstructed by poststructuralists. For me, the interstitial mode of production has still been adopted by many filmmakers around the world, but the works might be changed, exemplified from the study of Apichatpong's cinema.

Apichatpong's Interstitial Mode of Film Production

Writing in 2001, Hamid Naficy defines the term "interstitial" mode of production as one of the two categories of "accented cinema"[3]— which is considered as the alternative filmmaking practices adopted by exilic and diasporic filmmakers. For Naficy, the mode of cinematic production is closely associated with the mode of production in society in the sense that it is influenced and remodelled by the mode of social production.[4] In the same way as the mode of social production, it manifests a relationship between the forces and social relations of production. As a result, alternative approaches and imaginations still arise from "many cracks, tensions, and contradictions" that erupt

[3] The other group is collective mode of production which refers to the works that are collectively made by a group of filmmakers or organizations. The concept does not account only the collaborative productions of the films, but also their collective reception. Hamid Naficy, *An Accented Cinema: Exilic and Diasporic Filmmaking* (New Jersey: Princeton University Press, 2001), 43, 63.

[4] Naficy, 2001, 40–42.

from the centralization of the global economic and media powers controlled by a few hands. Nevertheless, many new forms of "accented cinema", such as the "author-based cinema"—in which Naficy borrows Red Stoneman's concept in clarifying the cinema that was "artisanal in scale, in intention, and in mode of production"[5]—the "black British" films and France's *"beur* cinema" are some of the alternative options of postindustrial works. Accented cinema is not situated only on the marginalized side of the industry and society, but also, as Naficy puts it, constructed in a capital of "mixed economy"—here referring to a variety of "market forces within media industries", incorporating "personal, private, public, and philanthropic funding resources; and ethnic and exilic economies".[6] In short, they are "rhizomatically interlinked" with independent, non-profit, political, and ethnoreligious organizations. It characterizes "small-scale, viewer-oriented technologies of production and consumption", "decentred", "schizophrenic", "ephemeral", minor, "interstitial", "multifunctional". In other words, it is "a cinema of alterity", which is also seen in both of Apichatpong's filmmaking process and cinematic endeavor. In terms of production, we can see that he has chosen to work completely outside the Thai film industry by connecting with all possible funding agencies around the world— both the mainstream and alternative, government and nongovernment, public and private agencies. His movies can be considered as "minor" and "decentred" or as *the international art cinema* type—one of many kinds of "small cinemas" that are categorized as some of the elements of Thai cinema by the criteria of geography and its reception. They are divided into urban cinema, provincial cinema, special interest cinema, and international art cinema—in contrast to global cinema, Asian regional cinema, mass cinema.[7] International art cinema refers to the films that are shown everywhere around the world but limited to a small group of audience. In terms of aesthetics, his works embraces the other kinds of cultures that are blended by both high and low, as well as Eastern and Western origins.

In the same way as Naficy's definition of "interstitial", Apichatpong's works are not fixed only on the marginal elements. To be interstitial, for Naficy, is to "operate both within and astride the cracks of the

---

[5] Naficy, 2001, 42.
[6] Naficy, 2001, 43–46.
[7] See more details in Anchalee Chaiworaporn, "Border-crossings and the Cinemas of Thai Arthouse Directors", Ph.D. diss., University of Southampton, 2022, 44–49.

system, benefiting from its contradictions, anomalies, and heteroge-neity".[8] It also means being "located at the intersection of the local and the global, mediating between the two contrary categories—the so-called 'subalternity' and 'superalternity'" (emphasis original). These forces still exist today, but I argue contemporary modes of film practice move into the paradigm of decentralization and fragmentation. The rise of independent filmmakers around the world, including southeast Asia, in the last two decades can be cited as some of the alternative movements that have emerged in opposition to the dominance of generic cinema both at home—popular genre films—and the world—the Hollywood products. This mode of film practices is also taken by several global art filmmakers around the world, including Apichatpong. In his two decade-plus filmmaking journey, he has mobilized several kinds of "interstitial" practices to finance his movies—ranging from a "homemade" filmmaking style, Wikanda Phromkhuntong's[9] theory of emotional capital and Bourdieu's social capital, Anne Jäckel's "variegated film industries",[10] and a combination of visual arts background, to construct a "democratic art"[11] network that allows him to maintain his hybrid avant-garde style, mixing contrasting artistic styles, but that might not adhere to the diasporic representation or identity crisis.

We start with what the director calls "home-made" filmmaking style, referring to the working practices where everyone pitched in and joined together like a family.[12] Apichatpong used this mode of practice during the shooting of his feature *Mysterious Object at Noon* (*Dokfa Nai Mueman*, 2000)—a documentary on Thai lives in four regions of the country. As a young film graduate who wanted to make his first feature-length documentary outside the studio-based industry at a time when there were only a few full independent filmmakers in Thailand, Apichatpong tried all possible ways to raise funds and cut technical costs. All of his film crew were volunteers or were recommended by

---

[8] Naficy, 2011, 46.
[9] Wikanda Phromkhuntong, "The East Asian Auteur Phenomenon: Context, Discourse and Agency Surrounding the Transnational Reputations of Apichatpong Weerasethakul, Kim Ki-duk and Wong Kar-wai", Ph.D. diss., Aberystwyth University, 2017, 41.
[10] Anne Jäckel, *European Film Industries* (London: British Film Institute, 2003), 25.
[11] Daren C. Brabham, *Crowdsourcing* (New York: MIT Press, 2013), 39, https://ieeexplore-ieee-org.soton.idm.oclc.org/servlet/opac?bknumber=6517605.
[12] Apichatpong Weerasethakul, "Introduction to the Film by Its Director", *Blissfully Yours (Sud Sanehha)*, directed by Apichatpong Weerasethakul (London: Second Run, 2006), DVD.

someone with a clear declaration that no payment would be given.[13] The director had doubted that it would be possible to bring back that kind of on-set atmosphere to the contemporary mode of filmmaking. Many of them had just graduated, had little experience of making movies, and usually took responsibility for more than one job. The two producers—Gridthiya Gaweewong and Mingmongkol Sonakul—were fellow friends. Financial support came from several non-cinema organizations like the US-based James Nelson Foundation, Bangkok-branched Toshiba, and Fuji Film, before the International Film Festival of Rotterdam's Hubert Bals Fund became involved. The Rotterdam funding meant he was able to continue and transfer from 16 millimeter to 35 millimeter.[14]

These characteristics of social bonding between the director and related stakeholders have often been repeated in Apichatpong's film practices, especially during the formative years of his career, firstly among the crew of *Mysterious Object at Noon* and later *Blissfully Yours* (*Sud Saneha*, 2002)—a day in the life of a Burmese worker and his Thai girlfriend, who try to balance his illegal migration status with their love life. Eric Chan, a Taiwanese factory owner, invested in the film, while his factory was also used as a shooting location by the director. Chan was someone who loved arts and music and sometimes supported artists.[15] Producers Simon Field and Charles de Meaux have also long supported Apichatpong, Field being one of the first people in the international film world with whom the director became acquainted during his first attempt to gain funding from the International Film Festival of Rotterdam (IFFR), where Field was the festival director. Meaux became known to the director through French artists he met during a residency in Paris.[16] *Blissfully Yours* was submitted to the Cannes International Film Festival by one of his French friends during his residency in Paris—otherwise he might not have had an opportunity to try with the festival.[17] Apichatpong accepted these kinds of connections as an important aspect of his filmmaking career, irrespective of whether they happened in Thailand or elsewhere.[18] This kind of relationship is

---

[13] Sonthaya Subyen and Teekhadhet Vacharadhanin, *Pa-Ti-Bat-Karn-Nang-Thun-Kham-Chat* [Transnational Funded Film Operation] (Bangkok: Openbooks, 2010), 201.

[14] Sudarat Musikawong, "Working Practices in Thai Independent Film Production and Distribution", *Inter-Asia Cultural Studies* 8, no. 2 (2007): 255, doi: 10.1080/14649370701238722.

[15] Subyen and Vacharadhanin, 2010, 204–206.

[16] Subyen and Vacharadhanin, 2010, 204–205.

[17] Subyen and Vacharadhanin, 2010, 207.

[18] Subyen and Vacharadhanin, 2010, 205.

conceptualized by Wikanda Phromkhuntong as "emotional capital",[19] which she develops from Bourdieu's discussion of the forms of capital that underpin social relations. Emotional capital, in her words, is found among Apichatpong's supporters, ranging from the IFFR to the filmmaker's artist friends, in many forms, from verbal and non-verbal recommendations of his works by other filmmakers, to the financial assistance in filmmaking. In this way, the director and his films have been continually maintained in the public.

Bourdieu's notion of affective expression and connection between people has been interrogated by numerous theorists, either in terms of "social capital", or "cultural capital", or even "emotional capital". Bourdieu himself never refers explicitly to the concept of emotional capital in his theory of social capital,[20] but it has been taken up by his followers. Helga Nowotny defines the term emotional capital as a variant of social capital, which can be accumulated according to length of time and can have some dominance in other forms of capital. But he suggests to use it in the private rather than the public sphere.[21] Marci D. Cottingham prefers to look at it as a form of cultural capital that incorporates "emotion-specific, trans-situational resources that individuals activate and embody in distinct fields".[22] For Zembylas, this concept of emotional capital should be integrated with many other "resources" such as politics, culture and society—covered by Bourdieu's other forms of capital. By doing so, emotional capital can "blend with them to facilitate or prevent certain practices and discourses".[23] It can be argued that the collaboration with Chinese director Jia Zhangke in *Memoria* is partly influenced by this capital. The directors have long supported each other. During the pandemic, they together published open letters to fans around the world for the Dutch film magazine *Film Krant*. They also convened a masterclass together during the Shanghai International Film Festival in 2021.[24] Through this collaboration,

---

[19] Phromkhuntong, 2017, 91.

[20] Michalinos Zembylas, "Emotional Capital and Education: Theoretical Infights from Bourdieu", *British Journal of Educational Studies* 55, no. 4 (2007): 450, doi: 10.1111/j.1467-8527.2007.00390.x.

[21] Helga Nowotny, "Women in Public Life in Austria", in *Access to Power: Cross-National Studies of Women and Elites*, ed. Cynthia Fuchs Epstein and Rose Laub Coser (London: Routledge, 1981), 148.

[22] Marci D. Cottingham, "Theorizing Emotional Capital', *Theory and Society* 45, no. 5 (2016): 451, https://www.jstor.org/stable/44981841.

[23] Zembylas, 2007, 457.

[24] "MasterClass | Dialogue between Apichatpong and Jia Zhangke: Through

other China-based companies also joined the group, including the big streaming provider, IQiyi Pictures.

As a result, emotional/social capital alone could not enable Apichatpong to thrive in the art cinema industry, especially when the director encountered, like many other global arthouse directors that are dependent on European funds, the complex network of "variegated film industries"[25] after he received the first Cannes prize in 2002 for *Blissfully Yours*. Jäckel does not define the term exactly. But it can be understood as the European film financing model that is constituted of several sources, from pan-European, national, and regional public funding institutions and small-scale production companies.[26] The "variegated film industries" surrounding Apichatpong's works are more complex, integrating both private and public film agencies, a variety of philanthropic supporters—those involved in the promotion of the arts, cinema and social issues—and then make his oeuvre like a kind of nongovernmental project for a better world. Much of the money comes from sales companies that do not invest much in the first place and recoup the money from rentals in other countries.[27] Since *Tropical Malady*, each project has comprised between seven and 30 local, national and international agencies. *Memoria* is a good case study to explain this phenomenon. Twenty-nine organizations[28] and companies from 14 countries supported the film, covering Thailand, China, Hong Kong, Japan, Taiwan, Qatar, France, Germany, Netherlands, Switzerland, United Kingdom, United States, Colombia and Mexico, under the four categories of "production companies", "co-production companies", "with the support of", or "with the participation of". It is not clear what criteria determine the type of credit for each organization, except that the "production companies" category includes only Apichatpong's Kick the Machine and Simon Field's Illuminations Films (Past Lives), before a third, Colombo-based Burning S.A.S., joined them in *Memoria*. The "variegated film industries" are exemplified from many levels of public integration, from the national French bodies

the lens, the 'love and hatred' towards the hometown is expressed", Shanghai International Film Festival, 16 June 2021.

[25] Jäckel, 2003, 25.

[26] Nuno Bararadas Jorge, *ReFocus: The Films of Pedro Costa. Producing and Consuming Contemporary Art Cinema* (Edinburgh: Edinburgh University Press, 2020), 65, doi: 10.3366/Edinburgh/9781474444538.001.0001.

[27] Tilman Baumgärtel, *Southeast Asian Independent Cinema: Essays, Documents, Interviews* (Hong Kong: Hong Kong University Press, 2012), 189, https://www-jstor-org.soton.idm.oclc.org/stable/j.ctt1xwgkr.

[28] See Table 1.

the Centrenational du cinéma et de l'image animée (CNC), the Institut Français for the Aide aux cinémas du monde, Universidad Nacional de Colombia (Colombia), Estudios Churubusco Azteca (Mexico), Doha Film Institute, to regional institutes such as Beijing Contemporary Art Foundation and Medienboard Berlin-Brandenburg. Several private funding agencies are also involved in supporting the making of his ninth feature from his home country (Purin Pictures and 100 Tonson Foundation) to Netherlands' Hubert Bals Fund and philanthropic organizations such as Danny Glover's Louverture Films that supports films with "historical relevance, social purpose, commercial value and artistic integrity",[29] while New York-based Field of Vision commissions innovative, artistic and critical works through a cinematic lens.[30]

Apichatpong's global financing model operates more like a patchwork investment structure, or what I define as personal distributed financing. Borrowing from Daren C. Brabham's notion of "distributed financing",[31] he uses this idea to synthesize the American independent cinema's crowdfunding and fundraising methods. In Apichatpong's case, his distributed financing is taken from all possible fundraising specifically from the director's contacts.

In line with Naficy's notion about the filmmakers' mobility in the interstices, Apichatpong's mode of production should not be examined only as the opposite of the Thai mainstream film industry and Hollywood, but becomes interstitial as he stands at the intersection of the local, region and the global, through the various modes of financing and production. Although *Memoria* does not have support from local studios, several of his earlier projects were coinvested by one of Thailand's biggest entertainment corporations, Grammy Entertainment (through its affiliates GMM Pictures, and TIFA), varying from *The Adventures of Iron Pussy* (2003), *Tropical Malady* (2004) and *Syndromes and a Century* (2006). The collaboration with the Thai film industry, according to Sudarat Mukikapong, can make him "remain true to his 'independent' aesthetic and content",[32] while using his cultural capital to access his international audience. The support he received from Asian conglomerates stopped a few years after their collaboration. Both studios that supported his productions during

[29] "About Us", Louverture Films, accessed 11 June 2022, https://www.louver-turefilms.com/about-us.
[30] "About Field of Vision", Field of Vision, accessed 11 June 2022, https://fieldofvision.org/about.
[31] Brabham, 2013, 39.
[32] Musikawong, 2007, 256.

his early years closed down their programs after a few years. His filmmaking finance conforms to Asuman Suner's assertion[33] about the interstitial filmmaker, in that they "resonate against prevailing cinematic production practices, as well as benefits from them". Placing Apichatpong within the discourse of "interstitial mode of production", we can see that he has worked both alongside and outside the dominant players at the global level—not only in one region, but also across the world and across disciplines.

Into the Paradigm of Post-interstitial Authorship

Some limitations exist in justifying Apichatpong's works purely by adopting Hamid Naficy's textual development on the concept of interstitiality. Using the terms "interstitial" and "accented" cinema interchangeably, the scholar integrates the interstitial theme with the inscription of "a private story of an individual and a social and public story of exile and diaspora".[34] Interstitial filmmakers for most scholars usually act out the role of "intercultural or accented filmmaker",[35] who raises a crisis of identity as their concern, resulting from "intercultural, diasporic, exilic, post-colonial, or accented subjects inhabit the interstices, a no-mans-land in-between indigenous and exogenous cultures, nations, histories, territories, languages, and identities". Arezou Zalipour also supports the ideology and the politics of representation as the common themes that are focused on these works,[36] while Will Higbee and Song Hwee Lim position "diasporic/transnational" filmmaking only as the interstitial and marginal spaces of national cinemas.[37]

Two questions may arise in this regard: should the notion of interstitiality be taken into the analysis of Apichatpong's works? And what are

---

[33] Asuman Suner, "Outside in: 'Accented Cinema' at Large", *Inter-Asia Cultural Studies* 7, no. 3 (2006): 368, doi: 10.1080/14649370600849223.

[34] Naficy, 2001, 31.

[35] Emma Louise Leather, "Interstitial Cinema: The Liminal Visions of Jose Luis Guerin and March Recha", Ph.D. diss., Manchester Metropolitan University, 2008, 101.

[36] Arezou Zalipour, "Interstitial and Collective Filmmaking in New Zealand: The Case of Asian New Zealand Film", *Transnational Cinemas* 7, no. 1 (2016): 102, https://doi.org/10.1080/20403526.2016.1111670.

[37] Will Higbee and Song Hwee Lim, "Concepts of Transnational Cinema: Towards a Critical Transnationalism in Film Studies", *Transnational Cinemas* 1, no. 1 (2010): 9, 10, doi: 10.1386/ trac.1.1.7/1.

the characteristics of Apichatpong's works that have made it different from most interstitial cinemas? Naficy's theme of interstitiality has been used sometimes to study the works of some southeast Asian filmmakers such as Indonesian director Edwin's *Postcards from the Zoo* (2012). Malaysia scholar Miaw Lee Teo finds the indirect exploration of Edwin's accented style in the ongoing implications of the long-term marginalization, erasure, displacement and trauma of Indonesia's Chinese community. Edwin also has accessed both local and international financial support, allowing him more freedom of expression, as well as wider distribution for his works.[38]

Nuno Barradas Jorge also uses Naficy's interstitial mode of production in his study on Pedro Costa's works, and concludes the term can be justified to any form of filmmaking that relies on low budgets and the use of digital video, not only the "exilic and diasporic".[39] Jorge develops the idea by proposing the concept of "independence and codependence"—a codependence of national and international public funding that can facilitate creative independence is often adopted by small-scale production companies.[40] Southeast Asian independent filmmakers also follow these "artisanal practices" and "negotiated dependence" in their access to the contemporary filmmaking system. Those who can reach the global art cinema arena, in particular, have to deal with "a more complex kind of interdependence".[41]

Naficy's concept of interstitiality, in my opinion, needs to be reconceptualized, especially if it is considered within the changing paradigm of the global emergence of art filmmakers and Asian migratory patterns in the last two decades. Contemporary migratory filmmakers do not need to suffer from their accented, dislocatory, migratory, and exilic characteristics, due to their temporary rhythm of movement. In fact, Thai filmmakers who had overseas educational experience and travel these days for their filmmaking mostly came from an upper-class family background. They are praised as important persons who bring fame to the country. Apichatpong, for example, was brought up by his physician parents before going to study at the Art Institute of Chicago. Female

---

[38] Miaw Lee Teo, "Interstitial Filmmaking, Spatial Displacement and Quasi-Family Ties in *Postcards from the Zoo* (2012)", *Journal of Chinese Cinemas* 15, no. 1 (2021): 4, https://doi.org/10.1080/17508061.2021.1926155.

[39] Jorge, 2020, 57.

[40] Jorge, 2020, 54.

[41] May Adadol Ingawanij, "Introduction: Dialectics of Independence", in *Glimpses of Freedom: Independent Cinema in Southeast Asia*, ed. May Adadol Ingawanij and Benjamin McKay (New York: Cornell University Press, 2012), 4–5.

director Anocha Suwichakornpong was supported by her family, which runs a jewellery business, and now she has moved to live in New York to teach at Columbia University. Senior fellow Pen-ek Ratanaruang has educated parents, who once worked with the BBC in London. Arguably, all of these cultural capitals affect the themes and stories that are chosen to be presented. Nevertheless, it does not mean that these directors will propose projects with no social concerns. They merely present their world into a new kind of "interstitial" cinema that does not necessarily tackle the ideology of diaspora and migration. Apichatpong's works still prioritize the lives of northeastern working class and disadvantaged groups who are not from Bangkok. His characters are a mixture of the professional middle class, the lower class and minorities—soldiers (*Tropical Malady*; *Cemetery of Splendour*), a farm owner (*Uncle Boonmee Who Can Recall His Past Lives*), a Burmese migrant (*Blissfully Yours*), factory workers (*Blissfully Yours*; *Tropical Malady*), the wife of a civil servant and an expat (*Blissfully Yours*, *Cemetery of Splendour*). Educated characters are also seen in his movies—ranging from two doctors in *Syndromes and a Century*—in which he pays homage to his parents—filmmakers, as well as an orchidologist in *Memoria*.

Apichatpong's works fit more into what I define as post-interstitial characteristics. Post-interstitial, in my term, should remain with Naficy's idea on the mode of production that incorporates both within and astride the cracks of the system, leading to the diversification of film finances, production, distribution and exhibition. But they might project more diversity of themes and stories. In my opinion, if we look at the cinematic trajectory of Apichatpong, there have been four phases of experimental and thematic developments. First is the observatory mode of address in *Mysterious Object at Noon*, where he uses exquisite corpse techniques to explore his cinematic and Thai roots. In the second stage, he tried to find his directing and cinematic styles by proposing and experimenting with different kinds of moviemaking methods and by blending his northeastern urban roots and the language of American structural film into a new kind of hybrid aesthetics in *Blissfully Yours*, *Tropical Malady*, and *Syndromes and a Century*. At this stage, he is more responsive to what Arezou Zalipour calls "personal/creative articulation" and "a professional commitment to filmmaking".[42] Childhood memories and experiences are often cited as the main resources of expression. His hometown, Khon Kaen, has been used as the main location until recently, though he has already moved to settle down in the north of Thailand, Chiang Mai province, for more than a decade. However, this

[42] Zalipour, 2016, 102.

relationship has been constructed in a "feeling of intertwined 'love and hatred'" (emphasis original), as he puts it: "I had a free childhood there. It taught me a lot of knowledge and also gave me many opportunities to dream [sic]. Of course, my hometown has always been a source of inspiration, and I also hope to see how the experience of the new generation of people who grew up there differs from me."[43] Scholars in the region interpret these northeastern references in a variety of ways. Singapore-based arts scholar David Teh sees that Apichatpong's northeastern experience has consistently been "under-represented in national historiography and politics apropos Thailand", despite the region's role as supplier of labor and popular culture to the rest of the country.[44] London-based theorists May Adadol Ingawanij and Richard Lowell MacDonald note the "unrepresentative[ness] of the economic marginality of the provincial underclass in Apichatpong's works, despite the expression of provincial cultural insecurity".[45] For Apichatpong, I argue, his cinematic world is not reproduced by a specific culture—like northeastern dance or music that is often treated as representing the region—as he admits that he is not what people might think of as a typical northeasterner: "Actually, I do not want to disintegrate what is Isaan, what is not. I am middle-class, half-Chinese, and a son of physicians. It is better to call it 'provincial people, provincial film'. And why does Bangkok have to be centralized in almost everything? How can we live in this space and our voices are heard?"[46] Here, it can be argued that Apichatpong's identity crisis had already taken place in his homeland, not the encounter against his temporary migration to the United States. It is urban provincial politics or national marginalized inequality that inspires him to make his movies.

What we see in Apichatpong's works are more associated with urban provincial culture that happen to be in the northeast of Thailand, different from the "northeastern-themed" movies—known as "Nang Isaan"—that have become popular in the region since the mid-2010s. To

---

[43] "MasterClass | Dialogue".

[44] David Teh, "Itinerant Cinema", *Third Text* 25, no. 5 (2011): 600, https://doi.org/10.1080/09528822.2011.608973.

[45] May Adadol Ingawanij and Richard Lowell MacDonald, "Blissfully Whose? Jungle Pleasures, Ultra-modernist Cinema and the Cosmopolitan Thai Auteur", in *The Ambiguous Allure of the West: Traces of the Colonial in Thailand*, ed. Rachel Harrison and Peter Jackson (Hong Kong: Hong Kong University Press, 2010), 120, https://www.jstor.org/stable/j.ctt1xwbmf.12.

[46] The Isaan Record, "Kwam chuea nai phumiphab Isan kong Apichatpong Weerasethakul [Faith in the Northeast of Apichatpong Weerasethakul]", *Isan Creative Festival*, Khon Kaen University, 10 January 2019, MP file.

some extent, the images of Khon Kaen and the jungles of the northeast, as well as the representations of media and cultural reproductions that are highlighted in his works, could be anywhere outside the capital city. He had never used northeastern Thai dialect until the making of *Cemetery of Splendour* and felt uncomfortable—before going to Chicago—by its association with low-class "café comedy".[47]

In my view—like the interstitial aesthetics that are mixed and in-between the states of things—Apichatpong's filmmaking style conforms more to the arts of hybridity, combining several binary realms of culture—East and West, high and low, and any kinds of visual arts, pertaining to be, as Professor Daniel Eisenberg evaluates, "someone who builds bridges between different kinds of cultural position".[48] In making these art pieces, Apichatpong uses a strategy of what US-based scholar Jihoon Kim addresses as "blending his feeling of the memory with the present", and "paint[ing] his fragments of memory with enhanced audiovisual senses".[49] As a result, the memories that are reflected in Apichatpong's movies are constructed in the mode of diaries on his town—Khon Kaen, people around him—his parents, his cast and his crew—the culture and the process. Even when he decides to depend on someone else's story, as in the background of *Uncle Boonmee Who Can Recall His Past Lives*, the film still contains tributes to the director's father, the land, and the movies that he grew up with.[50] Thai culture and folklore, ranging from entertainment experienced through old media like television, radio, cinema and comics to primitive folklore, rituals and beliefs, become commonly presented in his early works. The song that is used in the intermission between two sections of *Blissfully Yours* is adapted from Marcos Valle's *Summer Samba* and sung by modern Thai artist Nadia. In his earlier shorts, several forms of pop culture enjoyed among the working class were reinvented in a new form of experimental

---

47 "Café comedy" refers to the stand-up comedy that used to be found in cheap pubs or bars, which was popular during the 1990s and early 2000s. Comedians often used regional dialects to deliver crude jokes. Source: Isaan Record, 2019.

48 Daniel Eisenberg, interview message with the author, 3 February 2016, his office at the Art Institute of Chicago.

49 Jihoon Kim, "Between Auditorium and Gallery: Perception in Apichatpong Weerasethakul's Films and Installations", in *Global Art Cinema: New Theories and Histories* ed. Rosalind Galt and Karl Schoonover (New York: Oxford University Press, 2010), 134.

50 Apichatpong Weerasethakul, "Interview with Apichatpong Weerasethakul", *Uncle Boonmee Who Can Recall His Past Lives*, dir. Apichatpong Weerasethakul (London: New Wave Films, 2010), DVD.

work/video art. For example, parts of TV series were remixed with new casts and black-and-white shots for a short called *Haunted Houses* (2001). Footage from television series or old Thai movies were often inserted to interrupt the narrative. In the ending scene of *Uncle Boonmee Who Can Recall His Past Lives*, Tong (Sakda Kaewbuadee) and Jen (Jenjira Pongpas) are sitting motionlessly watching television series, like they are in the entry point of meditation. The image of the monkey ghost in the same movie is actually inspired from a cheap one-baht comic book[51] that had been popular among working-class readers. The shape of the film is more important than the content—the common characteristics of structural film in the American avant-garde tradition. Here, the shape of the whole film is "predetermined" and "simplified". This shape is constructed to offer the "primal impression" of the film, like what is known as the American avant-garde quality.[52]

This characteristic of overall film shape is clearly noticeable in the structure of bifurcated narrative in the director's trilogy *Blissfully Yours*, *Tropical Malady*, and *Syndromes and a Century*. *Blissfully Yours* is divided into two sections, with the first part focusing on the protagonists' attempt to get the man an ID card, and the second following them on a picnic in the jungle. Similarly, *Tropical Malady* invokes memories of the director's life in its story of the love affair between two gay men in Apichatpong's hometown Khon Kaen. At the halfway point, the characters suddenly become a hunter and a tiger-man in the jungle, and remain as such for the remainder of the film. *Syndromes and a Century* can be seen in terms of his hometown's encounter with modernity, the decline of the city being seen from the point of view of two doctors in a hospital—the doctors being homages to the director's parents. This duality is read by scholars with different levels of engagement—from a simplified reading as an encounter between a mystical and modern life,[53] as well as a shift between reality and imagination.[54] Others contemplate it organically and interpret it as "a cinema of odd conjunctions" where confusion and frustration, as well as dazzlement and seduction, interact against each other.[55] Jihoon Kim adopts a temporal means to evaluate this duality,

[51] Less than one cent in British pound.

[52] Adams P. Sitney, *Visionary Film: The American Avant-Garde, 1943–2000* (Oxford: Oxford University Press, 2002), 348.

[53] Michael Sicinski, "Bifurcated Time: Ulrich Köhler / Apichatpong Weerasethakul", in *The Berlin School and Its Global Contexts: A Transnational Art Cinema*, ed. Jaimey Fisher and Marco Abel (Detroit: Wayne State University Press, 2018), 196.

[54] Sicinski, 2018, 196–204.

[55] Brett Farmer, "Apichatpong Weerasethakul, Transnational Poet of the New

as an interstice between two "time zones" and two "types of durations". The first connection of time refers to the imitation of a two-screen installation inside the gallery wall, while the latter connection refers to the duration of the director's memory in the diegetic space; and the duration of images on the screen space embodied by the viewer's perception and attentiveness.[56] In my view, this bifurcated structure implies the director's encounter with the double identity that he had at that time—between the derogatory northeastern and imperceptible high-end subcultures, in which he elaborates them into the form of cinematic experimentation.

What is interesting is the third stage of his filmmaking journey, in which he is more engaged with political and economic subtexts in Thailand both through the screen world and his activities. Although social connections are sometimes hidden in his earlier works, they are presented as a social background, rather than as a main discourse of political actions. *Blissfully Yours* shows some of the difficulties of an illegal worker in obtaining an ID card, but the struggle is left behind when the two lovers decide to spend pleasurable time in the jungle. In *Tropical Malady*, Apichatpong creates one of the lead protagonists as a soldier, who does not exercise any power. *Syndromes and A Century* shows no political issues except the decline of his hometown upon its encounter with modernity. This has changed totally since the making of *Uncle Boonmee Who Can Recall His Past Lives, Mekong Hotel* (2012), *Cemetery of Splendour* (2015) and *10 Years Thailand* (2018), in which political subtexts are expressed cinematically and thematically. *Uncle Boonmee Who Can Recall His Past Lives* portrays the director's memory of the film's location Nabua, where there was a violent army cracked down in 1965. The sex scene between the ugly princess and the catfish can be read as a form of deconstruction against the old hierarchy of royalty in Thai popular culture—known in Thai as *lakorn jak jak wong wong*—where a handsome prince and beautiful princess indulge in their love affair. *Mekong Hotel* shifts between different realms, fact and fiction portraying the living and undead along the Mekong river dividing the border between Thailand and Laos. According to the Prince Claus Fund's home page, through the images of reality and fantasy, the film depicts "layers of demolition, politics, and a drifting dream".[57] Through the

Thai Cinema: Blissfully Yours/Sud Sanaeha', *Senses of Cinema* 38 (2006): para. 2, accessed 4 January 2021, https://www.sensesofcinema.com/2006/cteq/blissfully_yours/.

[56] Kim, 2010, 126.

[57] Prince Claus Fund, "Mekong Hotel by Apichatpong Weerasethakul", accessed 4 May 2023, https://princeclausfund.org/mekong-hotel-apichtapong-weerasethakul.

theme of sickness, sleep and memory, *Cemetery of Splendour* represents three levels of politics in Thailand. At first sight, the old hospital associates all of Apichatpong's memories with the setting—which used to be an old school—his city Khon Kaen, and his connection to medical lives. At the middle ground level, the sickness and sleep can be read as the foreground of Thailand's political condition at that time, where the country has long suffered from military occupation and long ongoing protests from democratic groups. Under the clinic lies the mythic ancient site, which in some ways signifies connections with the monarchy, especially if the film is considered together with its contexts and paratexts at that time. King Rama IX was at the time suffering from illness—he died in October 2016—and the fractions between loyalists and liberals have remained high in the country. The film's former title, *Cemetery of the King*, somehow shows that this contextual and paratextual relevance is not a coincidence.

During this time, like many activists and artists supporting one another, Apichatpong also showed his interest to support the pro-democratic groups through collaborations and activism. Since the premiere of *Uncle Boonmee Who Can Recall His Past Lives* in Cannes, he has often criticized and protested against the military governments in several ways. He is a key figure in the protest against section 112 of the Criminal Code or the *Lèse Majesté* law, which is designed to protect the king, queen, heir-apparent, and regent from being defamed, insulted or threatened with harm. He has never been reluctant to support the young people who have long protested the government for reform. His critique of the political establishment during this period has led to many public anti-sentiment reactions against him.

In terms of cinematic language, the duality of time, space and narration that we have seen in his autobiographical trilogy are developed into a paradigm of the multiplicity on several levels. First is the transfiguration of beings. In *Uncle Boonmee Who Can Recall His Past Lives*, the protagonist's past lives have seen him take many forms: human, animal and ghost, which are interpreted in different ways. Michael Sicinski sees them as "multiple temporal and cinematic disruptions",[58] while Apichatpong has admitted that they reflect his own interests and beliefs: "I believe in the transmigration of souls between humans, plants, animals, and ghosts."[59] The binary contrast between his provincial lifestyle and the high-art language of avant-garde/European

---

[58] Sicinski, 2018, 197.
[59] The Match Factory, *Uncle Boonmee Who Can Recall His Past Lives*, English Press Kit (n.p., 2010), last page.

cinema is now complicated by the use of mixed media in film, ranging from the reinvention of Thai popular entertainment (comics, Thai costume dramas, television series), new media (the use of stills) and the aesthetic traditions of avant-garde cinema. By combining this profusion of formats and media platforms into the texts and contexts of *Uncle Boonmee Who Can Recall His Past Lives*, Apichatpong sets an example for a new type of cinematic authorship deriving from various forms of "interstitial" activity that are performed not simply in duality, but in multiplicity. Furthermore, the format of structural films that is seen in his earlier works has now reached another phase of design by combining feature films and video installations.

According to Jihoon Kim, Apichatpong redefines cinema by allowing it to be "mutated through redistributing its properties"[60] into other forms of visual art. With his educational background in architecture in Thailand, he adopts two "cinematic" tendencies of video art into his filmmaking: "deepened durational space", or long takes; and the "spatialized form of broken narratives". In creating his "cinematic" video installations, he also uses new aesthetic forms and techniques that are originated in the video installation medium back to filmmaking. *Screen International* critic Allan Hunter also suggests that some of the scenes in *Cemetery of Splendour*, such as the scene of glowing electric lights used for the experimental treatment of soldiers with sleeping sickness, can be compared to an art gallery installation.[61] The combination between feature world and video installation is partly affected by the collaboration of his visual arts network that had multiplied by the time he made *Uncle Boonmee Who Can Recall His Past Lives*, including such visual arts organization as Munich's Haus der Kunst, Liverpool's Foundation for Art and Creative Technology (FACT) and London's Animate Projects. In *Cemetery of Splendour*, the Gwangju-based Asian Arts Theatre, which specializes in performance arts, also offered him funding on the condition that the director also produces a piece of performing art for the theater.[62] In *Memoria*, several public and private visual arts agencies were involved—from the Beijing Contemporary Art Foundation, the Hong Kong-based Edouard Malingue Gallery, the Tokyo-based SCAI The Bathhouse and the Bangkok-based 100 Tonson Foundation.

[60] Kim, 2010, 138.
[61] Allan Hunter, "Cemetery of Splendour Review", *Screen International*, 18 May 2015, https://www.screendaily.com/reviews/cemetery-of-splendour/5087447.article.
[62] Atsushi Sasaki, "Apichatpong Weerasethakul—Fever Room", *Asia Hundreds*, 5 July 2017, 1, https://jfac.jp/en/culture/features/f-ah-tpam-apichatpong-weerasethakul.

In fact, one of the most prominent members of his film network is not a common production company in the film industrial sense but is more identified with visual art. His longtime co-producer, Paris-based Anna Sanders Films, aims to support a new breed of cinema—one that is made by visual artists and shown mostly in galleries and at film festivals.[63] Several members of its executive team are also active visual artists themselves. His longtime supporter Simon Field, who has officially produced his works since 2006, sets up his company Illuminations Films due to their joint interest in "exploring this terrain between the art world and the film world".[64]

This visual arts connection is heightened both in the mode of production and cinematic endeavors in *Memoria*, which manifests the director's fourth stage of filmmaking transformation. The film is much more integrated with visual artistic signatures and a strong view of political resistance. *Memoria* has developed the notion of sickness, sleep and memory as the main theme of the movie, this time—I argue—in a more complex paradigm of accented cinema, where both the director and protagonist suffer from their dislocatory, migratory and exilic characteristics. In fact, if we want to discover the traditional concept of interstitial cinema, *Memoria* is more conjured up with those elements than are his previous films. Firstly, the director, some of the crew and the protagonist share the same identity as "accented filmmakers" in the foreign land—using some other languages more than their own mother tongue—English for Apichatpong and the crew, Spanish for Jessica (Tilda Swinton). Both of them—the director and the protagonist—share the same identities as outsiders who look into Colombian politics and history. Throughout the film, Jessica is framed by the use of long or extremely long shots, which also manifests the traits of theater performance used in the film, in addition to the common use of video installations. Secondly, both the director and Jessica share the same "trauma, rupture, and coercion",[65] which is understood as the starting point for those in diaspora or exile. In Jessica's case, it is the strange noise that nobody hears and might come from her mental state. In the director's case, his trauma is caused by his homeland's chronic political insecurity and censorship, which caused him to stop making films

---

[63] "Anna Sanders Films—The In-Between", *les presses du réel*, accessed 10 December 2020, https://www.lespressesdureel.com/EN/ouvrage.php?id=378.

[64] Geoffrey Macnab, "Keith Griffiths & Simon Field—Nurturing Creativity", *Screen International*, 20 March 2009, https://www.screendaily.com/keith-griffiths-and-simon-field-nurturing-creativity/4043703.article.

[65] Naficy, 2001, 14.

there.[66] While Naficy defines the accented filmmakers only as those who are "situated but universal" figures working in the interstices of social formation and cinematic practices,[67] post-interstitial filmmakers might be globetrotting and universal, due to their temporary migration. They might not be officially forced into exile, but they leave the countries voluntarily. Naficy points out an interesting aspect of the exilic filmmaker as someone who constructs his vertical and primary relationship with his homeland. His films are then accented by a "binarism and duality" rule of identity.[68] For a temporary exile like Apichatpong, the relationship and identity are constructed in a more complex process. On the surface, *Memoria* seems to be accented at two levels—between the Global North (British or Scottish) and Global South (Colombian identity). But as we investigate more, we find that there is the third identity in the film—the Thai identity—that is attached to the director.

In the first place, Jessica is connected to Colombian society through her mind and then the memories of Colombian pastness are recalled in her dream or subconsciousness, signified by many excavation scenes throughout the film. Everything in the movie is connected. Relationships do not take place only with ourselves, but also with others—the Colombians—and even the earth. Through Jessica and the director, himself, Colombian and Thai people are connected since they share the same political suffering. Although we do not know about the political details there, the people associated (Jessica, Colombian and Thai) share the same inequality and suffering that have long affected them. In other words, by making *Memoria*, Apichatpong "let[s] the origin return within the present, to make the present a repetition of the past and by that recreate the union with one's origin. The present has to get its depth through one's origin, one's Heimat."[69] As a result, Apichatpong's *Memoria* is accented in plurality and multiplicity, the qualification that Naficy prefers to assign to the diasporan filmmakers.

This incorporation and assemblage of the visual arts and Thai cultural production alongside the American avant-garde and European art film

---

[66] Chris Baker, "Death by a Thousand Cuts", *Bangkok Post*, 9 July 2021, https://www.bangkokpost.com/life/arts-and-entertainment/2146087/death-by-a-thousand-cuts.

[67] Naficy, 2001, 10.

[68] Naficy, 2001, 14–15.

[69] Andreas Niehaus and Tine Walravens, "Home Work: Post-Fukushima Constructions of Furusato by Japanese Nationals Living in Belgium", in *Diasporic Constructions of Home and Belonging*, ed. Florian Klager and Klaous Stierstorfer (Berlin: De Gruyter, 2015), 131.

traditions has raised the question of purity that is often expected from the works of avant-garde filmmakers. Barrett Hodsdon[70] argues that, in creating such works, the projection of the personal equates to "filmmaker's eyes = cinema apparatus = visual field = representational scheme", and then becomes "an extremely fluid one enmeshed in a sphere which often aspires to negotiate pure forms of phenomenological visualization". In Apichatpong's context, I argue, the discourse of purity becomes a complex issue that needs more consideration of how the *mind* perceives changing environments. It is his mind that works with cinema, and is then sent to viewers. As a result, the process is more important for Apichatpong to create a film, and not his thoughts or visual perceptions alone. In an interview given in 2016 after the screening of *Cemetery of Splendour* in Chicago, his teacher supports this:

> He enjoys the process more—the process that becomes what the work is—rather than the execution of what his thoughts are. He is changing his relationship to the work it was. He opens for different kinds of changing, opens up for what happen in the moment. He opens to shifting the script to the movement in the work. And that means a very sophisticated relationship with cinema.[71]

Apichatpong's "perception" can be considered as pure *projection*, but in a different way than other avant-gardists. His memories and filmmaking methods can be considered as hybrid, due to his multiple backgrounds in arts and culture—East and West, low and high, cinema and visual art—normally in the realms of duality and later multiplicity. He has to encounter and negotiate internally with those diverse forces in constructing his fluid perceptive projection and deliver without the interference of external forces. The equation becomes the filmmaker's (voluntary) hybrid "perception" = hybrid cinema apparatus = hybrid "sensual" field = hybrid representational scheme. Accordingly, he has observed that his movies are hybrid like Thai society and made from the memories of an adult who happens to be a filmmaker.[72]

In these senses, those forces that he has constructed through his life originate from his upbringing, childhood, lifestyle and education. Sitting

---

[70] Barrett Hodsdon, *The Elusive Auteur: The Question of Film Authorship throughout the Age of Cinema* (North Carolina: McFarland & Company, 2017), 93.

[71] Daniel Eisenberg, interview.

[72] Ekkasat Sapphachang, "Apichatpong Weerasethakul: Kabot Nang Thai [Thai film rebel]", *GM Magazine*, August 2010, 132.

POST-INTERSTITIAL AUTHORSHIP IN WEERASETHAKUL'S CINEMA   269

in the interstices between many spheres of contrasts, as mentioned above, Apichatpong has also employed these in-between states of things in making his works, both aesthetically and financially. Just as his mode of authorship defines a new perspective on hybrid art/avant-garde cinema, Apichatpong's financial strategies have also generated a new paradigm of global film financing that might be adopted as a model for contemporary art cinema, especially those working beyond Europe. He has become what I prefer to identify as a post-interstitial art filmmaker, open to all possible financial resources that have emerged among the cracks of global film financing so that the financial risks will be distributed among multiple partners and public institutions. Under this co-dependence of mixed and various film industries and visual arts, he can maintain his creative independence to the greatest extent. This chapter also shows that with changing migratory patterns, the reconceptualised theory is more complicated and region-specific than in the original theory conceived by Naficy.

Table 1 Supporters of Apichatpong Weerasethakul Films

Mysterious Object at Noon, 2000
Hubert Balls Fund in association with 9/6 Cinema Factory and
    Firecracker Film
Support from Toshiba and Fuji Photo Film (Thailand), Chateau Post
    (Thailand), The James Nelson Award (USA)
Tele-cine at the Fame Post-Production Co Lit, with support from Ms.
    Pornanong Mujalin, Sumet Amornworapon, William Watts
Edited at Chateau Post Bangkok with support from Tony Morias, Peter
    Jones, Book, Beum, Oi, Pluffy Omo
Post production laboratory: Siam Film Development. With support
    from Sa-nga Janjarasskul; Sound mixed by Karun Peaukjaipeaw
Producer: Gridthiya Gaweewong (Project 304), Mingmongkol Sonakul
    (Firecracker Film)
Source: The company's press material and the movie's credit lines.

Blissfully Yours, 2002
Production Company: La-Ong Dao / Kick the Machine
In association with: Anna Sanders Films
Produced by Eric Chan and Charles de Meaux
Source: Kick the Machine's English press material.

***Iron Pussy**, 2003
Production Companies: Kick the Machine & G Gate Production
Produced by Piyanan Chanklom G-Gate Production for GMM Pictures
    & Ray Pictures Peeraya Prommachat Kick the Machine
Source: GMM Pictures' brochure.

***Tropical Malady**, 2004
With the support of Fonds Sud Cinema France, Fondazione
    MonteCinemaVerita Switzerland, Hessen Invest Film, with the
    participation of Backup Films
Anna Sanders Films, TIFA, Downtown Pictures and Thoke + Moebius
    Film
In association with Rai Cinema, Fabrica Cinema
Co-production TIFA, Downtown Pictures, Thoke Moebius Film
Source: From the movie's credit lines.

***Syndrome and Century**, 2006
New Crowned Hope Festival Vienna 2006 (present)
In association with Fortissimo Films and Backup Films
In co-production with ANNA SANDERS FILMS and TIFA
With the participation of Fonds Sud Cinema
Source: From the company's credit line.

***Uncle Boonmee Who Can Recall His Past Lives**, 2010
Illuminations Films present A Kick the Machine Films (Thailand) and
    Illuminations Films Past Lives (UK) Production
In co-production with Anna Sanders Films (France); The
    Match Factory (Germany); GFF Geissendoerfer Film-und
    Fermschproduktion KG (Germany); Eddie Saeta, S.A. (Spain)
With the participation of Fonds Sud Cinema (France); Ministère de
    la culture et de la communication CNC (France); Ministère des
    Affaires Etrang reset Europennes (France)
With the Support of World Cinema Fund (Germany) ; The Hubert Bals
    Fund, International Film Festival of Rotterdam (Netherlands); Office
    of Contemporary Art and Culture, Ministry of Culture (Thailand)
In association with ZDF/Arte (Germany); Louverture Films (USA)
And with Haus der Kunst, Munich (Germany); FACT (Foundation for
    Art and Creative Technology), Liverpool (UK); Animate Projects,
    London (UK)
Source: The Match Factory's press kit.

***Mekong Hotel**, 2012
Illuminations Films (UK) and Kick the Machine Films (Thailand) present
In association with ARTE France—La Lucarne
With the participation of The Match Factory (Germany)
Post production supported by Jacob Burns Film Centre
With additional support from Fuori Orario (Rai Tre)
Source: The Match Factory's press kit.

Cemetery of Splendour, 2015

A Kick the Machine Films (Thailand) and Illuminations Films (Past Lives) Production (UK)

In co-production with Anna Sanders Films (France); Geißendörfer Film- und Fernsehproduktion KG (Germany); Match Factory Productions (Germany); ZDF/arte (Germany), and Astro Shaw (Malaysia); Asia Culture Centre-Asian Arts Theatre (South Korea); Detalle Films (Mexico); Louverture Films (USA); Tordenfilm (Norway)

With the participation of Aide aux cinémas du monde; Centre national du cinéma et de l'image animée; and Ministère de l'Europe et des Affaires étrangères; Institute Francais (France)

With the support of Sørfond (Norway), World Cinema Fund (Germany), Hubert Bals Fund (Netherland), Hong Kong—Asia Film Financing Forum

Source: The Match Factory's press kit.

Memoria, 2021

Production Companies: Burning S.A.S (Columbia); Kick the Machine (Thailand), Illuminations Films (Past Lives) (UK)

Co-production Companies: Anna Sanders Films (France), Match Factory Productions (Germany); Piano (Mexico); X stream Pictures (China); IQiYi Pictures (China), Titan Creative Entertainment (China); Rediance (China), ZDF/arte (Germany), Louverture Films (USA), Doha Film Institute (Qatar), Beijing Contemporary Art Foundation (China), Bord Cadre films (Switzerland), Sovereign Films (UK), Field of Vision (USA), 185 Films (Thailand)

With the support of: Fondo Fílmico Colombia, EFICINE 189 (Mexico), Medienboard Berlin- Brandenburg (Germany), Edouard Malingue Gallery (Hong Kong), SCAI The Bathhouse (Japan), Universidad Nacional de Colombia (Colombia), Hubert Bals Fund (Netherlands), Purin Pictures (Thailand), 100 Tonson Foundation (Thailand), Estudios Churubusco Azteca (Mexico)

With the Participation of: L'Aide aux Cinémas du Monde Centre national du cinéma et de l'image animée—Ministère des Affaires étrangères et du Développement international—Institut Français (France)

Source: The Match Factory's press kit.

Bibliography

"Anna Sanders Films—The In-Between". *les presses du réel*. Accessed 10 December 2020. https://www.lespressesdureel.com/EN/ouvrage.php?id=378.

Apichatpong Weerasethakul. "Introduction to the Film by Its Director". *Blissfully Yours* [*Sud Sanehha*]. Dir. Apichatpong Weerasethakul. London. Second Run. 2006. DVD.

Apichatpong Weerasethakul. "Interview with Apichatpong Weerasethakul". *Uncle Boonmee Who Can Recall His Past Lives*. Dir. Apichatpong Weerasethakul. London. New Wave Films. 2010. DVD.

Baker, Chris. "Death by a Thousand Cuts". *Bangkok Post*. 9 July 2021. https://www.bangkokpost.com/life/arts-and-entertainment/2146087/death-by-a-thousand-cuts.

Baumgärtel, Tilman. *Southeast Asian Independent Cinema: Essays, Documents, Interviews*. Hong Kong. Hong Kong University Press. 2012. https://www-jstor-org.soton.idm.oclc.org/stable/j.ctt1xwgkr.

Brabham, Daren C. *Crowdsourcing*. New York. MIT Press. 2013. https://ieeexplore-ieee-org.soton.idm.oclc.org/servlet/opac?bknumber=6517605.

Chaiworaporn, Anchalee. "Border-crossings and the Cinemas of Thai Arthouse Directors". Ph.D. diss. University of Southampton. 2022.

Cottingham, Marci D. "Theorizing Emotional Capital". *Theory and Society* 45, no. 5 (2016): 451–470. https://www.jstor.org/stable/44981841.

Farmer, Brett. "Apichatpong Weerasethakul, Transnational Poet of the New Thai Cinema: Blissfully Yours/Sud Sanaeha". *Senses of Cinema* 38 (2006). https://www.sensesofcinema.com/2006/cteq/blissfully_yours/.

First Look Institute. "About Field of Vision". Accessed 11 June 2022. https://fieldofvision.org/about.

Higbee, Will and Song Hwee Lim. "Concepts of Transnational Cinema: Towards a Critical Transnationalism in Film Studies". *Transnational Cinemas* 1, no. 1 (2010): 7–21. Doi: 10.1386/ trac.1.1.7/1.

Hodsdon, Barrett. *The Elusive Auteur: The Question of Film Authorship throughout the Age of Cinema*. North Carolina. McFarland & Company. 2017.

Hunter, Allan. "Cemetery of Splendour Review". *Screen International*. 18 May 2015. https://www.screendaily.com/reviews/cemetery-of-splendour/5087447.article.

Ingawanij, May Adadol. "Introduction: Dialectics of Independence". In *Glimpses of Freedom: Independent Cinema in Southeast Asia*. Ed. May Adadol Ingawanij and Benjamin McKay. New York. Cornell University Press. 2012. 1–14.

Ingawanij, May Adadol and Richard Lowell MacDonald. "Blissfully Whose? Jungle Pleasures, Ultra-modernist Cinema and the Cosmopolitan Thai Auteur". In *The Ambiguous Allure of the West: Traces of the Colonial in Thailand*. Ed. Rachel Harrison and Peter Jackson. Hong Kong. Hong Kong University Press. 2010. 119–134. https://www.jstor.org/stable/j.ctt1xwbmf.12.

Iordanova, Dina. "East Asia and Film Festivals: Transnational Clusters for Creativity and Commerce". In *Film Festival Yearbook 3: Film Festivals and East Asia*. Ed. Dina Iordanova and Ruby Cheung. St Andrews. St Andrews Film Studies. 2011. 1–33.

Isaan Record, The. "Kwam Chuea Nai Phumiphab Isan Kong Apichatpong Weerasethakul [Faith in the Northeast by Apichatpong Weerasethakul]". *Isaan Creative Festival*. Khon Kaen. Khon Kaen University. 10 January 2019.

Jäckel, Anne. *European Film Industries*. London. British Film Institute. 2003.

Jorge, Nuno Bararadas. *ReFocus: The Films of Pedro Costa: Producing and Consuming Contemporary Art Cinema*. Edinburgh. Edinburgh University Press. 2020. Doi: 10.3366/Edinburgh/9781474444538.001. 0001.

Kim, Jihoon. "Between Auditorium and Gallery: Perception in Apichatpong Weerasethakul's Films and Installations". In *Global Art Cinema: New Theories and Histories*. Ed. Rosalind Galt and Karl Schoonover. New York. Oxford University Press. 2010. 125–141.

Leather, Emma Louise. "Interstitial Cinema: The Liminal Visions of Jose Luis Guerin and March Recha". Ph.D. diss. Manchester Metropolitan University. 2008.

Louverture Films. "About Us". Accessed 11 June 2022. https://www.louverturefilms.com/about-us.

Macnab, Geoffrey. "Keith Griffiths & Simon Field—Nurturing Creativity". *Screen International*. 20 March 2009. https://www.screendaily.com/keith-griffiths-and-simon-field-nurturing-creativity/4043703.article.

Match Factory, The. *Uncle Boonmee Who Can Recall His Past Lives* [English press kit]. [n.p.], 2010.

Musikawong, Sudarat. "Working Practices in Thai Independent Film Production and Distribution". *Inter-Asia Cultural Studies* 8, no. 2 (2007): 248–261. DOI: 10.1080/14649370701238722.

Naficy, Hamid. *An Accented Cinema: Exilic and Diasporic Filmmaking*. New Jersey. Princeton University Press. 2001.

Niehaus, Andreas and Tine Walravens. "Home Work: Post-Fukushima Constructions of Furusato by Japanese Nationals Living in Belgium". In *Diasporic Constructions of Home and Belonging*. Ed. Florian Klager and Klaous Stierstorfer. Berlin. De Gruyter. 2015. 125–145.

Nowotny, Helga. "Women in Public Life in Austria". In *Access to Power: Cross-National Studies of Women and Elites*. Ed. Cynthia Fuchs Epstein and Rose Laub Coser. London. Routledge. 1981. 147–156.

Phromkhuntong, Wikanda. "The East Asian Auteur Phenomenon: Context, Discourse and Agency Surrounding the Transnational Reputations of Apichatpong Weerasethakul, Kim Ki-duk and Wong Kar-wai". Ph.D. diss. Aberystwyth University. 2017.

Prince Claus Fund. "Mekong Hotel by Apichatpong Weerasethakul". https://princeclausfund.org/mekong-hotel-apichtapong-weerasethakul.

Sapphachang, Ekkasat. "Apichatpong Weerasethakul: Kabot Nang Thai [Thai film rebel]". *GM Magazine*. August 2010. 130–140.

Sasaki, Atsushi. "Apichatpong Weerasethakul—Fever Room". *Asia Hundreds*. 5 July 2017. https://jfac.jp/en/culture/features/f-ah-tpam-apichatpong-weerasethakul.

Shanghai International Film Festival. "MasterClass | Dialogue between Apichatpong and Jia Zhangke: Through the lens, the 'love and hatred' towards the hometown is expressed". Accessed 1 November 2022. https://www.siff.com/english/content?aid=3f3baca9-60e1-4e6a-bf10-b68372623e21/.

Sicinski, Michael. "Bifurcated Time: Ulrich Köhler / Apichatpong Weerasethakul". In *The Berlin School and Its Global Contexts: A Transnational Art Cinema*. Ed. Jaimey Fisher and Marco Abel. Detroit. Wayne State University Press. 2018. 193–210.

Sitney, Adams P. *Visionary Film: The American Avant-Garde, 1943–2000*. Oxford. Oxford University Press. 2002.

Subyen, Sonthaya and Teekhadhet Vacharadhanin. *Pa-Ti-Bat-Karn-Nang-Thun-Kham-Chat* [Transnational Funded Film Operation]. Bangkok. Openbooks. 2010.

Suner, Asuman. "Outside in: 'Accented Cinema' at Large". *Inter-Asia Cultural Studies* 7, no. 3 (2006): 363–382. Doi: 10.1080/14649370600849223.

Teh, David. "Itinerant Cinema". *Third Text* 25, no. 5 (2011): 595–609. https://doi.org/10.1080/09528822.2011.608973.

Teo, Miaw Lee. "Interstitial Filmmaking, Spatial Displacement and Quasi-Family Ties in *Postcards from the Zoo* (2012)". *Journal of Chinese Cinemas* 15, no. 1 (2021): 1–17. https://doi.org/10.1080/17508061.2021.192 6155.

Zalipour, Arezou. "Interstitial and Collective Filmmaking in New Zealand: The Case of Asian New Zealand Film". *Transnational Cinemas* 7, no. 1 (2016): 96–110. https://doi.org/10.1080/20403526.2016.1111670.

Zembylas, Michalinos. "Emotional Capital and Education: Theoretical Infights from Bourdieu". *British Journal of Educational Studies* 55, no. 4 (2007): 443–463. Doi: 10.1111/j.1467-8527.2007.00390.x.

Filmography

10 Years Thailand. Dir. Aditya Assarat, Wisit Sasanatieng, Chulayarnnon Siriphol, Apichatpong Weerasethakul. Ten Years Studio. 2018.

The Adventure of Iron Pussy [*Hua jai tor ra nong*]. Dir. Apichatpong Weerasethakul and Michael Shaowanasai. GMM Pictures. 2003.

Blissfully Yours [*Sud sanaeha*]. Dir. Apichatpong Weerasethakul. Kick the Machine. 2002.

Cemetery of Splendour [*Rak Ti Khon Kaen*]. Dir. Apichatpong Weerasethakul. The Match Factory. 2015.

Haunted Houses. Dir. Apichatpong Weerasethakul. Kick the Machine. 2001.

Mekong Hotel. Dir. Apichatpong Weerasethakul. The Match Factory. 2012.

Memoria. Dir. Apichatpong Weerasethakul. The Match Factory. 2021.

Mysterious Object at Noon [*Dokfa Nai Meuman*]. Dir. Apichatpong Weerasethakul. Kick the Machine. 2000.

Syndromes and a Century [*Saeng sattawat*]. Dir. Apichatpong Weerasethakul. Kick the Machine. 2006.

Tropical Malady [*Sud Pralad*]. Dir. Apichatpong Weerasethakul. Kick the Machine. 2004.

Uncle Boonmee Who Can Recall His Past Lives [*Lung Boonmee raluek chat*]. Dir. Apichatpong Weerasethakul. The Match Factory. 2010.

Notes on Contributors

Alessandro Ferraro, art historian, recently earned a Ph.D. in Contemporary Arts from the University of Genoa, Italy. In 2017 he received a research fellowship at the Stiftung Hans Arp in Berlin and in 2022 he obtained a research grant at the C.M. Lerici Stiftelsen (Stockholm) and at the Hilma af Klint Archive (Moderna Museet, Stockholm). His research focuses on the impact of contemporary theory of abstraction in contemporary art and visual studies. From 2019 he taught "History of exhibitions and curatorial practices" at the University of Genoa. He is currently working on an edited volume titled *Representing and Understanding Abstraction Today* (forthcoming, 2023).

Anchalee Chaiworaporn has been active both in the film industries and academia in Thailand and the region, teaching at Thailand's University of Mahidol and Malaysia's Multimedia University. For more than two decades, she has received numerous foreign grants—from such bodies as the Japan Foundation and the Rockefeller-attached Asian Cultural Council—to undertake research on Asian cinema in Japan, South Korea, the Philippines, Malaysia, Indonesia, and New York. She has contributed more than ten books on the cinemas of Thailand and Asia in several languages. Through the University of Southampton's Vice-Chancellor's Award, she finished her Ph.D. in Film Studies, specializing on transnational cinema, art and popular cinema, auteur cinema, film festival, and film industrial studies. She has also been invited to several film festivals around the world—in Busan, Seoul, Hong Kong, Bangkok, Estonia, Karlovy Vary, and Vladivostok, to name just a few.

Anik Sarkar is Assistant Professor at Salesian College Siliguri. His forthcoming book is *Fabulating Ecologies* (Lexington Books). He is a contributor to books such as *Science Fiction in India* (Bloomsbury), *The Portrait of an Artist as a Pathographer* (Vernon Press), and

Environmental Postcolonialism (Lexington Books). His research areas include surveillance studies, film studies, the dystopian novel, and medical humanities.

Çağatay Emre Doğan researches, teaches, and writes on art, architectural and urban history, photography, and cinema. He holds a Ph.D. in art history. Coming from an architectural background, he follows an interdisciplinary research agenda, which involves topics like modern and contemporary art and architecture, history of design, art criticism, photography, film studies, urban history, new materialisms, and posthumanism. He is currently affiliated with Rutgers University School of Communication and Information.

Duncan Caillard is an early career researcher at the University of Melbourne, where his research investigates how filmmakers, artists and activists use moving images to negotiate identity and enact political resistance in the Asia-Pacific. His Ph.D. explored the forms and effects of emptiness across Apichatpong Weerasethakul's features, short films and installations. He is the Vice President of the *Senses of Cinema* film journal, an academic programmer at *Screening Ideas* and the author of *Apichatpong Weerasethakul: Contemplation and Resistance* (forthcoming with Edinburgh University Press).

Elizabeth Sikes, Ph.D., LMHC, is a psychotherapist in private practice in Seattle, Washington and a faculty member of the New School for Analytical Psychology. She taught philosophy at Seattle University for 14 years and has published in the areas of philosophy and art and the environment. She is the founder of PsychoCinematics, a nine month-long seminar course for psychotherapists and analysts exploring the intersection of psychoanalytical theory and film, and its implications for practice.

Francesco Quario is an independent researcher and filmmaker, who graduated with an MA in Film and Philosophy from King's College, London in 2021. Their research focuses on the intersection between temporality and media philosophy. Most recently, they presented a paper at the 2022 Society for Cinema and Media Studies conference on the works of director Tsai Ming-liang, exploring the relation between the spectatorial affect of Slow Cinema, and digital modes of production and distribution. These concerns are echoed in their creative work, which includes digital short films and educational video essays distributed through online streaming platforms.

NOTES ON CONTRIBUTORS

Jade de Cock de Rameyen is a Ph.D. graduate in Film Studies and Literature from the Université Libre de Bruxelles. In 2021–22 she was visiting researcher at Universidad Autónoma de Madrid, and in 2018–19 at Yale University. Her thesis focused on narrative ecology in contemporary artists' cinema. Her peer-reviewed articles are published in *Film Philosophy*, *New Review of Film and Television Studies* and *Revue Belge de Philologie et d'Histoire*. She holds MA's in Languages and Literature (ULB), Philosophy (ULB), and British Studies (Humboldt Universität Berlin).

Jayjit Sarkar is an Assistant Professor at the Department of English, Raiganj University, India. He is the author of the monograph *Illness as Method: Beckett, Kafka, Mann, Woolf and Eliot* (Vernon Press, 2019). He is also the co-editor of books like *Border and Bordering: Poetics, Politics, Precariousness* (ibidem Press, 2020); *The Portrait of an Artist as a Pathographer: On Writing Illnesses and Illnesses in Writing* (Vernon Press, 2021); and *Geographia Literaria* (ibidem Press, 2021). In the past, he has also written for India Independent Films, *Live Wire*, *Newslaundry*, and *We the World* magazines.

Jeffner Allen is Professor of Philosophy and Africana Studies at Binghamton University, State University of New York. A philosopher and creative writer, her book publications include *SINUOSITIES: Lesbian Poetic Politics* (Indiana University Press, 1996) and *r e v e r b e r a t i o n s across the shimmering CASCADAS* (SUNY Press, 1994), which was performed in collaboration at Lincoln Center. *Reef Passions: Postcolonial Aesthetics Between Coral Reefs* (forthcoming) engages postcolonial, environmental, and aesthetic dimensions of coral reef communities, especially those of Sulawesi and Bonaire.

Palita Chunsaengchan is an Assistant Professor of Southeast Asian cinema and media cultures in the Department of Asian and Middle Eastern Studies at the University of Minnesota, Twin Cities. Her current book manuscript, entitled *A History of Chimeric Cinema: Thai Film Culture (1880–1942)*, draws together the beginnings of Thai cinema from its intermedial relationships with prose, poetry, and theatre. The book also traces cinema's complex intertwinement with questions of sovereignty and modernity. Her past publications appeared in *The Complete Guide to Thai Cinema* (I.B. Tauris, 2018), *Asian Cinema* (Intellect, 2021), and *SOJOURN* (ISEAS–Yusof Ishak Institute, 2022). Her upcoming article and review are currently in production at the *Journal of Modern Periodical Studies* and *Journal of Asian Studies* respectively.

Patrícia Sequeira Brás concluded her doctoral research in 2015 at the Department of Iberian and Latin American Studies at Birkbeck, University of London. She has taught at Queen Mary, University of London, Birkbeck, University of London and at the University of Exeter in the UK. She held a research position at Universidade Lusófona in Lisbon, before accepting the invitation to hold a position as a Visiting Assistant Professor at Universidade de Coimbra, where she currently teaches film. She is an integrated researcher at CEIS20. The relationship between politics and cinema that motivated her doctoral work continues to shape her new research projects. Her current research interests include documentary film genre, feminism and gender studies, filmic temporality, and visual coloniality.

Sivaranjini is an independent filmmaker and research scholar. She is currently pursuing her Ph.D. in Communication Design from the IDC School of Design, IIT Bombay. Her practice-based research is about hybrid cinema-cinematic narratives in the interstices between fiction and non-fiction. Her research interests are around phenomenology and realism in film. Sivaranjini did her Master's at the National Institute of Design (NID), Ahmedabad, in Film and Video Communication, where she occasionally teaches now as visiting faculty. Her films have been selected and screened at multiple film festivals.

Index

Aikham 168
Ajahn Buddhadasa Bhikkhu 198
Akerman, Chantal 13
anthropocentric 16, 17, 89, 90, 92, 95, 96, 104, 108, 109, 169, 198
Antonioni, Michelangelo 75

Baroni, Raphaël 183, 191, 192, 193, 195, 199, 204, 206
Bazin, André 31, 238
Benjamin, Walter 71, 138
Bergson, Henri 15, 48
beur cinema 251
Brahmanism 167
Braidotti, Rosi 91
Bryant, Levi 102
Buñuel, Luis 233, 234
Burch, Noel 235, 238
Butler, Judith 73

cadaver exquisite 35
Cahiers du Cinéma 199, 206, 211
Cannes 2, 8, 10, 12, 20, 22, 23, 40, 105, 112, 119, 155, 163, 164, 165, 174, 209, 210, 213, 219, 227, 253, 255, 264
Carels, Edwin 133, 150
Carrion-Murayari, Gary 86, 159, 162, 174, 182, 188, 205
Cartesian 58, 63, 96
Casetti, Francesco 135, 194
Chan, Eric 253, 269
Chan-ocha, Prayuth 77, 231

Chion, Michel 99, 186, 189, 194
cinematic time 15, 89, 196, 205, 232
Cottingham, Marci D. 254
Crary, Jonathan 147, 148
Creed, Barbara 10, 16, 70, 71

Diaz, Lav 13

Eisenstein, Sergei 138, 150
Elwes, Catherine 185,
escapism 80, 230
Ettinger, Bracha 18, 126
exquisite corpse 10, 76, 233, 259
EYE Film Institute 150

Field, Simon 253, 255, 266, 273
Fuhrman, Anika 82
Fukushima Daiichi 155

Garcia, Dora 183
Gaweewong, Gridthiya 230, 253, 269
Gioni, Massimiliano 159, 174, 182, 188, 205
Goodall, Jane 164
Griffith, David 150
Grusin, Richard 91, 106, 110, 112, 244, 246
Gunning, Tom 134, 143

Halberstam, Jack 79
Haus der Kunst 181, 265, 270

INDEX

Hayles, Katherine 91
Horn, Eva 91

Ingawanij, May Adadol 79, 106, 163, 258, 260, 272
Iordanova, Dina 249, 273

Jeong, Seung-Yoon 107
Jeppesen, Travis 4, 151
Jihoon, Kim 51, 52
joint deep attention 137, 145, 153
Joo, Eungie 183, 188, 206
Jorge, Nuno Barradas 28, 29, 44, 47, 55, 64, 93, 99, 110, 111, 258

Kalayanamitr, Akritcharlerm 190
Kaweewattana, Chalermrat 190
Khmer 19, 105, 168, 170, 198
Khon Kaen 4, 15, 36, 51, 57, 60, 87, 104, 118, 158, 233, 259, 260, 261, 262, 264, 273, 275
Kiarostami, Abbas 93, 99, 111, 236

Lamas, Salome 183
Lan Xang 167
late capitalism 14, 27, 29, 32, 147, 148, 152
Lèse Majesté 221, 222, 226, 231, 264
Levinas, Emmanuel 16, 70, 72, 86
Lomnoi, Banlop 104, 171, 239
LomoKino 13, 22, 219, 220
Lovatt, Philippa 99, 111, 190, 191, 205, 242, 246
Lynch, David 2, 22, 135, 146

Magritte, René 1
Mahayana 167
Makhmalbaf, Mohsen 236
Malee and the Boy 237
Meaux, Charles de 253, 269
Ming-liang, Tsai 13
Musser, Charles 196
Mutterleib complex 126
Mysterious Objects at Noon 2, 10, 13, 21, 233

Nabua 3, 11, 12, 20, 78, 115, 118, 119, 122–127, 130, 131, 158, 181–190, 194, 195, 199, 201, 202, 206, 207, 209, 210, 225, 227, 244, 245, 263
Naficy, Hamid 249, 250, 257
New Museum (New York) 78, 86, 159, 174, 182, 184, 185, 186, 187, 205
Nong Khai 170, 171, 243
Nowotny, Helga 254

O'Flaherty, Wendy Doniger 146
October Rumbles 208, 226
ontological 73, 74, 90, 91, 92, 94, 95, 103, 107, 112, 141, 142, 191, 204, 215

Palme d'Or 11, 2, 40, 119, 155, 161, 174, 209, 212
Phangkhi 168
photogenie 5, 22, 240
Photophobia 116, 117, 124, 126, 160
Phromkhuntong, Wikanda 252, 254
Phu Phan 164
post-humanism 90, 91
posthumanism 90, 92, 109, 112, 278

Rancière, Jacques 29, 117, 133
Rivers, Ben 183

Sakamoto, Ryuicki 148
Schoonover, Karl 28, 31, 41, 52, 64, 94, 111, 183, 205, 246, 261, 273
Segal, Eyal 195
Shaviro, Steven 14, 30, 106
Sica, Vittorio De 75
Sicinski, Michael 262, 264
slow cinema 14, 15, 27, 30, 44, 47
slowness 47, 48, 50, 51, 55, 63, 64, 93, 94, 111
social hierarchy 84
Sonakul, Mingmongkol 253, 269
Stern, Daniel 192
Sternberg, Meir 190
subaltern 85, 252

INDEX

subalternity 252
superalternity 252
Swinton, Tilda 2, 69, 148, 210, 227, 266

Teh, David 75, 234, 260
Teo, Miaw Lee 258
territory-sounds 189
Theravada Buddhism 167
time-image 49, 64, 93, 121, 124, 195, 205
Toolan, Michael 193

uncertainty principle 238

Valle, Marcos 261
Vejjajiva, Abhisit 222

Walker Art Center (Minneapolis, Minnesota) 101, 112, 213, 214, 215, 216, 227
Ward, Paul 146
Warhol, Andy 44, 50, 55
Wollen, Peter 238

Printed in the USA
CPSIA information can be obtained
at www.ICGtesting.com
CBHW071047211124
17624CB00015B/206